MODERN BIOLOGY

Chapter Tests with Answer Key

HOLT, RINEHART AND WINSTON
Harcourt Brace & Company
Austin • New York • Atlanta • San Francisco • Boston • Dallas • Toronto • London

Art Credits
Pedro Julio Gonzalez/Melissa Turk & The Artist Network; pages 74, 75, 115, 118, 119, 158, 176, 178. Wendy Smith-Griswold/Melissa Turk & The Artist Network; pages 59, 63. David Kelly/Woody Coleman Represents; pages 60, 68, 95, 96, 100, 103, 123, 124, 132, 144, 152, 166, 168, 170, 172, 174, 183.

Printed in the United States of America

ISBN 0-03-051762-1

1 2 3 4 5 6 023 02 01 00 99 98

CONTENTS

Name ______________________ Class ______________ Date ______________

CHAPTER 1 TEST

THE SCIENCE OF LIFE

MATCHING **Write the correct letter in the blank before each numbered term.**

_____ **1.** metabolism

_____ **2.** magnification

_____ **3.** autotroph

_____ **4.** reproduction

_____ **5.** resolution

_____ **6.** TEM

_____ **7.** heterotroph

_____ **8.** SEM

a. an organism that must take in food

b. produces greatly magnified images of surface details

c. increase of an object's apparent size

d. production of offspring

e. produces a greatly magnified image of internal detail

f. sum of all chemical processes of an organism

g. capability of showing clear details

h. an organism that makes its own food

TRUE-FALSE **If a statement is true, write *T* in the blank. If a statement is false, write *F* in the blank, and then in the space provided, explain why the statement is false.**

_____ **9.** Scientists have identified all species of organisms on Earth.

____

_____ **10.** Many nonliving things, such as rock crystals, display greater organization than do the structures found in living things.

____

_____ **11.** Growth in living things occurs by cell division and cell enlargement.

____

_____ **12.** In a scientific investigation, experimenting generally precedes the steps of hypothesizing and predicting.

____

_____ **13.** A light microscope has greater magnification and resolving powers than an electron microscope.

____

Name ______________________ Class ____________ Date ____________

MULTIPLE CHOICE **Write the letter of the most correct answer in the blank.**

______ **14.** To maintain their internal organization, all living things must have a constant supply of

a. oxygen. **b.** carbon dioxide. **c.** water. **d.** energy.

______ **15.** Reproduction involves the transfer of genetic information from

a. autotroph to heterotroph.
b. parents to offspring.
c. offspring to parents.
d. unicellular organisms to multicellular organisms.

______ **16.** The stable internal environment maintained by living things is called

a. homeostasis. **b.** differentiation. **c.** adaptation. **d.** interdependence.

______ **17.** The most important driving force in evolution is

a. natural selection.
b. heterotrophy.
c. autotrophy.
d. asexual reproduction.

______ **18.** The scientific process that involves using the five senses is

a. inference. **b.** analyzing. **c.** modeling. **d.** observation.

______ **19.** Data that are quantitative are always

a. described in words.
b. represented by numbers.
c. duplicated for verification.
d. the most accurate kind of data.

______ **20.** A hypothesis is a statement that

a. is always true.
b. is usually true.
c. is the same as a theory.
d. can be tested.

______ **21.** A broad and comprehensive statement of what is believed to be true is a(n)

a. model. **b.** theory. **c.** prediction. **d.** inference.

______ **22.** A small part used to represent an entire population is called a

a. portion. **b.** tract. **c.** statistic. **d.** sample.

______ **23.** The organism shown at the right is a

a. unicellular autotroph.
b. unicellular heterotroph.
c. multicellular autotroph.
d. multicellular heterotroph.

Name ____________________ Class ____________ Date ____________

SHORT ANSWER **Answer the questions in the space provided.**

24. List six major themes of biology. ____________________

____

____

25. List six major characteristics of life. ____________________

____

____

26. Would a field biologist who studies the ecology of a bird species necessarily use the same scientific methods as a laboratory biologist who studies how a virus infects cells? Why or why not?

____

____

27. Why is it important for scientists to communicate about their work, and what are two common ways that they do so? ____________________

____

____

28. Why do scientists use SI (Système International d'Unités) rather than the system of measurement adopted for use in their own country? ____________________

____

____

29. Which step in the scientific methods does the chart below represent? ____________________

____

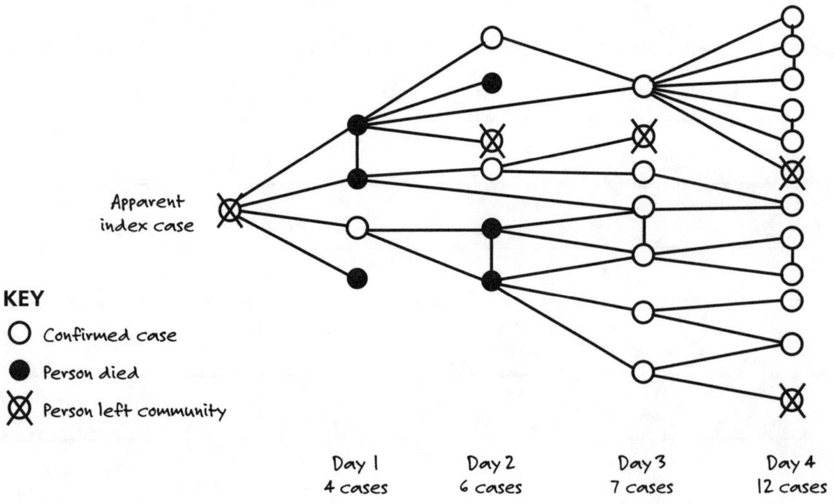

DRAWING CONCLUSIONS **Follow the directions given below.**

30. A microbiologist tested the rate of reproduction (called growth) of a bacterial species in two kinds of bacterial food (called media). The data were organized on the graph below. Analyze the data, and answer the following questions.

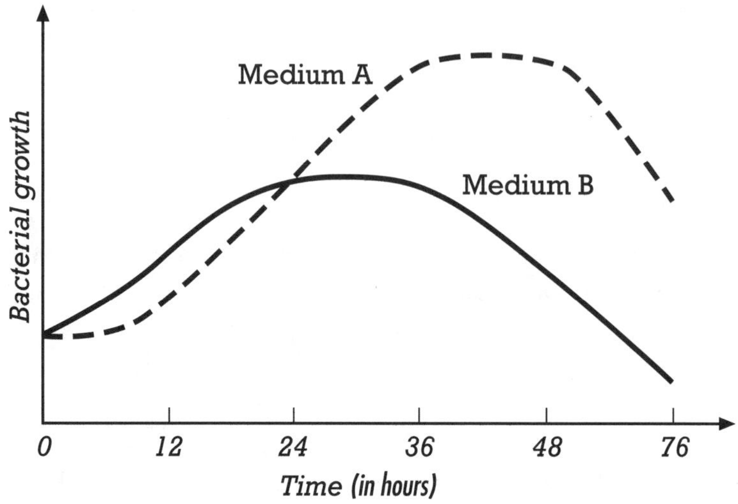

a. At what time was the growth rate equal for the bacteria in both media? ______________

____

____

b. Which medium produced the most rapid growth initially? ______________

____

____

c. Which medium produced the most growth overall? ______________

____

____

d. What does the descending part of the curves represent? What may have caused this effect?

____

____

____

e. What can you predict about the results of a similar experiment run for one week? ______________

____

____

Name ______________________ Class ____________ Date ____________

CHAPTER 2 TEST

CHEMISTRY

MATCHING **Write the correct letter in the blank before each numbered term.**

_____ **1.** exergonic reaction

_____ **2.** atom

_____ **3.** reduction

_____ **4.** compound

_____ **5.** molecule

_____ **6.** endergonic reaction

_____ **7.** oxidation

_____ **8.** element

a. absorbs free energy

b. loss of an electron

c. pure substance that cannot be broken down

d. releases free energy

e. a pure substance composed of two or more elements

f. gain of an electron

g. simplest part of an element

h. particle composed of one or more atoms

TRUE-FALSE **If a statement is true, write *T* in the blank. If a statement is false, write *F* in the blank, and then in the space provided, explain why the statement is false.**

_____ **9.** Elements tend to undergo chemical reactions that decrease their stability.

____

_____ **10.** Sodium chloride (table salt) is an example of a compound formed by ionic bonding.

____

_____ **11.** Matter can change from one state to another by the addition of energy, which makes the particles in the matter move faster.

____

_____ **12.** When pure water dissociates, it contains an equal number of hydroxide ions and hydronium ions.

____

_____ **13.** A solution that contains more hydroxide ions than hydronium ions is acidic.

____

MULTIPLE CHOICE **Write the letter of the most correct answer in the blank.**

_____ **14.** Charged particles that move around an atom's nucleus are

a. electrons. **b.** protons. **c.** ions. **d.** neutrons.

_____ **15.** Chemical bonds are broken, atoms are rearranged, and new bonds are formed during

a. changes of state.
b. chemical reactions.
c. the addition of energy to an element.
d. measurement of pH of a solution.

_____ **16.** Atoms with filled outermost energy levels tend to

a. participate in chemical reactions.
b. not participate in chemical reactions.
c. participate only in redox reactions.
d. dissociate in water.

_____ **17.** In an ionic bond,

a. two atoms of opposite charge are held together by electrical attraction.
b. two uncharged atoms share one or more pairs of electrons.
c. molecules of water are broken into hydroxide ions and hydronium ions.
d. both atoms involved in the bond become negatively charged.

_____ **18.** Which of the following represents the correct order of states of matter from that having the slowest moving particles to that having the fastest moving particles?

a. gas, liquid, solid. **b.** liquid, solid, gas. **c.** solid, gas, liquid. **d.** solid, liquid, gas.

_____ **19.** An attachment between atoms that results from the atoms sharing one or more pairs of electrons is a(n)

a. ionic bond.
b. covalent bond.
c. reduction reaction.
d. oxidation reaction.

_____ **20.** A redox reaction

a. involves the transfer of electrons between atoms.
b. occurs between atoms with filled outer energy levels.
c. results in a net gain of electrons for the reactants.
d. does not involve transfer of energy.

_____ **21.** The amount of energy needed to start a chemical reaction is the reaction's

a. mechanical energy.
b. chemical energy.
c. free energy.
d. activation energy.

_____ **22.** A substance that neutralizes small amounts of acids or bases added to a solution is a(n)

a. alkaline substance.
b. solvent.
c. catalyst.
d. buffer.

_____ **23.** A chemical reaction that can proceed forward or backward is a(n)

a. reversible reaction.
b. ionic reaction.
c. endergonic reaction.
d. exergonic reaction.

Name ____________________ Class __________ Date __________

SHORT ANSWER **Answer the questions in the space provided.**

24. Why is it necessary for oxidation and reduction reactions to occur as paired reactions? ____________

25. What is the role of enzymes in chemical reactions occurring in living things? ____________

26. Describe the relationship between the solute, the solvent, and the concentration of a solution.

27. List two characteristics of acids and two characteristics of bases. ____________

28. What is the pH scale, and what does its range of values mean? ____________

29. What is the atomic number of the atom shown below? Is this a stable atom or an unstable atom? How can you tell? ____________

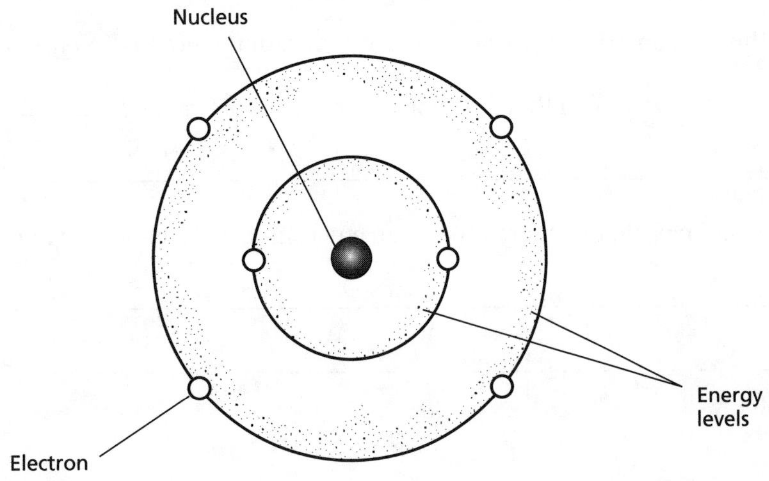

Name ______________________ Class ____________ Date ____________

DRAWING CONCLUSIONS **Follow the directions given below.**

30. The graph below depicts the rate of enzyme activity in relation to pH for two enzymes, pepsin and trypsin. Both enzymes break down molecules in food taken into the human body, but the enzymes act in series. Pepsin breaks some bonds in very large molecules. Trypsin acts on the fragments produced by the action of pepsin, breaking them into smaller units. Answer the questions based on the graph.

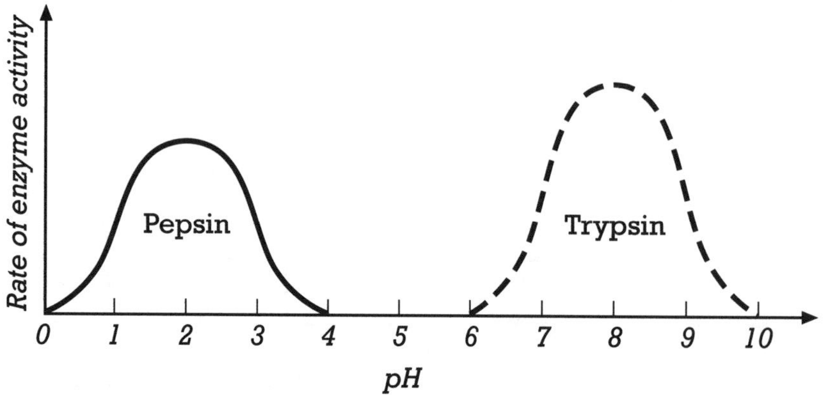

a. The liquid in the stomach has a pH of about 2. Which of the two enzymes would be active in the stomach? ______________________

____

b. The liquid in the small intestine has a pH of about 8. Which of the two enzymes would be active in the small intestine? ______________________

____

c. What must happen to the liquid as it passes from the stomach to the small intestine for digestion to occur normally? ______________________

____

____

d. Consider the data on pH and enzyme activity shown in the graph. Do enzymes typically function only at a specific pH, or can they function at a range of pH values? ______________________

____

e. Can pepsin and trypsin function in the same environment? Why or why not? ______________________

____

____

Name ______________________ Class ____________ Date ____________

CHAPTER 3 TEST

BIOCHEMISTRY

MATCHING **Write the correct letter in the blank before each numbered term.**

_____ **1.** nucleotide

_____ **2.** hydrolysis

_____ **3.** adhesion

_____ **4.** amino acid

_____ **5.** condensation reaction

_____ **6.** glucose

_____ **7.** cohesion

_____ **8.** fatty acid

a. forms large molecules from smaller ones

b. attractive force between like particles

c. monomer of many polysaccharides

d. component of many lipids

e. monomer of nucleic acids

f. attractive force between unlike particles

g. monomer of proteins

h. breaks large molecules into smaller ones

TRUE-FALSE **If a statement is true, write *T* in the blank. If a statement is false, write *F* in the blank, and then in the space provided, explain why the statement is false.**

_____ **9.** The angled shape of the water molecule contributes to its property of polarity.

____

_____ **10.** A functional group changes the structure of a compound but does not alter its chemical properties.

____

_____ **11.** In a triple bond, three pairs of electrons are shared between two atoms.

____

_____ **12.** Amino acids become linked together by peptide bonds during hydrolysis reactions.

____

_____ **13.** Nucleic acids function primarily to carry genetic instructions and direct cellular activities.

____

Name ______________________ Class ____________ Date ____________

MULTIPLE CHOICE **Write the letter of the most correct answer in the blank.**

______ **14.** Water is an effective solvent because

a. it is a polar molecule.
b. it dissolves other polar substances.
c. it dissolves ionic compounds.
d. All of the above

______ **15.** The presence of four electrons in the outermost energy level of a carbon atom enables

a. carbon atoms to form four covalent bonds with atoms of other elements.
b. carbon atoms to form covalent bonds with other carbon atoms.
c. carbon atoms to form double bonds with other atoms.
d. All of the above

______ **16.** The breakdown of polymers into monomers occurs through a process known as

a. hydrolysis.
b. condensation.
c. dissociation.
d. removal of a functional group.

______ **17.** Organic molecules that catalyze reactions in living systems are

a. phospholipids.
b. enzymes.
c. polysaccharides.
d. steroids.

______ **18.** Lipids are good energy-storage molecules because

a. they can absorb a large amount of energy while maintaining a constant temperature.
b. they have many carbon-hydrogen bonds.
c. they are composed of many simple sugars.
d. they cannot be broken down by enzymes.

______ **19.** A compound found in living things that supplies the energy in one of its chemical bonds directly to cells is

a. phosphate. **b.** RNA. **c.** ATP. **d.** alcohol.

______ **20.** Enzymes lower activation energy by

a. linking to the substrate and weakening bonds within the substrate.
b. becoming chemically changed and reacting with the substrate.
c. changing the temperature and pH of the substrate's environment.
d. linking to the substrate permanently, creating a very large molecule.

______ **21.** A compound that is stored as glycogen in animals and as starch in plants is

a. alcohol. **b.** cellulose. **c.** glucose. **d.** phosphate.

______ **22.** The three molecules shown below are

a. phosphates. **b.** isomers. **c.** not organic. **d.** steroids.

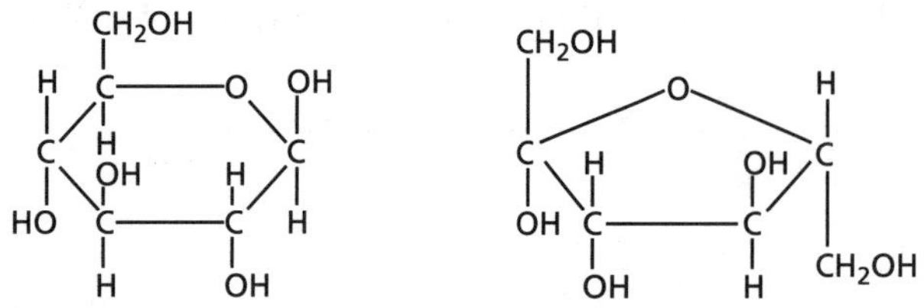

______ **23.** A bond that forms between a positively charged hydrogen atom of one molecule and a negatively charged region of another molecule is a(n)

a. ionic bond.
b. hydrogen bond.
c. covalent bond.
d. basic bond.

SHORT ANSWER **Answer the questions in the space provided.**

24. Describe the structure of a water molecule, and explain how electrical charge is distributed over the molecule. ______________________

____

25. How does a condensation reaction differ from a hydrolysis reaction? ______________________

____

____

26. What are the structural differences between monosaccharides, disaccharides, and polysaccharides?

____

____

____

27. Living things contain many different proteins of vastly different shapes and functions. What determines the shape and thus the function of a particular protein?

____

____

28. How does the structure of phospholipids, linear molecules with a polar end and a nonpolar end, relate to their function in the cell membrane? ______________________

____

____

29. In the diagram of the molecule below, draw in lines as necessary to indicate the presence of any double bonds.

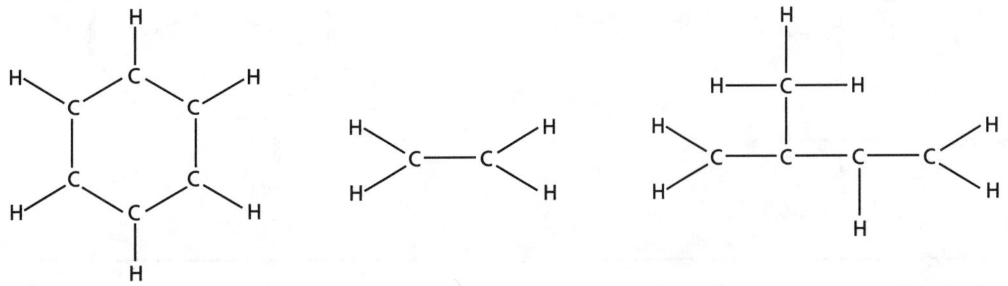

Name ______________________ Class ____________ Date ____________

DRAWING CONCLUSIONS **Follow the directions given below.**

30. The diagrams below illustrate a variety of chemical structures. Write the correct name from the following list in the blank below each diagram. Not every name will be used.

alcohol
dipeptide
disaccharide
enzyme/substrate complex
fatty acid
nucleotide
polysaccharide
water

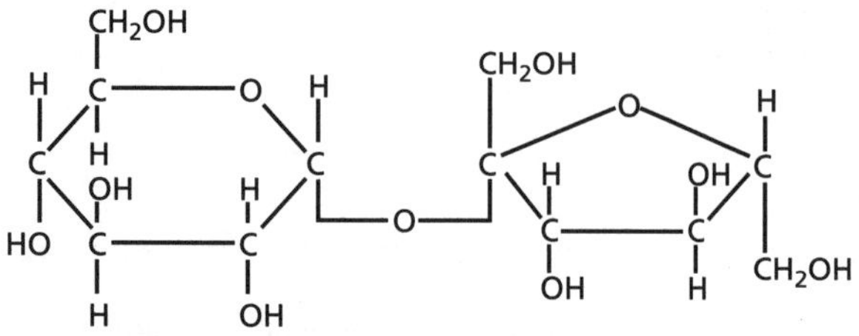

a ______________________

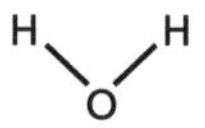

c ______________________

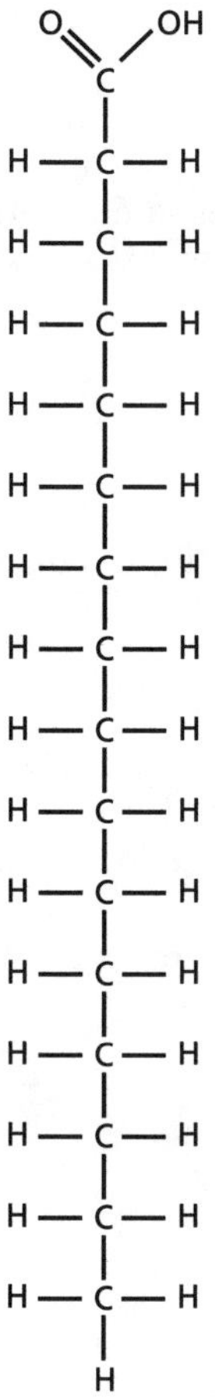

b ______________________

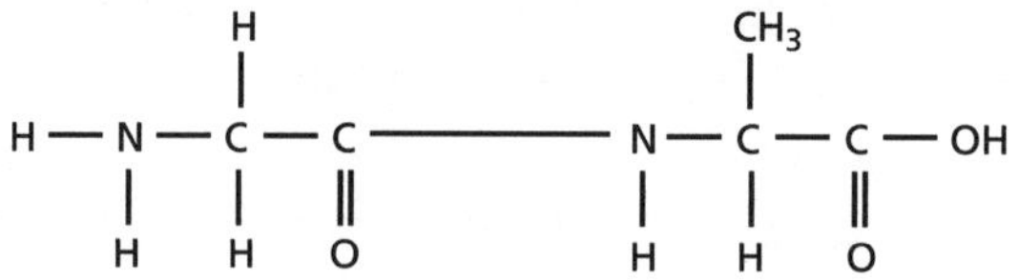

d ______________________

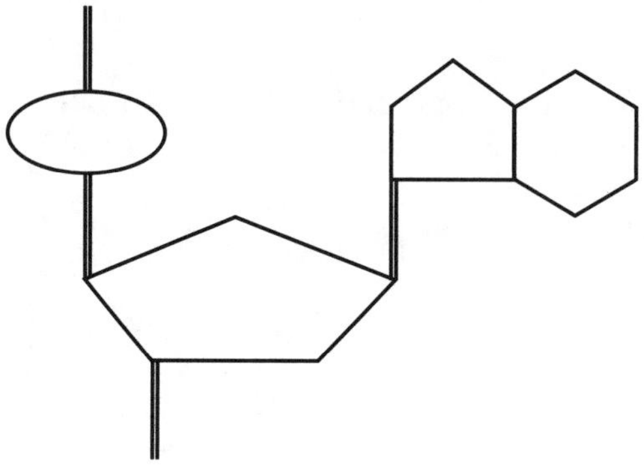

e ______________________

Name ______________________ Class ____________ Date ____________

CHAPTER 4 TEST

STRUCTURE AND FUNCTION OF THE CELL

MATCHING **Write the correct letter in the blank before each numbered term.**

______ **1.** mitochondrion

______ **2.** endoplasmic reticulum

______ **3.** cell membrane

______ **4.** ribosome

______ **5.** cell

______ **6.** Golgi apparatus

______ **7.** nucleus

______ **8.** lysosome

a. stores DNA and synthesizes RNA

b. digests molecules, old organelles, and foreign substances

c. organizes protein synthesis

d. processes and packages substances produced by the cell

e. prepares proteins for export and synthesizes steroids

f. regulates movement of substances into and out of cell

g. transfers energy to ATP

h. the basic unit of life

TRUE-FALSE **If a statement is true, write *T* in the blank. If a statement is false, write *F* in the blank, and then in the space provided, explain why the statement is false.**

______ **9.** The nucleus is the smallest unit that can carry out all the processes of life.

____

______ **10.** The cell membrane behaves like a fluid, and the membrane's components can move laterally within it.

____

______ **11.** Ribosomes differ from other organelles in that they are membrane bound.

____

______ **12.** Chloroplasts in plant cells are functionally similar to lysosomes in animal cells.

____

______ **13.** A tissue is a group of related cells that carries out a specific function.

____

Name ______________________ Class ____________ Date ____________

MULTIPLE CHOICE Write the letter of the most correct answer in the blank.

______ **14.** The maximum size to which a cell may grow is limited mainly by the cell's

a. shape.
b. surface area.
c. function.
d. internal organization.

______ **15.** The discovery of cells is linked most directly with

a. early investigations of causes of diseases.
b. observations of large, unicellular organisms.
c. the development of the microscope.
d. efforts to reproduce organisms in the laboratory.

______ **16.** Which of the following are components of the cell membrane that have a significant role in its functioning?

a. lipids
b. proteins
c. carbohydrates
d. All of the above

______ **17.** In which of the following types of cells would you expect to find a large number of mitochondria?

a. bone
b. skin
c. muscle
d. blood

______ **18.** Microfilaments and microtubules

a. contain digestive enzymes.
b. function in cell structure and movement.
c. are sites of protein synthesis.
d. are sites of photosynthesis.

______ **19.** Which of the following is the correct order of structures in living things, from the simplest to the most complex?

a. cells, tissues, organs, organ systems
b. cells, organs, tissues, organ systems
c. cells, organs, organ systems, tissues
d. organ systems, organs, tissues, cells

______ **20.** An example of an organ is

a. connective tissue.
b. the digestive system.
c. nerve cells.
d. the stomach.

______ **21.** Short, hairlike organelles that can move and may cover a unicellular organism or line the respiratory tract are called

a. chromatin strands.
b. flagella.
c. cilia.
d. spindle fibers.

______ **22.** The first cells on Earth were likely

a. colonial algae.
b. eukaryotes.
c. prokaryotes that did not make their own food.
d. prokaryotes that made their own food.

______ **23.** Name two functions of the proteins embedded in the cell membrane.

a. They transport substances across the membrane and aid in protein synthesis.
b. They store wastes and form the outer layer of the membrane.
c. They serve as attachment sites for molecules in the extracellular fluid and transport substances across the membrane.
d. They aid in cell movement and serve as attachment sites for molecules in the extracellular fluid.

SHORT ANSWER **Answer the questions in the space provided.**

24. What are the three parts of the cell theory?

____

____

____

25. Name two different kinds of animal cells, and describe how their shape is related to their function.

____

____

____

26. Describe two differences between prokaryotic cells and eukaryotic cells.

____

____

____

27. The diagram below depicts a plant cell. Write the names of structures *a–e* in the blanks. Which of these structures are found in plants but not in animals?

____

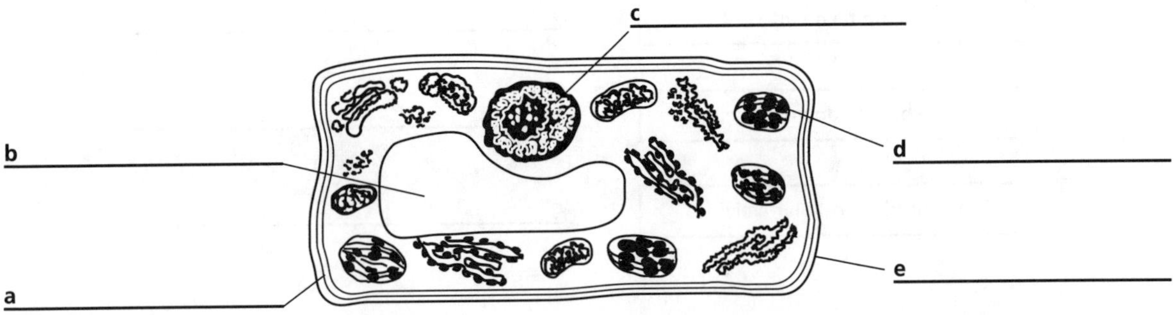

Name ______________________ Class ____________ Date ____________

28. What are the major roles of the nucleus, and what parts of the nucleus carry out these roles?

____

____

____

____

29. What is a colonial organism, and what does it have in common with a multicellular organism?

____

____

____

DRAWING CONCLUSIONS Follow the directions given below.

30. The flow charts below depict two important processes that occur in cells: protein synthesis and energy conversion. Each step in the two processes is numbered. For each process step, identify the location in the cell where the step occurs.

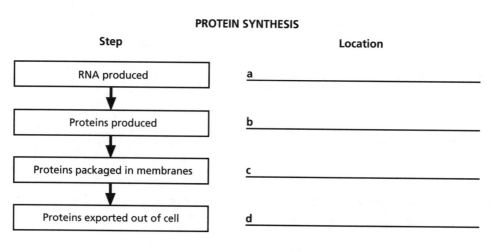

PROTEIN SYNTHESIS

Step	Location
RNA produced ↓	a ____________
Proteins produced ↓	b ____________
Proteins packaged in membranes ↓	c ____________
Proteins exported out of cell	d ____________

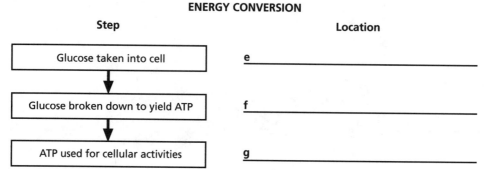

ENERGY CONVERSION

Step	Location
Glucose taken into cell ↓	e ____________
Glucose broken down to yield ATP ↓	f ____________
ATP used for cellular activities	g ____________

Name ______________________ Class ____________ Date ____________

CHAPTER 5 TEST

Homeostasis and Transport

MATCHING **Write the correct letter in the blank before each numbered term.**

______ **1.** plasmolysis

______ **2.** vesicle

______ **3.** hypertonic

______ **4.** concentration gradient

______ **5.** cytolysis

______ **6.** hypotonic

______ **7.** phagocytosis

______ **8.** pinocytosis

a. relatively low solute concentration

b. membrane-bound organelle

c. uptake of large particles

d. shrinking of cells

e. uptake of solutes or fluids

f. bursting of cells

g. concentration difference across space

h. relatively high solute concentration

TRUE-FALSE **If a statement is true, write *T* in the blank. If a statement is false, write *F* in the blank, and then in the space provided, explain why the statement is false.**

______ **9.** The random movement of molecules in diffusion requires energy in the form of ATP.

____

______ **10.** When a solution is in equilibrium, all movement of its molecules stops.

____

______ **11.** Sodium-potassium pumps cause positive charge to accumulate inside cells.

____

______ **12.** In a plant cell, water molecules exert turgor pressure on the cell membrane.

____

______ **13.** Molecules diffuse down their concentration gradient.

____

Name ________________ Class ________ Date ________

MULTIPLE CHOICE Write the letter of the most correct answer in the blank.

______ **14.** The process of diffusion requires

a. a cell membrane.
b. an aqueous solution.
c. a difference in the concentration of molecules throughout a space.
d. All of the above

______ **15.** If the molecular concentration of a substance is the same throughout a space, the substance

a. has a large concentration gradient.
b. is in equilibrium.
c. will undergo diffusion.
d. will undergo osmosis.

______ **16.** A type of transport in which water moves across a membrane and down its concentration gradient is

a. simple diffusion.
b. facilitated diffusion.
c. diffusion through ion channels.
d. osmosis.

______ **17.** Net movement of water across a cell membrane occurs

a. from a hypotonic solution to a hypertonic solution.
b. from a hypertonic solution to a hypotonic solution.
c. from an isotonic solution to another isotonic solution.
d. through gated water channels.

______ **18.** All forms of passive transport depend on

a. energy from the cell in the form of ATP.
b. the kinetic energy of molecules.
c. ion channels.
d. carrier proteins.

______ **19.** Sodium-potassium pumps

a. move Na^+ ions and K^+ ions into cells.
b. move Na^+ ions and K^+ ions out of cells.
c. move Na^+ ions out of cells and K^+ ions into cells.
d. move Na^+ ions into cells and K^+ ions out of cells.

______ **20.** Which of the following processes is illustrated in the diagram at right?

a. the action of the sodium-potassium pump
b. pinocytosis
c. phagocytosis
d. exocytosis

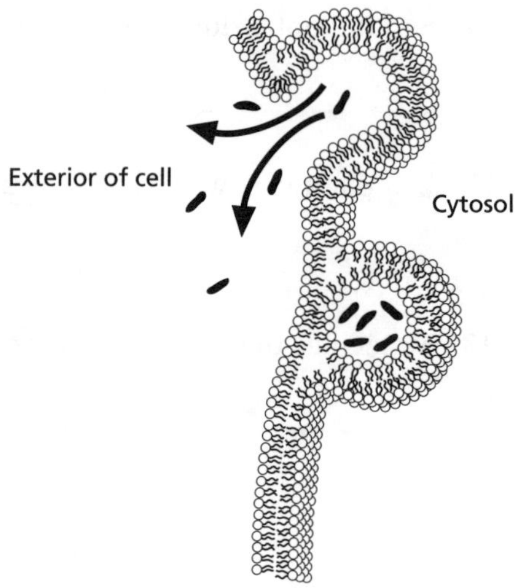

_____ **21.** A structure that can move excess water out of unicellular organisms is a

a. carrier protein.
b. contractile vacuole.
c. ion channel.
d. cell membrane pump.

_____ **22.** Most of the time, the environment that plant cells live in is

a. isotonic.
b. hypertonic.
c. hypotonic.
d. None of the above

_____ **23.** Plasmolysis of a human red blood cell would occur if the cell were

a. in an isotonic solution.
b. in a hypertonic solution.
c. in a hypotonic solution.
d. None of the above

SHORT ANSWER **Answer the questions in the space provided.**

24. Name three types of passive transport and three types of active transport.

____

____

____

____

25. Describe what would happen to the molecules in a drop of ink dropped into a beaker of water. What is this process called?

____

____

26. What is the fundamental difference between carrier proteins that participate in facilitated diffusion and carrier proteins that function as pumps?

____

____

____

27. How do ions cross the lipid bilayer of the cell membrane?

____

____

Name ______________________ Class ____________ Date ____________

28. Describe the action of the sodium-potassium pump.

____

____

____

____

29. Contrast endocytosis with exocytosis.

____

____

____

____

DRAWING CONCLUSIONS Follow the directions given below.

30. The diagrams below illustrate cells carrying out different types of transport across their cell membranes. Identify each process by writing the correct term in the blank below each diagram. Then answer the question.

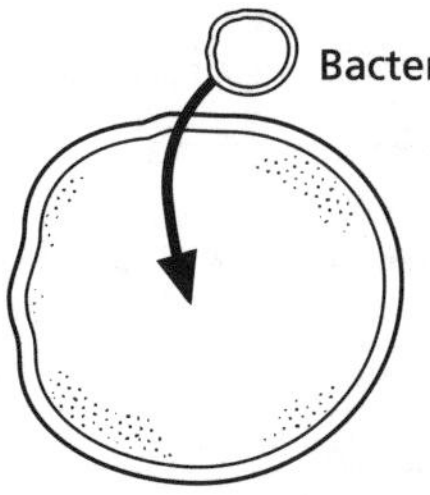

a ______________________

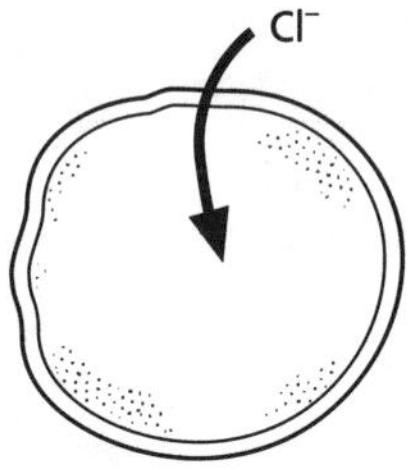

b ______________________

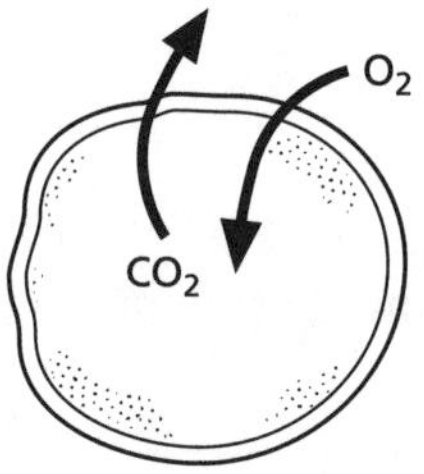

c ______________________

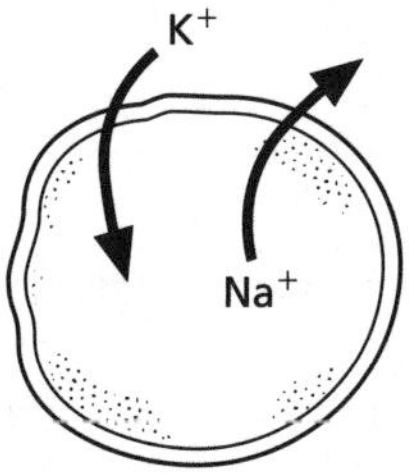

d ______________________

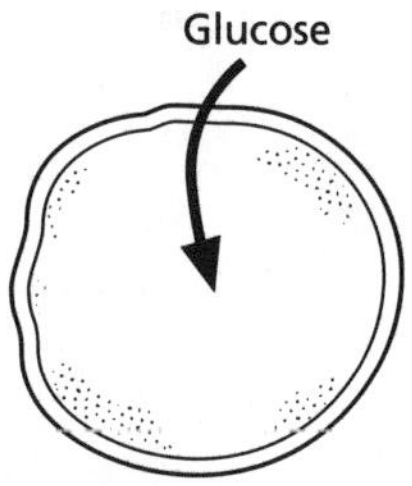

e ______________________

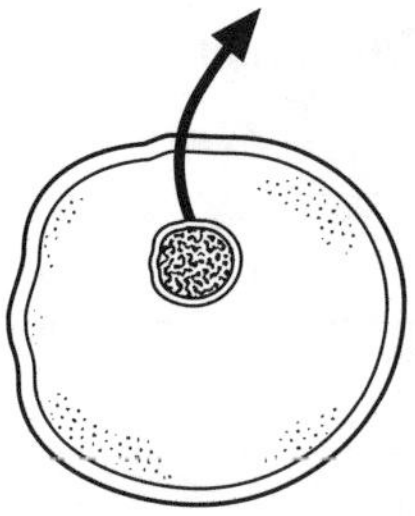

f ______________________

g. Which of the above processes are active-transport processes?

____

Name ______________________ Class __________ Date __________

CHAPTER 6 TEST

PHOTOSYNTHESIS

MATCHING Write the correct letter in the blank before each numbered term.

_____ **1.** carotenoids

_____ **2.** ATP synthase

_____ **3.** photosystem

_____ **4.** PGAL

_____ **5.** RuBP

_____ **6.** visible spectrum

_____ **7.** chlorophylls

_____ **8.** biochemical pathway

a. adds phosphate group to ADP

b. absorb violet, blue, and red light

c. component colors of white light

d. series of linked chemical reactions

e. three-carbon molecule in Calvin cycle

f. absorb blue and green light

g. five-carbon carbohydrate in Calvin cycle

h. cluster of pigment molecules

TRUE-FALSE If a statement is true, write *T* in the blank. If a statement is false, write *F* in the blank, and then in the space provided, explain why the statement is false.

_____ **9.** Light of different wavelengths is different colors.

____

_____ **10.** High-energy electrons move along the thylakoid membrane from photosystem I to photosystem II.

____

_____ **11.** The oxygen atoms in the oxygen gas produced in photosynthesis come from carbon dioxide.

____

_____ **12.** Compounds that can be produced from products of the Calvin cycle include amino acids, lipids, and carbohydrates.

____

_____ **13.** C_4 plants differ from C_3 plants in that they do not use the Calvin cycle for carbon fixation.

____

Name ______________________ Class ______________ Date ______________

MULTIPLE CHOICE **Write the letter of the most correct answer in the blank.**

______ **14.** What product of the light reactions of photosynthesis is released and does not participate further in photosynthesis?

a. ATP **b.** NADPH **c.** H_2O **d.** O_2

______ **15.** Where does the energy required for the Calvin cycle originate?

a. ATP and NADPH produced by the light reactions
b. O_2 produced by the light reactions
c. the sun's heat
d. photons of light

______ **16.** Protons are moved into the thylakoid using energy from

a. ATP.
b. NADPH.
c. electrons in the transport chain.
d. the sun's heat.

______ **17.** At the end of the photosystem I transport chain, electrons

a. combine with $NADP^+$ to form NADPH.
b. combine with ADP to form ATP.
c. are ejected out of the membrane, into the stroma.
d. enter photosystem II.

______ **18.** Carbon atoms are fixed into organic compounds in

a. the Calvin cycle.
b. the light reactions.
c. electron transport chains.
d. photosystems I and II.

______ **19.** To produce the same amount of carbohydrate, C_4 plants require less

a. ATP than C_3 plants.
b. carbon dioxide than C_3 plants.
c. water than C_3 plants.
d. RuBP than C_3 plants.

______ **20.** Which of the following environmental factors will cause a rapid decline in the photosynthesis rate if the factor rises above a certain level?

a. light intensity **b.** temperature **c.** carbon dioxide **d.** oxygen

______ **21.** In the diagram below of a chloroplast, the light reactions would occur in area

a. *a.* **b.** *b.* **c.** *c.* **d.** *d.*

______ **22.** In the diagram at right of a chloroplast, the reactions of the Calvin cycle would occur in area

a. *a.*
b. *b.*
c. *c.*
d. *d.*

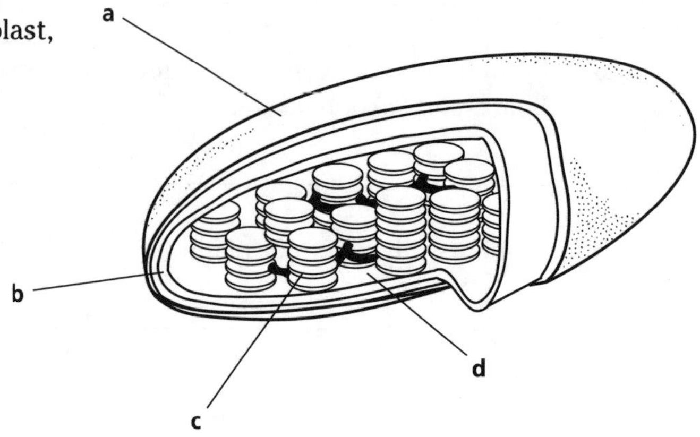

______ **23.** Accessory pigments differ from chlorophyll *a* in that they

a. absorb all wavelengths of light.
b. absorb only yellow and orange light.
c. are not directly involved in the light reactions of photosynthesis.
d. have no function in photosynthesis.

SHORT ANSWER Answer the questions in the space provided.

24. Describe the internal structure and the external structure of a chloroplast.

____

____

____

____

25. What happens to the components of water molecules that are split during the light reactions of photosynthesis?

____

____

____

26. How is ATP formed in photosynthesis?

____

____

____

27. What is the fate of most of the PGAL molecules in the third step of the Calvin cycle? What happens to the remaining PGAL molecules?

____

____

____

____

28. How do CAM plants differ from C_3 and C_4 plants? How does this difference allow CAM plants to exist in hot, dry conditions?

____

____

____

29. Photosynthesis is said to be "saturated" at a certain level of CO_2. What does this mean?

____

____

____

DRAWING CONCLUSIONS Follow the directions given below.

30. The diagram below illustrates the site of the light reactions in the thylakoid membrane. Identify the primary electron acceptors, photosystem I, photosystem II, and the electron transport chains by writing the correct term in each blank. Then answer the question.

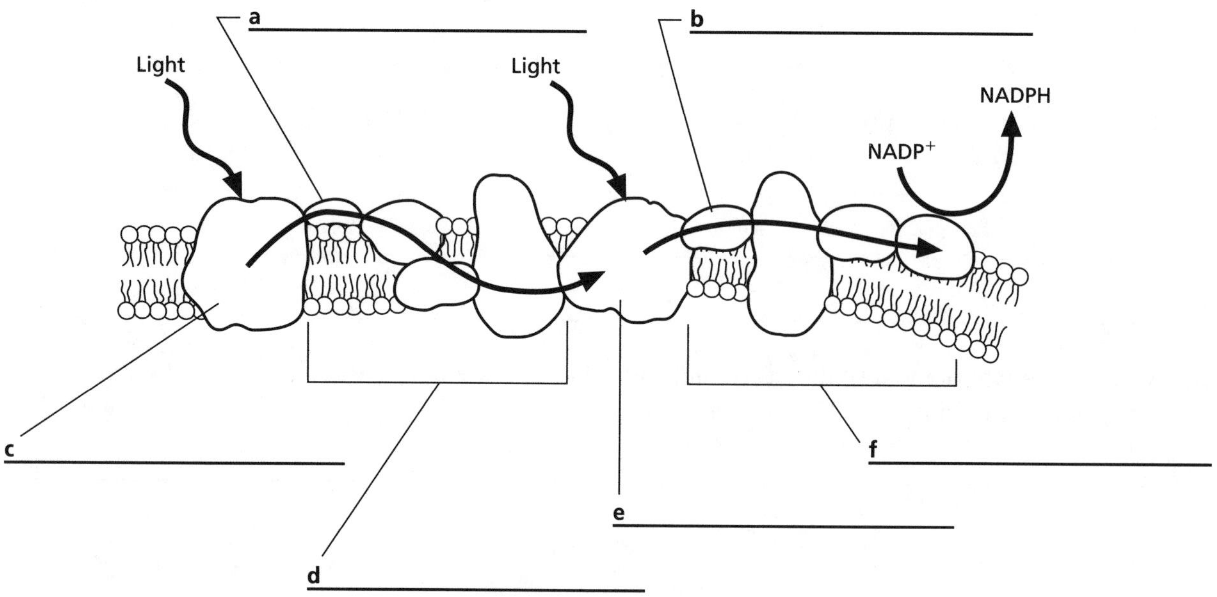

g. What structure that is found in the thylakoid membrane and is important to chemiosmosis is *not* shown in the diagram?

____

Name ______________________________ Class ______________ Date ______________

CHAPTER 7 TEST

CELLULAR RESPIRATION

MATCHING **Write the correct letter in the blank before each numbered term.**

_____ **1.** citric acid

_____ **2.** kilocalorie

_____ **3.** glycolysis

_____ **4.** aerobic respiration

_____ **5.** cell membrane

_____ **6.** cytosol

_____ **7.** NAD^+

_____ **8.** fermentation

a. first pathway of cellular respiration

b. glycolysis and anaerobic pathways

c. product of acetyl CoA and oxaloacetic acid

d. location of glycolysis

e. electron acceptor

f. location of electron transport chain in prokaryotes

g. unit of energy

h. cellular respiration in the presence of oxygen

TRUE-FALSE **If a statement is true, write *T* in the blank. If a statement is false, write *F* in the blank, and then in the space provided, explain why the statement is false.**

_____ **9.** In aerobic respiration, glucose molecules are converted into acetyl CoA molecules when they enter the Krebs cycle.

____

_____ **10.** Yeasts produce alcohol and CO_2 in the process of lactic-acid fermentation.

____

_____ **11.** In cellular respiration, glycolysis follows the Krebs cycle.

____

_____ **12.** In cellular respiration, more energy is transferred in the electron transport chain than in any other step.

____

_____ **13.** ATP and NADH donate electrons to the electron transport chain.

____

Name ______________________ Class ____________ Date ____________

MULTIPLE CHOICE Write the letter of the most correct answer in the blank.

______ **14.** The breakdown of organic compounds to produce ATP is known as

a. cellular respiration.
b. lactic-acid fermentation.
c. alcoholic fermentation.
d. photosynthesis.

______ **15.** Glycolysis begins with glucose and produces

a. PGAL. **b.** lactic acid. **c.** acetyl CoA. **d.** pyruvic acid.

______ **16.** An important molecule generated by both lactic acid fermentation and alcoholic fermentation is

a. ATP. **b.** NADH. **c.** CO_2. **d.** NAD^+.

______ **17.** In the first step of aerobic respiration, pyruvic acid from glycolysis produces CO_2, NADH, H^+, and

a. citric acid. **b.** acetyl CoA. **c.** oxaloacetic acid. **d.** lactic acid.

______ **18.** The electron transport chain is driven by two products of the Krebs cycle—

a. oxaloacetic acid and citric acid.
b. H_2O and CO_2.
c. NADH and $FADH_2$.
d. acetyl CoA and ATP.

______ **19.** What happens to electrons as they are transported along the electron transport chain?

a. They lose energy.
b. They gain energy.
c. They are pumped into the space between the inner and outer mitochondrial membranes.
d. They combine with O_2 and protons to form water.

______ **20.** The energy efficiency of aerobic respiration (including glycolysis) is approximately

a. 7 percent. **b.** 50 percent. **c.** 66 percent. **d.** 100 percent.

______ **21.** In the diagram below of a mitochondrion, the reactions of the Krebs cycle would occur in area

a. *a*. **b.** *b*. **c.** *c*. **d.** *d*.

______ **22.** In the diagram below of a mitochondrion, the electron transport chain is located in area

a. *a*. **b.** *b*. **c.** *c*. **d.** *d*.

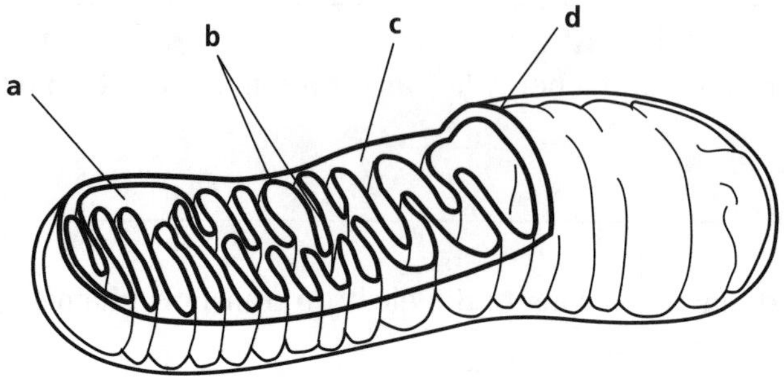

______ **23.** In alcoholic fermentation, ethyl alcohol is produced from

a. NAD^+.
b. NADH.
c. lactic acid.
d. pyruvic acid.

SHORT ANSWER Answer the questions in the space provided.

24. The fourth step of glycolysis yields four ATP molecules, but the *net* yield from glycolysis is only two ATP molecules. Explain this discrepancy.

____

____

____

25. Under what conditions would cells in your body undergo lactic-acid fermentation?

____

____

26. Glycolysis produces only 3.5% of the energy that would be produced if an equal quantity of glucose were completely oxidized. What has happened to the remaining energy in the glucose?

____

____

____

27. Explain the role of oxaloacetic acid with respect to the cyclical nature of Krebs cycle.

____

____

____

28. What happens to electrons that accumulate at the end of the electron transport chain?

____

____

Name ____________________ Class __________ Date __________

29. Where in the mitochondrion do protons accumulate, and what is the source of the protons?

____

____

____

DRAWING CONCLUSIONS Follow the directions given below.

30. The diagram below depicts the pathways of cellular respiration. Rectangles denote substances involved in cellular respiration and ovals denote processes. Identify the processes by writing the correct term in each blank.

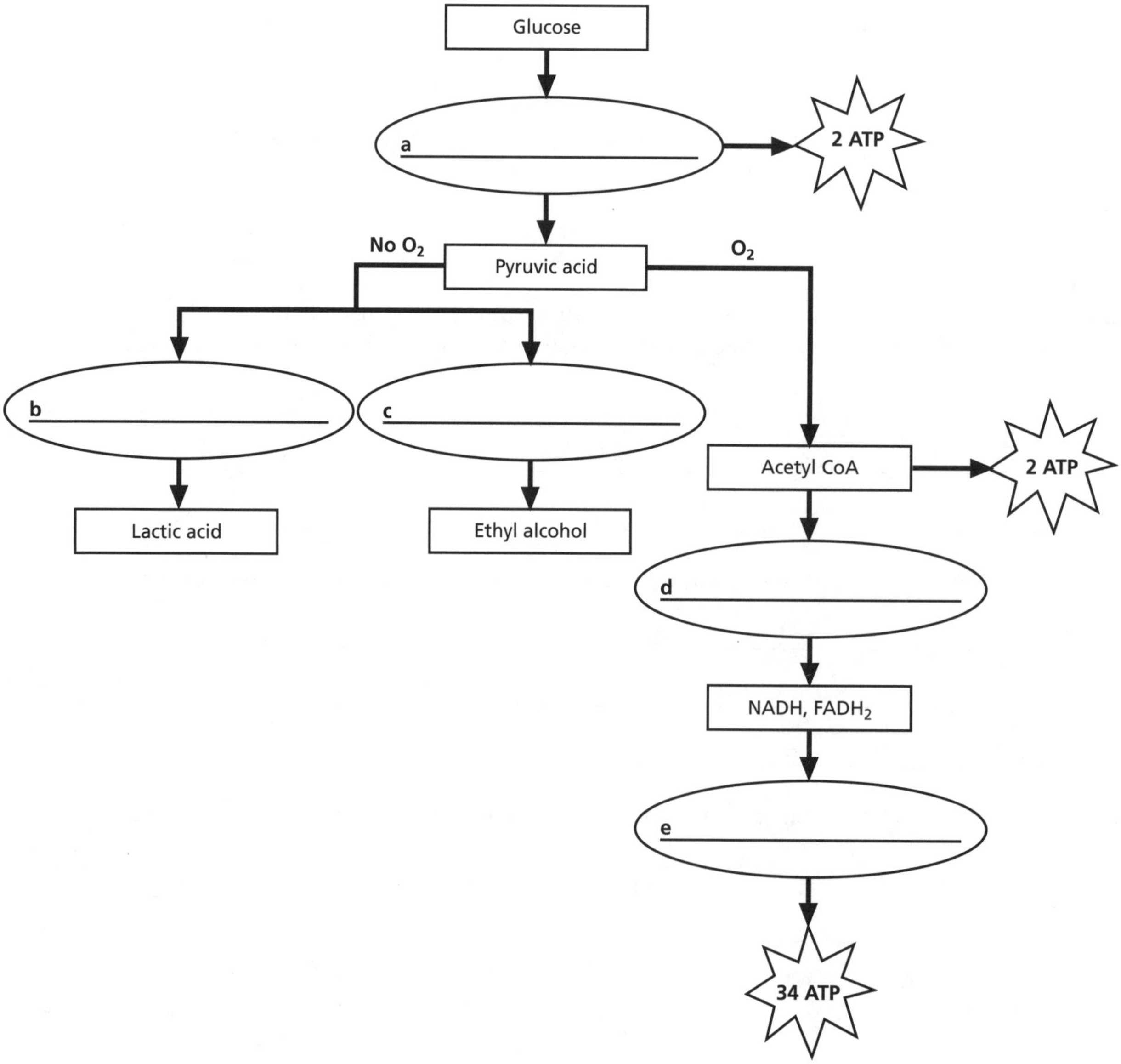

Name ______________________ Class ____________ Date ____________

CHAPTER 8 TEST

CELL REPRODUCTION

MATCHING Write the correct letter in the blank space before each numbered term.

_____ **1.** mitotic spindle

_____ **2.** prophase

_____ **3.** asexual reproduction

_____ **4.** S phase

_____ **5.** interphase

_____ **6.** G_1 phase

_____ **7.** cleavage furrow

_____ **8.** anaphase

a. the period during which DNA is copied

b. the first phase of interphase

c. the phase of mitosis during which chromosomes move to opposite poles

d. the time between cell divisions

e. equally divides chromatids between offspring cells

f. equally divides an animal cell into two offspring cells

g. the first phase of mitosis

h. the production of offspring from one parent

TRUE-FALSE If a statement is true, write *T* in the blank. If a statement is false, write *F* in the blank, and then in the space provided, explain why the statement is false.

_____ **9.** Each offspring cell that is produced by mitosis has half as many chromosomes as the original cell had.

____

_____ **10.** Chromatids form while DNA copies itself before cell division.

____

_____ **11.** During mitosis, centrioles are present in both animal cells and plant cells.

____

_____ **12.** Binary fission is the division of a prokaryotic cell into two offspring cells.

____

_____ **13.** Two of the 46 human chromosomes are sex chromosomes.

____

Name ______________________ Class ____________ Date ____________

MULTIPLE CHOICE **Write the letter of the most correct answer in the blank.**

_____ **14.** If an organism has 12 chromosomes in each body cell, how many chromosomes would you expect to find in the organism's gametes?

a. 4 **b.** 6 **c.** 10 **d.** 12

_____ **15.** During which phase of meiosis do tetrads form?

a. prophase **b.** telophase I **c.** metaphase II **d.** anaphase II

_____ **16.** The division of the cytoplasm of a eukaryotic cell is called

a. mitosis.
b. binary fission.
c. cytokinesis.
d. cytoplasmic streaming.

_____ **17.** Which of the following events occurs during synapsis?

a. replication of the DNA
b. appearance of spindle fibers
c. division of the cytoplasm
d. pairing of homologues

_____ **18.** During mitosis and meiosis, kinetochore fibers are thought to

a. control cytokinesis.
b. make centromeres.
c. move chromosomes.
d. join chromatids.

_____ **19.** Histones are proteins that

a. are found only in prokaryotic cells.
b. aid in the packing of DNA in eukaryotic cells.
c. aid in controlling the activity of regions of DNA.
d. All of the above

_____ **20.** Spermatogenesis results in

a. four haploid cells.
b. one haploid cell and three polar bodies.
c. four diploid cells.
d. two sperm cells and two polar bodies.

_____ **21.** Each offspring cell produced by binary fission contains

a. half the chromosomes of the original cell.
b. twice as many chromosomes as the original cell had.
c. an identical copy of the original cell's chromosome.
d. an independent assortment of the original cell's chromosomes.

_____ **22.** Crossing-over results in genetic recombination by

a. reducing the original cell's chromosome number by half.
b. randomly separating the maternal and paternal chromosomes.
c. mixing half the maternal chromosomes with half the paternal chromosomes.
d. permitting the exchange of genetic material between maternal and paternal chromosomes.

______ **23.** What structure not found in animal cells forms along the midline of a dividing plant cell?

a. cleavage furrow **b.** chloroplast **c.** cell plate **d.** kinetochore

SHORT ANSWER Answer the questions in the space provided.

24. Describe how you could determine if a dividing cell is a prokaryote or a eukaryote. What structures would you look for? ______________________________

____

____

____

25. List two ways that meiosis differs from mitosis. ______________________________

____

____

____

26. Compare the products of mitosis with those of meiosis II. ______________________________

____

____

27. In the space below, draw a diagram of the cell cycle. Label and briefly describe the events that take place during each phase of the cell cycle.

Name ____________________ Class __________ Date __________

28. How do the products of spermatogenesis and oogenesis differ? ____________________

____

____

____

29. What is independent assortment, and how does it affect the genetic makeup of offspring cells?

____

____

____

DRAWING CONCLUSIONS Follow the directions given below.

30. The diagrams below depict stages of cell reproduction. Identify the stages by writing the correct term in each blank. Indicate the correct sequence of the phases by writing a number next to the name of the phase. Then answer the question.

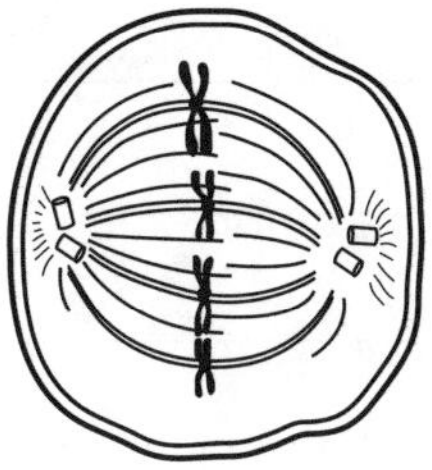

a ____________________

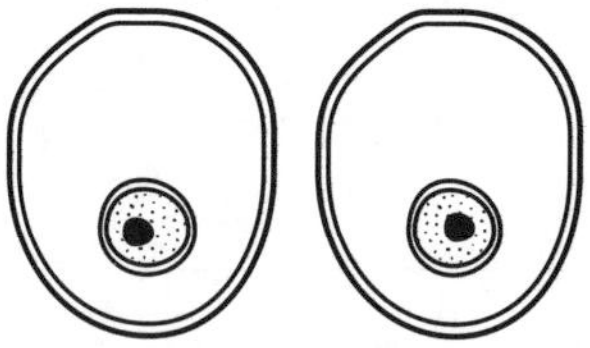

b ____________________

c ____________________

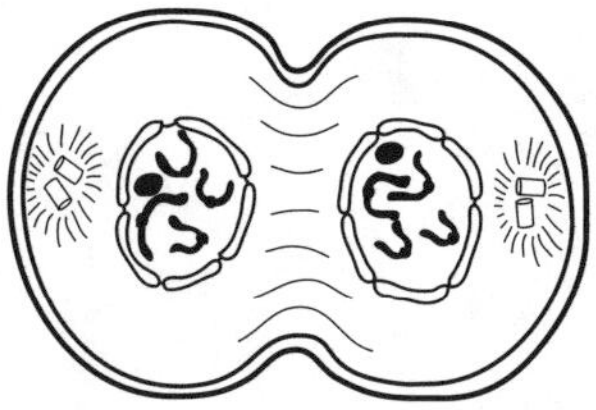

d ____________________

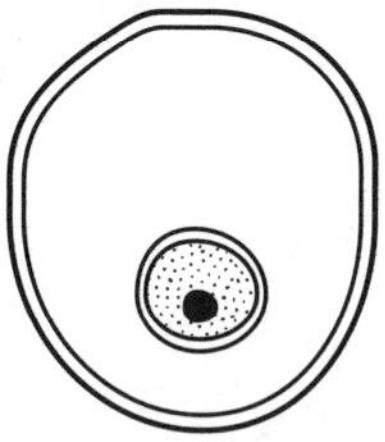

e ____________________

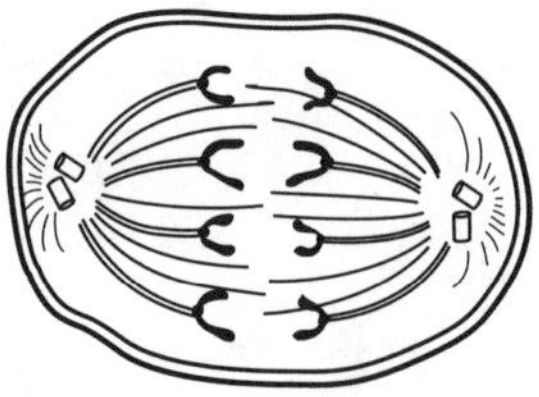

f ____________________

g. What type of cell division is depicted above? Justify your answer.

____

____

Name ______________________ Class ____________ Date ____________

CHAPTER 9 TEST

FUNDAMENTALS OF GENETICS

MATCHING **Write the correct letter in the blank before each numbered term.**

_____ **1.** homozygous dominant

_____ **2.** genotype

_____ **3.** monohybrid cross

_____ **4.** heredity

_____ **5.** allele

_____ **6.** heterozygote

_____ **7.** trait

_____ **8.** gene

a. a segment of DNA that controls a particular hereditary trait

b. a cross involving one pair of contrasting traits

c. an alternative form of a gene

d. an organism having two different alleles for a trait

e. the genetic makeup of an organism

f. a contrasting form of a hereditary characteristic

g. having two similar, dominant alleles for a trait

h. the transmission of characteristics from parents of offspring

TRUE-FALSE **If a statement is true, write *T* in the blank. If a statement is false, write *F* in the blank, and then in the space provided, explain why the statement is false.**

_____ **9.** Offspring of the P_1 generation are called F_2 generation.

____

_____ **10.** The law of segregation states that alleles separate during the formation of gametes.

____

_____ **11.** The law of independent assortment states that alleles for different characteristics are distributed to gametes in pairs.

____

_____ **12.** An organism that is homozygous for flower color could have the genotype *Qq*.

____

_____ **13.** Codominance occurs when both alleles for a gene are expressed in a heterozygous offspring, such as would be seen in pink four o'clock flowers.

____

Name ______________________ Class ______________ Date ______________

MULTIPLE CHOICE **Write the letter of the most correct answer in the blank.**

_____ **14.** A heterozygous individual would have the following genotype:

a. *pp* **b.** *YY* **c.** *Zz* **d.** None of these

_____ **15.** In a monohybrid cross between a homozygous dominant parent and a homozygous recessive parent, one would predict the offspring to be

a. 3:4 homozygous dominant.
b. 2:4 heterozygous.
c. 1:4 homozygous recessive.
d. all heterozygous.

_____ **16.** In a monohybrid cross between two heterozygous parents, one would expect the offspring to be

a. 1 *pp* : 3 *PP*. **b.** 3 *Pp* : 1 *pp*. **c.** 1 *PP* : 2 *Pp* : 1 *pp*. **d.** all *Pp*.

_____ **17.** In guinea pigs, black fur is dominant. A black guinea pig is crossed with a white guinea pig. If the litter contains a white offspring, the genotype of the black-haired parent is probably

a. homozygous dominant.
b. heterozygous.
c. homozygous recessive.
d. None of the above.

_____ **18.** Segregation of alleles occurs during

a. mitosis. **b.** meiosis. **c.** fertilization. **d.** pollination.

_____ **19.** If two parents with dominant phenotypes produce an offspring with a recessive phenotype, then probably

a. both parents are heterozygous.
b. one parent is heterozygous.
c. both parents are homozygous.
d. one parent is homozygous.

_____ **20.** A trait occurring in 400 offspring out of a total of 1,600 offspring has a probability of

a. .04. **b.** .25. **c.** .50. **d.** .75.

_____ **21.** Suppose you have found a new species of plant. Some of the plants have yellow flowers, and some have red flowers. You cross a red-flowering plant with a yellow-flowering plant. All of the offspring have orange flowers. Suggest a possible genotype for the offspring.

a. *RR*
b. *Rr*
c. *R′R′*
d. *rr*

_____ **22.** The diagram at right represents a Punnett square of a

a. dihybrid cross.
b. monohybrid cross.
c. homozygous × homozygous cross.
d. dominant × recessive cross.

	GI	Gi	gI	gi
GI				
Gi			X	
gI				
gi				

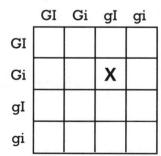

_____ **23.** Refer again to the diagram above. The genotype of the cell labeled *X* is

a. *GGII*. **b.** *GgIi*. **c.** *ggii*. **d.** *GGIi*.

Name ______________________ Class ____________ Date ____________

SHORT ANSWER **Answer the questions in the space provided.**

24. List the steps in Mendel's experiments on pea plants. Include the P generation, F_1 generation, and F_2 generation.

____

____

____

25. In the space below, write the equation for probability.

____

26. Distinguish between codominance and incomplete dominance. Give an example of each type of inheritance.

____

____

____

27. Purple flowers are completely dominant in pea plants. How can you determine the genotype of a purple-flowering pea plant? Draw a Punnett square for each of the possible genotypes.

____

____

28. In tomatoes, red fruit color is dominant to yellow fruit color. Predict the genotypic ratio of offspring produced by crossing a homozygous dominant parent with a homozygous recessive parent. Draw a Punnett square to illustrate your prediction.

____

____

29. In pea plants, yellow seeds are dominant to green seeds. Predict the genotypic ratio of offspring produced by crossing two parents heterozygous for this trait. Draw a Punnett square to illustrate your prediction.

____

____

Name ______________________ Class ____________ Date ____________

DRAWING CONCLUSIONS **Follow the directions given below.**

30. The Punnet square below illustrates a prediction of color and texture in garden peas. Refer to the Punnett square as you answer the following questions.

	QT	Qt	qT	qt
QT	QQTT	QQTt	QqTT	______
Qt	QQTt	QQtt	QqTt	______
qT	QqTT	QqTt	qqTT	______
qt	QqTt	Qqtt	qqTt	______

Q = green
q = yellow
T = smooth
t = wrinkled

a. Does the Punnett square represent a monohybrid cross or a dihybrid cross? How do you know?

____

____

____

b. List the genotypes of the parents.

____

c. Complete the Punnett square. Then list the genotypes predicted by the Punnett square.

____

____

d. Give the genotypic ratio predicted by the Punnett square for the cross.

____

____

e. Give the phenotypic ratio predicted by the Punnett square for the cross.

____

____

Name ______________________ Class ____________ Date ____________

CHAPTER 10 TEST

NUCLEIC ACIDS AND PROTEIN SYNTHESIS

MATCHING **Write the correct letter in the blank before each numbered term.**

______ 1. anticodon

______ 2. codon

______ 3. deoxyribose

______ 4. double helix

______ 5. nucleotides

______ 6. peptide bond

______ 7. ribosome

______ 8. uracil

a. site of translation

b. repeating subunits of DNA and RNA

c. group of three sequential bases of mRNA

d. substitutes for thymine in RNA

e. links together amino acids in a protein

f. identifies the specific amino acid for tRNA

g. sugar found in DNA

h. spiral shape of DNA

TRUE-FALSE **If a statement is true, write *T* in the blank. If a statement is false, write *F* in the blank, and then in the space provided, explain why the statement is false.**

______ 9. Replication starts at one end of the DNA molecule and proceeds to the other end.

____

______ 10. Transcription begins at a promoter region and continues until RNA polymerase reaches a stop codon.

____

______ 11. Translation is the process of assembling amino acids.

____

______ 12. In a eukaryotic cell, DNA carries the information for protein synthesis from the nucleus to the cytoplasm.

____

______ 13. In general, every organism has its own version of the genetic code.

____

Name ______________________ Class ______________ Date ______________

MULTIPLE CHOICE **Write the letter of the most correct answer in the blank.**

______ **14.** A large region of DNA that directs the formation of a protein is called a

a. promoter. **b.** nucleotide. **c.** monomer. **d.** gene.

______ **15.** Which of the following bonds to one specific type of amino acid?

a. mRNA **b.** tRNA **c.** rRNA **d.** DNA

______ **16.** New mRNA is made through the process of

a. duplication. **b.** transcription. **c.** translation. **d.** crystallography.

______ **17.** Complementary base pairing links

a. amino acids.
b. nitrogen-containing bases.
c. phosphate groups.
d. proteins.

______ **18.** Damaged DNA is usually repaired by

a. purines. **b.** nucleotides. **c.** enzymes. **d.** ribosomes.

______ **19.** During replication, the two strands of DNA separate at a point called a

a. helicase. **b.** ribosome. **c.** replication fork. **d.** mutation.

______ **20.** A section of one DNA strand has the sequence ACCGAGGTT. What is the sequence of an mRNA transcribed from this section of DNA?

a. ACCGAGGUU **b.** ACCGAGGTT **c.** TGGCTCCAA **d.** UGGCUCCAA

______ **21.** In the nucleic acid shown at right, the structure labeled *X* represents a(n)

a. nitrogen-containing base.
b. deoxyribose molecule.
c. amino acid.
d. phosphate group.

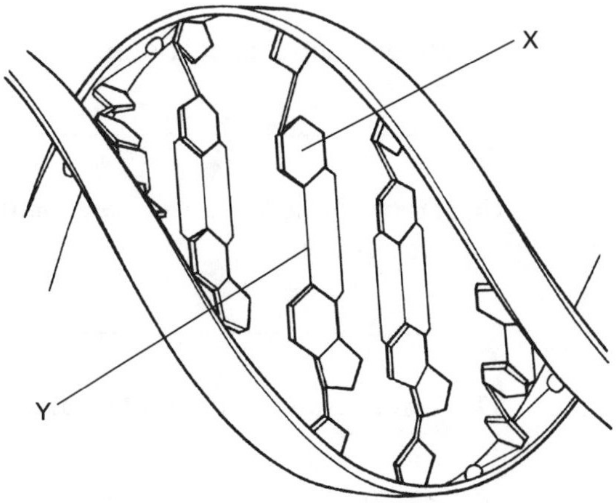

______ **22.** Which type bond will form at the point labeled *Y* in the figure shown at right?

a. peptide bond
b. covalent bond
c. hydrogen bond
d. nitrogen bond

______ **23.** Which type of molecule is shown in the diagram at right?

a. tRNA
b. mRNA
c. stop codon
d. methionine

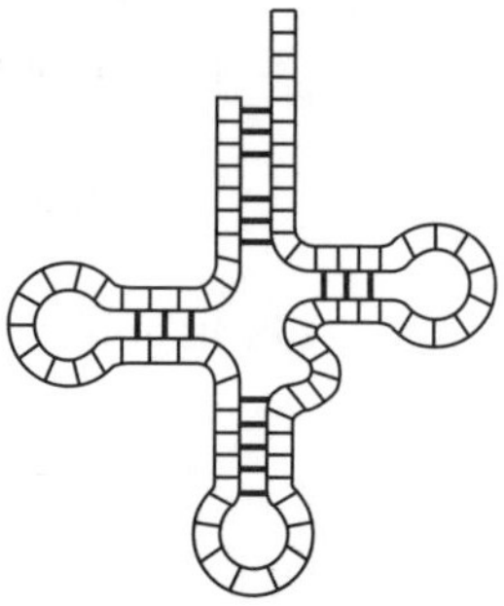

Name ______________________ Class ____________ Date ____________

SHORT ANSWER **Answer each question in the space provided.**

24. Describe the differences between transcription and translation.

25. Compare the structure of DNA with the structure of RNA.

26. Explain the significance of the start codon and the stop codons.

27. Describe the structure and function of three different types of RNA.

28. List the steps of DNA replication.

29. Distinguish between a termination signal and a stop codon.

Name ______________________ Class ______________ Date ______________

DRAWING CONCLUSIONS **Follow the directions given below.**

30. The data in the table below show the amount of each type of nucleotide by percentage found in samples of DNA taken from the organisms listed. Refer to the table as you answer the following questions.

Distribution (in percent) of Nitrogen-Containing Bases in Various Organisms

Organism	G	C	A	T
Mold	15.2	34.3	14.9	35.1
Plant	19.7	41.2	19.5	42.1
Mollusk	17.4	32.3	17.9	34.7
Reptile	12.9	35.6	13.2	35.7
Mammal	14.6	39.5	13.8	37.6

a. List the terms that the abbreviations G, C, A, and T refer to.

____

____

b. Describe the pairing behavior of nitrogen-containing bases in DNA and RNA.

____

____

____

c. Do the data support the base-pairing rules? Why or why not?

____

____

____

d. Do the data support the near-universality of the genetic code? Explain your answer.

____

____

e. What percentage of uracil would you expect to find in an mRNA molecule isolated from the mollusk referred to in the table? Explain your answer.

____

____

____

Name ______________________ Class ____________ Date ____________

CHAPTER 11 TEST

GENE EXPRESSION

MATCHING **Write the correct letter in the blank before each numbered term.**

_____ **1.** oncogene

_____ **2.** mutation

_____ **3.** euchromatin

_____ **4.** tumor suppressor gene

_____ **5.** enhancer

_____ **6.** morphogenesis

_____ **7.** homeotic gene

_____ **8.** carcinogen

a. prevents uncontrolled cell division

b. substance that increases the risk of cancer

c. noncoding control sequence in a eukaryotic gene

d. gene that causes cancer

e. development of an organism's form

f. regulates development during morphogenesis

g. changes in a cell's DNA

h. uncoiled form of DNA

TRUE-FALSE **If a statement is true, write *T* in the blank. If a statement is false, write *F* in the blank, and then in the space provided, explain why the statement is false.**

_____ **9.** Structural genes code for specific polypeptides.

____

_____ **10.** Exons do not code for amino acids and are not translated into proteins.

____

_____ **11.** Benign tumors usually invade healthy tissue.

____

_____ **12.** Introns are sections of a gene that are translated into proteins.

____

_____ **13.** A mutagen is a substance that causes mutations within a cell.

____

Name ______________________ Class ____________ Date ____________

MULTIPLE CHOICE Write the letter of the most correct answer in the blank.

_____ **14.** The spread of cancer cells beyond their original site is called

a. gene expression.
b. morphogenesis.
c. metastasis.
d. cell differentiation.

_____ **15.** Pre-mRNA is a form of RNA that contains

a. euchromatin.
b. prokaryotic transcription factors.
c. introns and exons.
d. only exons.

_____ **16.** Operons have been identified in

a. prokaryotes only.
b. eukaryotes only.
c. archaebacteria only.
d. both prokaryotes and eukaryotes.

_____ **17.** Liver cells differ from muscle cells in the same organism because of

a. different chromosomes.
b. morphogenesis.
c. crossing-over.
d. cell differentiation.

_____ **18.** Active transcription in eukaryotes occurs within

a. an operon. **b.** an operator. **c.** euchromatin. **d.** an enhancer.

_____ **19.** The activation of a gene that results in the formation of a protein is called

a. translation. **b.** gene expression. **c.** enhancement. **d.** gene repression.

_____ **20.** An operon consists of

a. a group of operators.
b. a group of structural genes.
c. an operator, a promoter, and structural genes.
d. lactose, polymerase, and operators.

_____ **21.** The structure labeled *X* in the diagram below is called

a. a repressor protein.
b. lactose.
c. a promoter.
d. RNA polymerase.

_____ **22.** The diagram below shows

a. activation. **b.** translation. **c.** repression. **d.** replication.

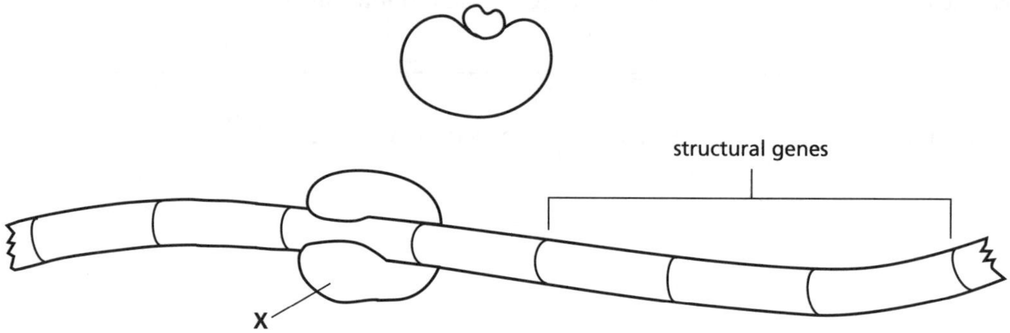

Name ______________________ Class ____________ Date ____________

______ **23.** Normal genes that control a cell's growth and differentiation are called

a. tumor-suppressor genes.
b. oncogenes.
c. proto-oncogenes.
d. growth factors.

SHORT ANSWER Answer the questions in the space provided.

24. How is it beneficial for cells to be able to control gene expression? ______________________

____

____

____

25. Describe the process shown in the diagram below. ______________________

____

____

____

Is this cell prokaryotic or eukaryotic? ______________________

What do the structures labeled *A* and *B* represent? ______________________

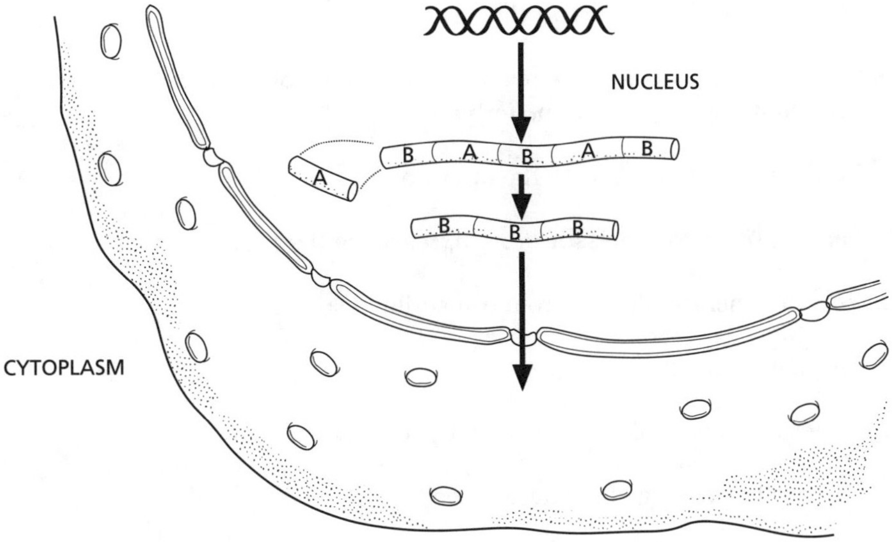

26. List three ways cancer cells differ from normal cells. ______________________

____

____

____

27. Describe how mutations in proto-oncogenes or tumor-suppressor genes could lead to cancer.

____

____

____

28. Describe the role of homeotic genes in the development of *Drosophila.* ______________________

____

____

____

29. Compare the genomes of prokaryotes with those of eukaryotes. ______________________

____

____

____

DRAWING CONCLUSIONS **Follow the directions given below.**

30. The list below represents steps in the regulation of the *lac* operon. Label the steps in the order they occur. The first one has been done for you.

a. ______ Repressor protein binds to the operator.

b. ______ Lactose binds to repressor protein, releasing the protein from the operator.

c. ______ RNA polymerase blocked from transcribing structural genes.

d. ______ Enzymes break down lactose.

e. ______ Structural gene mRNA is translated into enzymes.

f. __1__ Lactose is introduced to bacterial cell.

g. ______ RNA polymerase transcribes structural genes.

Name ______________________ Class ______________ Date ______________

CHAPTER 12 TEST

INHERITANCE PATTERNS AND HUMAN GENETICS

MATCHING Write the correct letter in the blank before each numbered term.

_____ **1.** genetic marker

_____ **2.** chromosome map

_____ **3.** Huntington's disease

_____ **4.** linked genes

_____ **5.** sex linkage

_____ **6.** point mutation

_____ **7.** nondisjunction

_____ **8.** ABO blood group

a. autosomal dominant gene

b. controlled by multiple alleles

c. substitution, deletion, or addition of a single nucleotide

d. piece of DNA closely associated with a gene

e. genes found on the same chromosome

f. determined by crossing-over data

g. failure of homologous chromosomes to separate during meiosis

h. presence of a gene on a sex chromosome

TRUE-FALSE If a statement is true, write *T* in the blank. If a statement is false, write *F* in the blank, and then in the space provided, explain why the statement is false.

_____ **9.** Down syndrome is also known as monosomy-21.

____

_____ **10.** A sex-linked gene is found on one sex chromosome, but not on the other.

____

_____ **11.** Somatic mutations occur in sex chromosomes and can be inherited.

____

_____ **12.** Polygenic traits are controlled by no more than three alleles.

____

_____ **13.** A frame-shift mutation occurs any time a gene mutation results in the insertion or deletion of a number of nucleotides that is not a multiple of three.

____

Name ______________________________ Class ______________ Date ______________

MULTIPLE CHOICE **Write the letter of the most correct answer in the blank.**

_____ **14.** In order to produce a male offspring, an egg must be fertilized by a sperm carrying a(n)

a. Y chromosome.
b. X and a Y chromosome.
c. X chromosome.
d. None of the above

_____ **15.** If two genes are closely arranged on a chromosome, they probably will

a. cross over.
b. segregate separately.
c. control the same trait.
d. be inherited together.

_____ **16.** Which of the following mutations does not affect an organism but can be passed on to offspring?

a. somatic cell **b.** translocation **c.** germ cell **d.** substitution

_____ **17.** Which of the following is a point mutation that does not result in a frame shift?

a. addition **b.** substitution **c.** deletion **d.** inversion

_____ **18.** If two genes cross over 35 percent of the time, how many map units apart are they on a chromosome map?

a. 15.5 **b.** 35 **c.** 50.5 **d.** 70

_____ **19.** Genetic disorders in human chromosomes can be determined by removing a small piece of tissue from a structure that lies between the uterus and the placenta. This procedure is called

a. amniocentesis.
b. fetoscopy.
c. chorionic villi sampling.
d. genetic counseling.

_____ **20.** If the parents of a child have the ABO blood group genotypes I^AI^B and *ii*, what are the possible blood types of the child?

a. A or B **b.** A only **c.** O **d.** AB

_____ **21.** A man and woman are both heterozygous for the pattern-baldness allele, but only the man loses his hair. This is an example of a(n)

a. Y-linked trait.
b. X-linked trait.
c. sex-influenced trait.
d. sex-linked trait.

_____ **22.** The chromosome map below indicates that

a. *X* and *Y* cross over about 15 percent of the time.
b. *X* and *Y* cross over more frequently than X and Z do.
c. *X* and *Z* cross over about 15 percent of the time.
d. *Y* and *Z* cross over about 15 percent of the time.

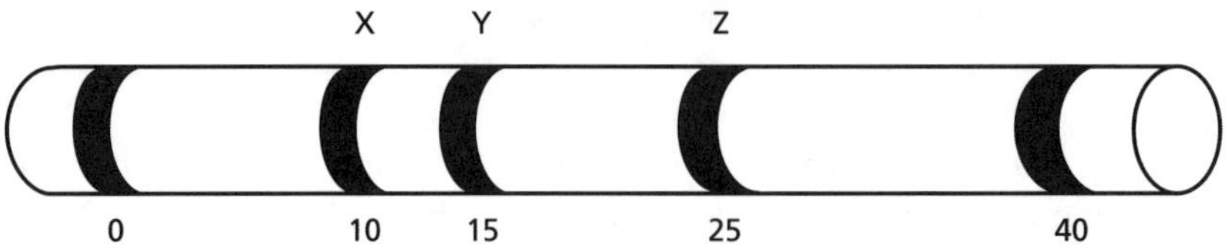

______ **23.** Which of the following genotypes is possible for a person whose ABO blood type is B?

a. I^BI^B
b. *ii*
c. Both a and b
d. None of the above

SHORT ANSWER **Answer the questions in the space provided.**

24. Why is hemophilia carried by females and yet rarely expressed in females?

____

____

25. Describe how linked genes are an exception to Mendel's principle of independent assortment.

____

____

____

26. Describe the difference between a chromosome mutation and a gene mutation.

____

____

____

27. Distinguish between multiple-allele traits and polygenic traits. ______________

____

____

____

28. Use the data table below to draw a chromosome map of traits A, B, and C. Include the number of map units between each trait in your chromosome map.

Crossing-Over Data

Trait	Percentage of cross-over
A and C	5
C and B	15
A and B	20

29. Explain the difference between a sex-linked trait and a sex-influenced trait.

____

____

____

DRAWING CONCLUSIONS Follow the directions given below.

30. Complete the pedigree below based on the information given in *a*. You may have to add shading and symbols to the diagram. Then follow the directions in *b* and *c*.

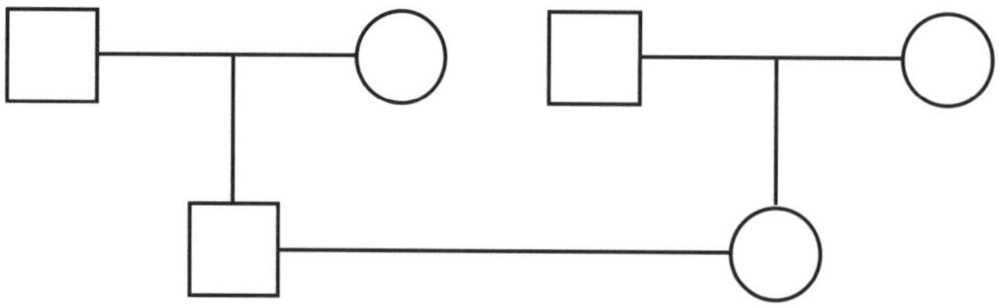

a. Cystic fibrosis is caused by a single-allele recessive trait.

- A husband and wife both have parents who are heterozygous for cystic fibrosis.
- The husband and wife are also heterozygous for the trait.
- Their son has cystic fibrosis.
- Their second child, a daughter, is normal for the trait.
- Their third child, another daughter, is a carrier of the trait.

b. Draw a key for the completed pedigree in the space below.

c. Predict the possible phenotypes of a child born to the F_2 son if the son marries a woman who does not carry the cystic-fibrosis trait.

____

Name ______________________ Class ____________ Date ____________

CHAPTER 13 TEST

DNA TECHNOLOGY

MATCHING Write the correct letter in the blank before each numbered term.

_____ **1.** recombinant DNA

_____ **2.** RFLP analysis

_____ **3.** sticky end

_____ **4.** genetic engineering

_____ **5.** gel electrophoresis

_____ **6.** transgenic organism

_____ **7.** plasmid

_____ **8.** PCR

a. separates DNA fragments by size and charge

b. ring of DNA found in bacteria

c. rapidly multiplies DNA segments

d. combination of DNA from different sources

e. compares different DNA fragments

f. single-stranded part of a DNA fragment that has been cut by restriction enzymes

g. application of molecular genetics

h. host that receives DNA from two different sources

TRUE-FALSE If a statement is true, write *T* in the blank. If a statement is false, write *F* in the blank, and then in the space provided, explain why the statement is false.

_____ **9.** A plasmid is an example of a cloning vector.

____

_____ **10.** A cloning vector has the ability to replicate its DNA and the DNA of a donor gene it may carry.

____

_____ **11.** A DNA fingerprint is a pattern of bands made up of specific fragments of an individual's DNA.

____

_____ **12.** PCR is used to cut DNA into many fragments.

____

_____ **13.** The goal of the Human Genome Project is to prevent any mutations in the human genome.

____

Name ______________________________ Class ______________ Date ______________

MULTIPLE CHOICE **Write the letter of the most correct answer in the blank.**

______ **14.** Which of the following is *not* a current application of genetic engineering?

a. the insertion of pest-resistance genes into crop plants
b. the production of human insulin by bacterial cells
c. the construction of genomic libraries and the identification of specific genes
d. the insertion of normal genes into human fetuses that carry defective genes

______ **15.** Restriction enzymes

a. cleave DNA between G and A in a GAATTC nucleotide sequence.
b. cleave DNA at specific sites within specific sequences of DNA.
c. recognize specific genes and cleave them out of a DNA molecule.
d. All of the above

______ **16.** Recombinant DNA is

a. plasmid DNA to which a piece of foreign DNA has been added.
b. any combination of DNA from a bacterium and a eukaryote.
c. any combination of DNA from two or more different sources.
d. bacterial DNA to which a cloning vector has been added.

______ **17.** A pattern of bands made up of specific DNA fragments is a

a. restriction enzyme.
b. cloning vector.
c. homeotic gene.
d. DNA fingerprint.

______ **18.** A process that separates DNA fragments according to size and charge is

a. gel electrophoresis.
b. RFLP analysis.
c. polymerase chain reaction.
d. the isolation of a gene.

______ **19.** Gene therapy currently

a. can be used to treat certain diseases, such as cystic fibrosis.
b. can be used to cure certain diseases, such as cystic fibrosis.
c. provides cures for diseases that can be passed on to the next generation.
d. All of the above

______ **20.** The purpose of the Human Genome Project is

a. to determine the nucleotide sequence of the entire human genome.
b. to answer fundamental questions about genome structure and function.
c. to map the location of every gene on each of the chromosomes of humans.
d. All of the above

______ **21.** An exact copy of a gene is called a

a. plasmid. **b.** donor gene. **c.** cloning vector. **d.** gene clone.

______ **22.** An advantage of genetically engineered vaccines over traditional vaccines is that they

a. are effective against unidentified pathogens.
b. are more specific to the disease they protect against.
c. may be safer.
d. are easier to produce.

Name ______________________ Class ____________ Date ____________

_____ 23. DNA technology is being used to produce medicines by

a. growing genetically engineered bacteria and collecting human DNA that they produce.
b. growing genetically engineered bacteria and collecting human proteins that they produce.
c. Neither a nor b
d. Both a and b

SHORT ANSWER Answer the questions in the space provided.

24. Describe the role of each of the following in a gene-transfer experiment:

cloning vector ______________________________

donor gene ______________________________

host organism ______________________________

25. What is gene therapy? How does it differ from traditional treatments? ______________________________

____

____

26. Describe two ways that DNA fingerprinting has been used. ______________________________

____

____

27. Discuss the accuracy of DNA fingerprints. ______________________________

____

____

28. List one potential advantage and one potential disadvantage of genetic engineering.

____

____

29. The diagrams below represent steps involved in making a DNA fingerprint. Sequence the steps by writing the appropriate numerals in the spaces provided.

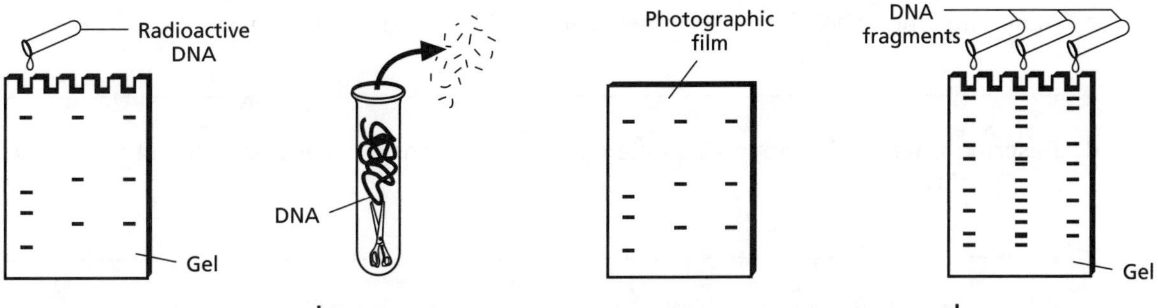

a ________ b ________ c ________ d ________

Name ________________________ Class ______________ Date ______________

DRAWING CONCLUSIONS **Follow the directions given below.**

30. The figure below represents some of the steps involved in making recombinant DNA. Step 1 shows a segment of DNA that is being cut by the restriction enzyme *Eco*R1. Answer the following questions based on the figure.

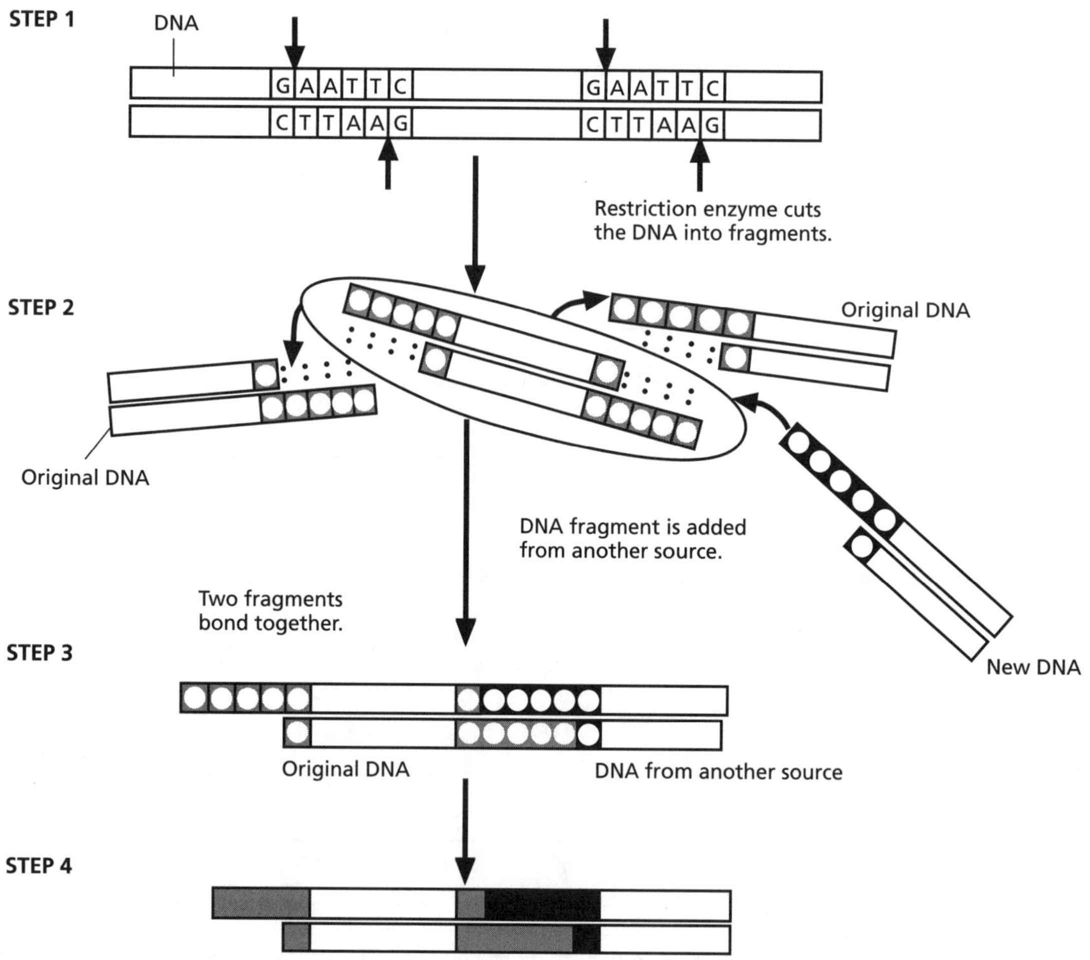

a. Complete Steps 2 and 3 by writing the first letter of each missing nucleotide in the blanks provided in the figure (A = adenine, G = guanine, T = thymine, C = cytosine).

b. What role do restriction enzymes play in genetic engineering? ______________________________

____

c. Name the type of bonds that form between the sticky ends in the figure.

____

d. Describe what would happen if a different restriction enzyme were used to cut the second source of DNA.

____

e. What bacterial structure becomes a cloning vector when DNA is inserted into it?

____

Name ______________________ Class __________ Date __________

CHAPTER 14 TEST

ORIGIN OF LIFE

MATCHING **Write the correct letter in the blank before each numbered term.**

_____ **1.** biogenesis

_____ **2.** endosymbiosis

_____ **3.** archaebacteria

_____ **4.** cyanobacteria

_____ **5.** ribozyme

_____ **6.** coacervates

_____ **7.** chemosynthesis

_____ **8.** spontaneous generation

a. photosynthetic, unicellular prokaryotes

b. production of organic molecules by oxidation of inorganic molecules

c. life arising from nonliving things

d. collections of droplets composed of various organic molecules

e. one organism living inside another in a mutually beneficial relationship

f. RNA that can act as a catalyst

g. life arising from other life

h. often chemosynthetic, unicellular prokaryotes

TRUE-FALSE **If a statement is true, write *T* in the blank. If a statement is false, write *F* in the blank, and then in the space provided, explain why the statement is false.**

_____ **9.** Heterotrophic prokaryotes evolved before autotrophic prokaryotes.

____

_____ **10.** Spontaneous generation occurs in microscopic organisms but not in visible organisms.

____

_____ **11.** Ribozymes can produce other ribozymes under controlled laboratory conditions.

____

_____ **12.** The proportions of gases in the atmosphere of Earth today are the same as they were 4 billion years ago.

____

_____ **13.** Earth is thought to have formed from repeated collisions of debris in space.

____

Name ______________________ Class ____________ Date ____________

MULTIPLE CHOICE **Write the letter of the most correct answer in the blank.**

_____ **14.** You are determining the age of an organic object using the carbon-14 dating technique and you know that the half-life of carbon-14 is 5,715 years. If only 25 percent of the original amount of carbon-14 is left in the object, approximately how old is the object?

a. 57,150 years **b.** 11,430 years **c.** 5,715 years **d.** 1,143 years

_____ **15.** A French botanist wrote in 1609, "There is a tree . . . in Scotland. From this tree leaves are falling; upon one side they strike the water and slowly turn into fishes, upon the other they strike the land and turn into birds." What biological hypothesis or principle was he describing?

a. spontaneous generation
b. endosymbiosis
c. biogenetic evolution
d. pasteurization

_____ **16.** Before life arose on this planet, which of these gases was present in the atmosphere?

a. oxygen **b.** ozone **c.** carbon **d.** nitrogen

_____ **17.** What type of organic molecules were Miller and Urey able to produce in their 1953 experiment?

a. proteins **b.** phospholipids **c.** carbohydrates **d.** amino acids

_____ **18.** Which of the following is true of microspheres and living cells?

a. Both have organelles.
b. Both have membranes.
c. Both grow and have genetic material.
d. Both use oxygen.

_____ **19.** Based on the conditions of early Earth and experimentation, scientists have inferred that the first cellular life-forms were anaerobic prokaryotes and that they used

a. photosynthesis to generate energy.
b. ozone for respiration.
c. organic molecules for food.
d. chemosynthesis for respiration.

_____ **20.** What role did ozone play in the evolution of early life on this planet?

a. The ozone layer protected Earth's surface from ultraviolet radiation, which damages DNA.
b. Early life was damaged by oxygen, but it used ozone as a means of respiration.
c. Ozone was an important element in the processes of chemosynthesis and photosynthesis.
d. Breaking the chemical bonds in ozone molecules released energy for use by cyanobacteria.

_____ **21.** Aerobic respiration may have protected early unicellular organisms from damage by

a. binding ozone.
b. binding oxygen.
c. capturing ultraviolet radiation from the sun.
d. slowing radioactive decay of important elements.

_____ **22.** Two types of autotrophy include

a. spontaneous generation and biogenesis.
b. chemosynthesis and photosynthesis.
c. biogenesis and photosynthesis.
d. biogenesis and chemosynthesis.

_____ **23.** The first life-forms arose sometime after the formation of Earth was complete and the planet surface cooled, probably less than

a. 4 million years ago.
b. 40 million years ago.
c. 400 million years ago.
d. 4 billion years ago.

SHORT ANSWER Answer the questions in the space provided.

24. Why is the carbon-14 dating technique used only for organic objects less than about 60,000 years old? ____

____

25. Francesco Redi's experiment was one of the first documented examples of a controlled experiment. Describe the control group, the experimental group, and the independent and dependent variables.

____

____

____

26. What were the objections to Spallanzani's experimental design and conclusions, and how did Pasteur address these criticisms in his own experiment? ____

____

____

____

27. How does the discovery of microspheres and coacervates support hypotheses of the origin of life?

____

____

28. In what respect are RNA molecules and proteins similar? ____

____

____

29. Explain the hypothesis of endosymbiosis with respect to the origins of two organelles found in eukaryotic cells. ____

____

____

____

Name ______________________ Class __________ Date __________

DRAWING CONCLUSIONS **Follow the directions given below.**

30. The figure below illustrates the Miller-Urey apparatus. Use the figure to answer the questions that follow.

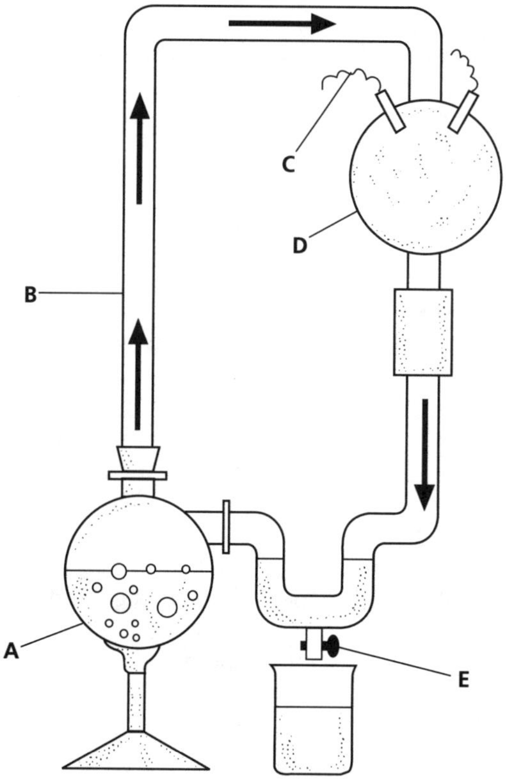

a. What substance is contained in the reaction chamber labeled *A?*

____

b. What substance travels through the tubing labeled *B?*

____

c. What is the structure labeled *C,* and what is its function?

____

____

d. What gases are present in the reaction chamber labeled *D?*

____

e. What is released at the valve labeled *E?*

____

Name ______________________ Class ____________ Date ____________

CHAPTER 15 TEST

EVOLUTION: EVIDENCE AND THEORY

MATCHING **Write the correct letter in the blank before each numbered term.**

_____ **1.** natural selection

_____ **2.** fitness

_____ **3.** acquired trait

_____ **4.** biogeography

_____ **5.** fossil

_____ **6.** law of superposition

_____ **7.** convergent evolution

_____ **8.** adaptive radiation

a. the lowest stratum in a cross section is the oldest

b. trace of long-dead organism

c. process which results in similar phenotypes

d. process in which many related species evolved from a single ancestral species

e. is not determined by genes

f. an organism's contribution to the next generation

g. differential reproductive success caused by the environment

h. study of geographical distribution of fossils

TRUE-FALSE **If a statement is true, write *T* in the blank. If a statement is false, write *F* in the blank, and then in the space provided, explain why the statement is false.**

_____ **9.** The relative age, but not the absolute age, of a fossil can be inferred using the law of superposition.

____

_____ **10.** Darwin was the first scientist to suggest a mechanism by which living things could evolve over time.

____

_____ **11.** Analogous structures in living organisms are a clue to common ancestry.

____

_____ **12.** The fossil record shows that organisms arise only in areas where identical organisms once lived.

____

_____ **13.** Darwin realized that environmental change is often gradual, therefore species modification may be gradual as well.

____

Name ______________________ Class ____________ Date ____________

MULTIPLE CHOICE **Write the letter of the most correct answer in the blank.**

_____ **14.** Analogous features

- **a.** look different and have dissimilar embryological origins.
- **b.** look similar and have dissimilar embryological origins.
- **c.** may look different or similar but have similar embryological origins.
- **d.** None of the above

_____ **15.** Although they do not have recent common ancestors, birds and bats have similar body shapes necessary for powered flight. What pattern of evolution does this relationship represent?

- **a.** divergent evolution
- **b.** convergent evolution
- **c.** vestigial structures
- **d.** conserved genotype

_____ **16.** The pattern of evolution that is usually a response to different habitats is

- **a.** artificial selection.
- **b.** coevolution.
- **c.** divergent evolution.
- **d.** convergent evolution.

_____ **17.** Which of the following is an acquired human characteristic?

- **a.** colorblindness in females
- **b.** sickle cell anemia
- **c.** the presence of a tailbone in humans
- **d.** large muscles from weight lifting

_____ **18.** Under which circumstance is adaptive radiation most likely to occur?

- **a.** The polar icecaps have melted, raising the level of the oceans and isolating species on mountaintops that are now islands.
- **b.** A hurricane has blown a single breeding pair of rats onto a deserted island that has many varied habitats.
- **c.** An asteroid has smashed into Earth and destroyed an isthmus that previously had joined two large continents.
- **d.** The jetstream has shifted, and a flock of birds have been stranded on an isolated island covered entirely with grass.

_____ **19.** Which of the following pairs of structures are analogous?

- **a.** horse's leg and human forearm
- **b.** insect's wing and bird's wing
- **c.** bat's wing and dolphin's flipper
- **d.** hummingbird's wing and seal's flipper

_____ **20.** The similarity in the body shape of a shark and of a porpoise is an example of

- **a.** divergent evolution.
- **b.** convergent evolution.
- **c.** coevolution.
- **d.** vestigial structures.

_____ **21.** What does the presence of a vestigial structure in a modern organism indicate?

- **a.** Natural selection prepares the anatomy of organisms so that in the future the vestigial structure can be used.
- **b.** The vestigial structure was not used by the modern organism, so it became nonfunctional within the organism's lifetime.
- **c.** A limited number of genes are expressed during the lifetime of an organism.
- **d.** The structure probably was functional in some ancestor of the modern organism.

______ **22.** Which of these pairs of fossils would you expect to find in the same sedimentary strata?

a. trilobites and early mammals
b. dinosaurs and humans
c. trilobites and dinosaurs
d. dinosaurs and early mammals

______ **23.** In order to be considered an evolutionarily favorable trait for an organism, a trait must increase the individual's

a. fitness.
b. health.
c. lifespan.
d. range.

SHORT ANSWER Answer the questions in the space provided.

24. Explain Lamarck's theory of evolution, and tell what he was right about and what he was wrong about.

____

____

25. Recount two of Darwin's observations made during the voyage of the *Beagle* that led to his hypothesis of species modification over time.

____

____

26. How is the breeding of domestic animals such as dogs similar or dissimilar to natural selection?

____

____

27. Briefly explain the first of Darwin's two major theories: descent with modification.

____

____

28. Briefly explain the second of Darwin's theories: modification by natural selection.

____

____

29. In the figure at right, what similarities would cause scientists to infer that these two organisms shared an evolutionary history?

____

____

____

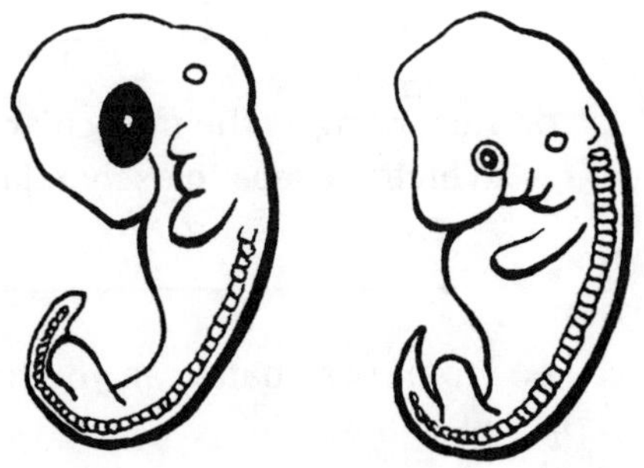

Name ______________________ Class ____________ Date ____________

DRAWING CONCLUSIONS **Follow the directions given below.**

30. Satellite photos recently revealed the existence of an unexplored group of islands, shown below, named the Latin Archipelago.

You are the leader of a natural-history expedition to seek out new life-forms on the islands. On your team are geologists, biogeographers, and molecular biologists. After extensive effort, they present you with data about three new animal species, which you name *A, B,* and *C.* Answer the following questions based on the cross-section of geological strata shown at top right and the table shown at bottom right.

Geological Cross-Sections

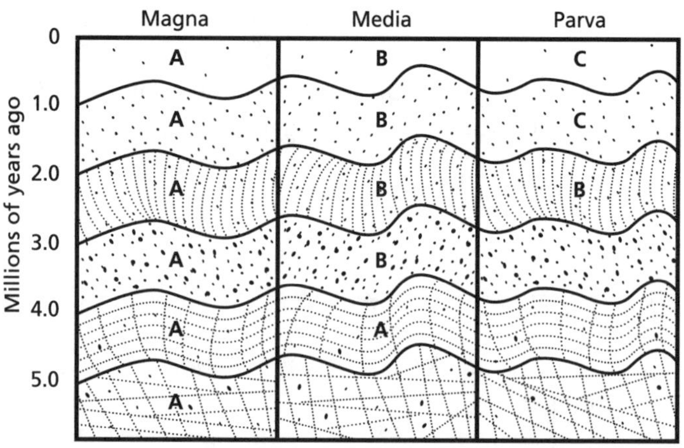

Hemoglobin—Amino Acid Differences

	Species A	Species B	Species C
Species A	0	5	10
Species B	5	0	5
Species C	10	5	0

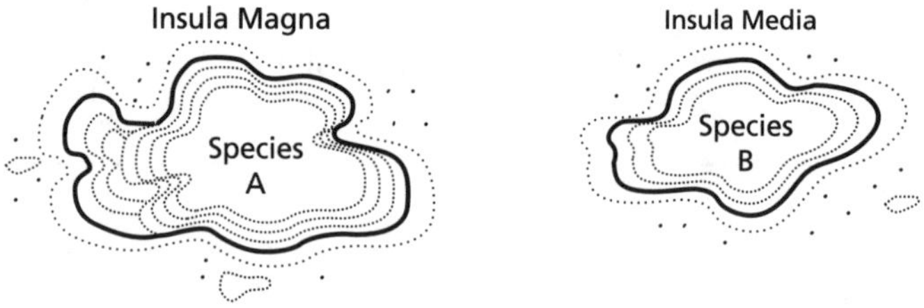

a. Which is the oldest species, and which is the youngest species?

____

b. Are the results of the molecular examination (the hemoglobin–amino acid differences) consistent with the geological-strata results?

____

c. Would you predict that the environments on the three islands are the same or different?

____

d. According to the molecular and geological data, which species are most closely related? Which are least closely related?

____

e. From these data, can you tell if the environment on each island is stable?

____

Name ______________________ Class ____________ Date ____________

CHAPTER 16 TEST

THE EVOLUTION OF POPULATIONS AND SPECIATION

MATCHING **Write the correct letter in the blank before each numbered term.**

_____ **1.** morphology

_____ **2.** reproductive isolation

_____ **3.** evolution

_____ **4.** gene flow

_____ **5.** sexual selection

_____ **6.** assortative mating

_____ **7.** mutation

_____ **8.** geographic isolation

a. changes in a population's genetic material

b. choosing a mate that resembles oneself

c. an organism's structure and appearance

d. alterations of DNA

e. females choosing a mate based on appearance

f. anatomincal barriers to successful breeding

g. physical separation of populations

h. movement of genes between populations

TRUE-FALSE **If a statement is true, write *T* in the blank. If a statement is false, write *F* in the blank, and then in the space provided, explain why the statement is false.**

_____ **9.** Individual organisms in a population evolve.

____

_____ **10.** Gene flow occurs as a result of immigration but not of emigration.

____

_____ **11.** Disruptive selection can lead to speciation.

____

_____ **12.** Genetic drift is most obvious in small populations.

____

_____ **13.** In stabilizing selection, one extreme of a range of phenotypes is favored.

____

Name ______________________ Class ____________ Date ____________

MULTIPLE CHOICE **Write the letter of the most correct answer in the blank.**

______ **14.** Genotypic variation in a population can increase through

a. maintenance of genetic equilibrium for many generations.
b. an increase of the quality and quantity of available food.
c. recombination of genes by independent assortment.
d. prevention of immigration and emigration between populations.

______ **15.** Genetic drift is

a. the movement of genes between populations.
b. changes in allele frequency caused by random events.
c. physical isolation of a population by geography.
d. immigration and emigration among populations.

______ **16.** What is a *consequence* of violating the Hardy-Weinberg genetic equilibrium assumptions?

a. evolution
b. reproductive isolation
c. mutation
d. sexual selection

______ **17.** The most common kind of selection, which results in the average form of a trait, is

a. sexual selection.
b. stabilizing selection.
c. direction selection.
d. disruptive selection.

______ **18.** The biological species concept is useful only for

a. extinct organisms.
b. organisms that reproduce asexually.
c. organisms that reproduce sexually.
d. None of the above

______ **19.** The morphological-species concept classifies organisms on the basis of their

a. ecological relationships.
b. structure and appearance.
c. ability to reproduce.
d. behavior.

______ **20.** Sexual selection is a form of

a. reproductive isolation.
b. morphological speciation.
c. genetic drift.
d. nonrandom mating.

______ **21.** Speciation often results from

a. directional selection.
b. sexual selection.
c. disruptive selection.
d. stabilizing selection.

______ **22.** Mice that have been separated into two populations by the construction of a new road through their range are considered

a. geographically isolated.
b. reproductively isolated.
c. prezygotically isolated.
d. morphologically isolated.

______ **23.** One source of genotypic variation that occurs within a single organism and that may be the result of environmental factors is

a. reproduction isolation.
b. gene flow.
c. assortative mating.
d. mutation.

Name ______________________ Class ____________ Date ____________

SHORT ANSWER **Answer the questions in the space provided.**

24. Explain why genetic drift is more likely to occur in a population with few members.

____

____

25. What are the five conditions that must be met to establish Hardy-Weinberg genetic equilibrium in a population?

____

____

____

26. What is the effect of gene flow between populations?

____

____

27. Explain the significance of the bell curve with respect to traits in a population.

____

____

____

28. Explain the difference between punctuated equilibrium and gradual evolutionary change.

____

____

____

29. The figure below shows a sample of four o'clock flowers. These flowers show incomplete dominance for color. Flowers with homozygous dominant genotype (*RR*) are red; flowers with homozygous recessive genotype (*rr*) are white, and flowers with heterozygous genotype (*Rr*) are pink. Compute the allele frequency and the phenotype frequency for the flowers shown.

____

____

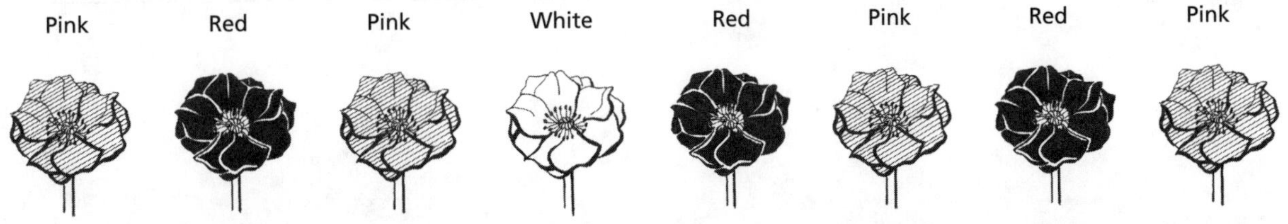

Name ______________________________ Class ______________ Date ____________

DRAWING CONCLUSIONS **Follow the directions given below.**

30. The graphs shown below show the distribution of size of leeches found in Carver Creek at the beginning and end of a 40-year period. Answer the following questions based on the graphs.

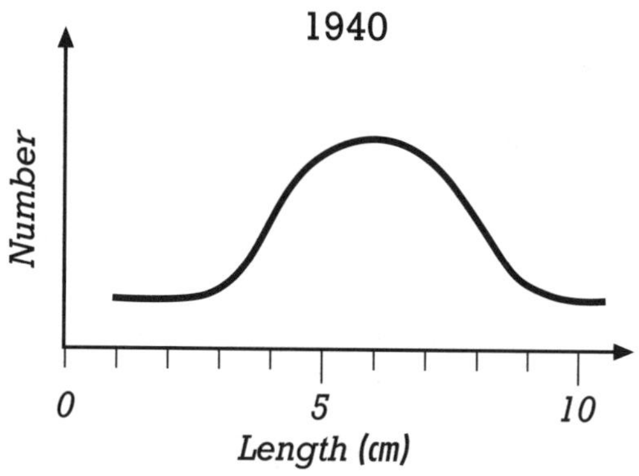

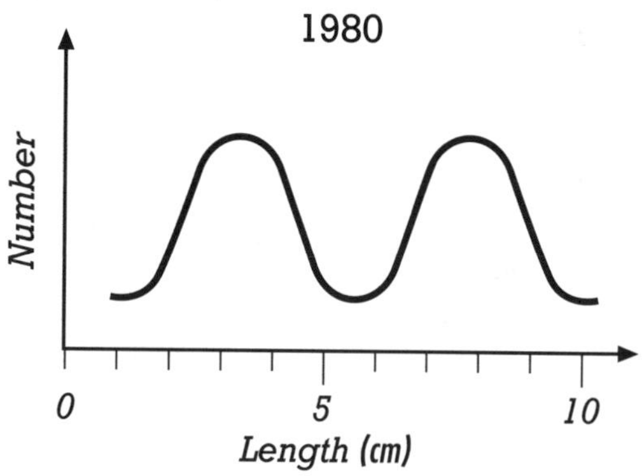

a. Which type of selection occurred in this leech population before 1940?

____

b. Which type of selection was occurring in this leech population between 1940 and 1980?

____

c. What is the most common body length of leeches in 1940 and in 1980?

____

____

d. In 1941, a species of fish that eats leeches was introduced to Carver Creek. Based on the data in the graph, what would be a logical hypothesis regarding the fish's food preference?

____

____

e. How would you test the hypothesis you proposed in item d?

____

____

____

____

Name ______________________ Class ____________ Date ____________

CHAPTER 17 TEST

HUMAN EVOLUTION

MATCHING **Write the correct letter in the blank before each numbered term.**

______ **1.** *Homo sapiens* (modern)

______ **2.** *Australopithecus afarensis*

______ **3.** *Homo erectus*

______ **4.** *Australopithecus robustus*

______ **5.** *Ardipithecus ramidus*

______ **6.** *Homo habilis*

______ **7.** *Australopithecus africanus*

______ **8.** *Homo sapiens* (Neanderthal)

a. cranial capacity (*cc*) of 600–800 cm^3; tool user; meat eater

b. *cc* of 1450 cm^3; protruding teeth and brow

c. *cc* of 450–600 cm^3; heavy skull; large teeth

d. *cc* unknown; might be bipedal

e. *cc* of 475 cm^3; bipedal; "Lucy"

f. *cc* of 1400 cm^3; tall; no brow ridge; language

g. *cc* of 700–1250 cm^3; tool and fire user

h. *cc* of 430–550 cm^3; no tools; bipedal

TRUE-FALSE **If a statement is true, write *T* in the blank. If a statement is false, write *F* in the blank, and then in the space provided, explain why the statement is false.**

______ **9.** Toolmaking and language apparently developed in the australopithecines.

____

______ **10.** *Homo erectus* was probably the first hominid to leave the African continent.

____

______ **11.** During the course of hominid evolution, walking upright, tool use, and language development occurred at the same time.

____

______ **12.** *Australopithecus afarensis* ("Lucy") is probably a human ancestor, whereas *Australopithecus robustus* is not.

____

______ **13.** On the average, *Homo sapiens* (Neanderthal) had a larger cranial capacity than modern *Homo sapiens.*

____

Name ______________________ Class ____________ Date ____________

MULTIPLE CHOICE **Write the letter of the most correct answer in the blank.**

_____ **14.** What two characteristics are common to all primates?

a. opposable thumbs and the same dental formula
b. opposable big toes and rotating shoulder joints
c. identical DNA and large brain capacity
d. color vision and movable fingers and toes

_____ **15.** Which of the following is a prosimian primate?

a. marmoset **b.** gorilla **c.** tarsier **d.** monkey

_____ **16.** Which of these hominid characteristics could be used by scientists to infer that a fossil primate was bipedal?

a. C-shaped spine
b. S-shaped spine
c. flat pelvis
d. opposable big toe

_____ **17.** Why was Donald Johanson's discovery of *Australopithecus afarensis* ("Lucy") so important to the understanding of human evolution?

a. Lucy was the first hominid whose species was thought to have language.
b. Stone tools found with Lucy indicated tool use by this species.
c. Lucy's teeth indicated that *A. afarensis* were meat-eaters and therefore hunters.
d. Lucy's cranial capacity was small, indicating that bipedalism preceded the evolution of a large brain.

_____ **18.** All members of the genus *Homo* share which of the following characteristics?

a. tool making
b. written language
c. opposable big toe
d. protruding brow ridge

_____ **19.** According to the hominid phylogenetic tree shown below, which three species would have coexisted about 100,000 to 50,000 years ago?

a. *Australopithecus afarensis, A. africanus,* and *Homo habilis*
b. *Homo erectus, H. sapiens* (modern), and *H. sapiens* (Neanderthal)
c. *Homo habilis, H. erectus,* and *Australopithecus robustus*
d. *Australopithecus anamensis, A. boisei,* and *A. robustus*

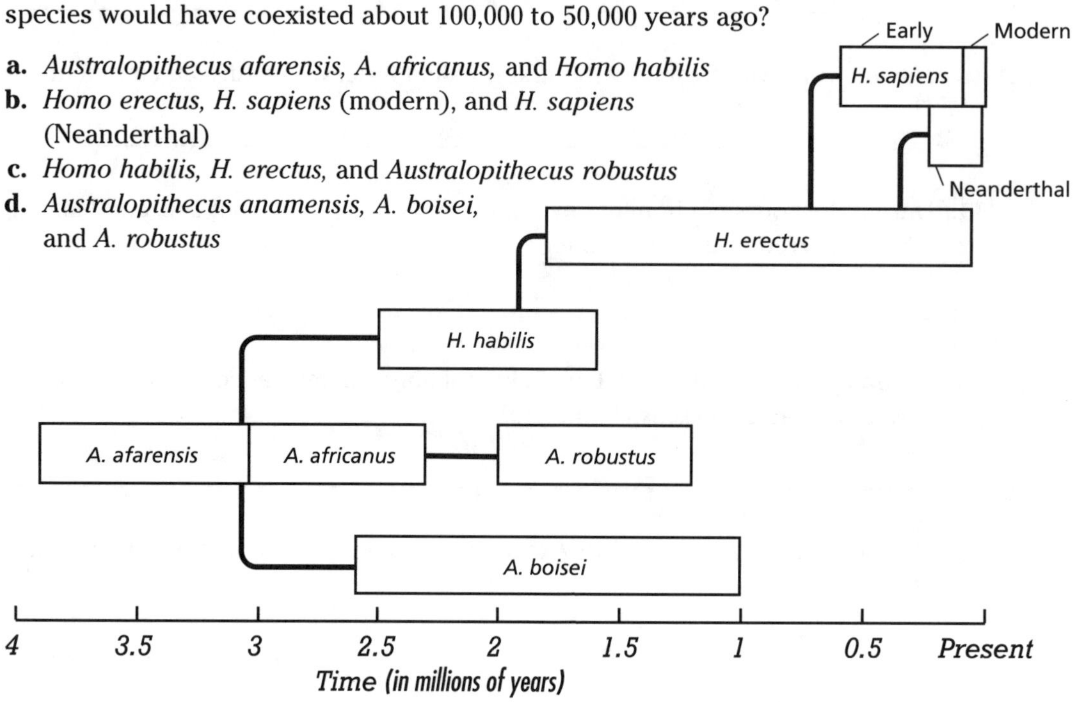

______ **20.** Which statement is true regarding the genus *Australopithecus?*

a. The size of the brain of *Australopithecus* was the same as that of members of the genus *Homo,* but the body size was much smaller.
b. Stone tools are commonly found with the fossil remains of *Australopithecus.*
c. Most members of this genus were quadrupedal.
d. Most members of the genus *Australopithecus* are not direct ancestors of modern humans.

______ **21.** What characteristic must *Ardipithecus ramidus* show to be considered a hominid?

a. tool use **b.** language **c.** bipedalism **d.** opposable thumb

______ **22.** Which of the following statements best describes the phylogenetic pattern of human evolution?

a. Humans evolved in a single, uninterrupted parade of increasingly humanlike forms.
b. The human phylogenetic tree resembles a bush, with many branches representing extinct forms.
c. Throughout human evolution only one hominid species has existed at any one time.
d. Modern humans have many ancestors of different species of hominids that interbred.

______ **23.** If the mitochondrial DNA of *Homo sapiens* showed an accumulation of mutational differences representing several millions of years, which hypothesis of human evolution would this support?

a. the recent-African-origin hypothesis
b. the Euroasian-origin hypothesis
c. the multiregional hypothesis
d. None of the above

SHORT ANSWER Answer the questions in the space provided.

24. What information can a paleoanthropologist infer from fossilized hominid skull fragments and teeth?

____

25. List three characteristics unique to anthropoid primates, including humans.

____

____

26. In 1995, two species were discovered that are older than *A. afarensis*. Name these two species, and state whether they demonstrate bipedalism or not.

____

____

27. The hallmarks of hominid evolution include bipedalism, tool use, and enhanced brain development and language. Which of these characteristics is seen in the genus *Australopithecus?*

____

____

28. Most paleoanthropologists agree that *Homo habilis* and *H. erectus* were meat eaters. What is the evidence?

____

____

29. Explain why the data from studies of mitochondrial DNA mutations support the recent-African-origin hypothesis as opposed to the multiregional hypothesis of human evolution.

____

____

DRAWING CONCLUSIONS **Follow the directions given below.**

30. Some events of the distant past, such as the evolution of human beings, cannot be tested directly. To study past events, scientists usually make inferences based on the available data or material evidence, such as fossils. Toolmaking and tool use are inferred from paleoanthropological finds. If you discovered the charred animal bone and stone tools shown below together in an early hominid excavation site, which of the following inferences would be supported and which would not be supported? Explain your answers.

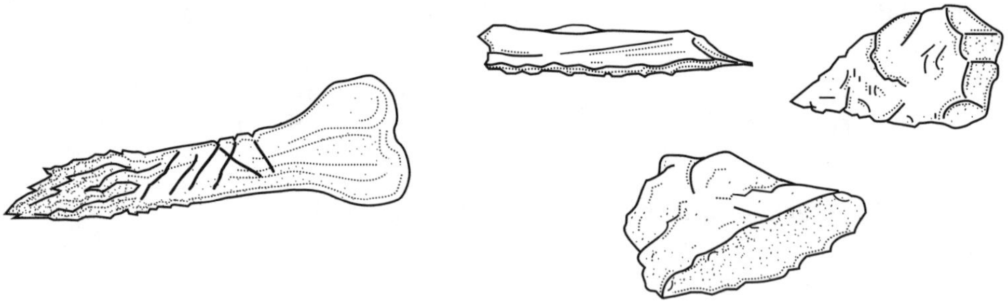

a. The species that made the tools were capable of language.

____

b. The species that made the tools used fire.

____

c. The species that made the tools were meat eaters.

____

d. The species that made the tools wore clothing.

____

e. The species that made the tools had an opposable thumb.

____

Name ______________________ Class ____________ Date ____________

CHAPTER 18 TEST

CLASSIFICATION

MATCHING **Write the correct letter in the blank before each numbered term.**

_____ **1.** Archaea

_____ **2.** Bacteria

_____ **3.** Eukarya

_____ **4.** Animalia

_____ **5.** Archaebacteria

_____ **6.** Eubacteria

_____ **7.** Fungi

_____ **8.** Protista

a. kingdom; includes *Euglena* and amoebas

b. domain; includes chemosynthetic bacteria

c. kingdom; includes mushrooms and molds

d. kingdom; includes humans and insects

e. kingdom; includes disease-causing bacteria

f. domain; includes both plants and animals

g. kingdom; includes chemosynthetic bacteria

h. domain; includes disease-causing bacteria

TRUE-FALSE **If a statement is true, write *T* in the blank. If a statement is false, write *F* in the blank, and then in the space provided, explain why the statement is false.**

_____ **9.** In Aristotle's system, the classification of animals was based on morphology and similarity of embryological development.

____

_____ **10.** According to cladistic taxonomy, dinosaurs are more closely related to birds than they are to lizards.

____

_____ **11.** Scientists think that archaebacteria, some of which live in extremely harsh environments, closely resemble the first kinds of organisms to live on Earth.

____

_____ **12.** Systematic taxonomists consider the habitat of an organism as their primary basis for classification.

____

_____ **13.** Recognition by scientists of two broad types of bacteria resulted in the establishment of two different kingdoms of bacteria.

____

Name ______________________ Class ____________ Date ____________

MULTIPLE CHOICE **Write the letter of the most correct answer in the blank.**

_____ **14.** Which of the following taxonomic categories refers only to plants?

a. phylum **b.** class **c.** division **d.** kingdom

_____ **15.** Linnaeus grouped structurally similar organisms of a single type into the category called a

a. species. **b.** genus. **c.** class. **d.** order.

_____ **16.** The species identifier denoting the species of the leopard frog, *Rana pipiens*, is

a. leopard. **b.** frog. **c.** *Rana.* **d.** pipiens.

_____ **17.** The main criterion used by Linnaeus to classify organisms is their

a. phylogeny. **b.** taxonomy. **c.** morphology. **d.** habitat.

_____ **18.** The branch of biology that names and groups organisms according to their characteristics and evolutionary history is

a. morphology. **b.** taxonomy. **c.** phylogeny. **d.** embryology.

_____ **19.** An ancestry diagram made by grouping organisms according to their shared derived characters is called a

a. phylogenetic tree.
b. taxonomic category.
c. phylum.
d. cladogram.

_____ **20.** A modern systematic taxonomist would likely consider the following when classifying an organism:

a. the fossil record, morphology, embryological development, and macromolecules
b. the fossil record, morphology, embryological development, and habitat
c. behavior, morphology, embryology, and habitat
d. the fossil record, macromolecules, habitat, and embryological development

_____ **21.** The evolutionary history of an organism is its

a. morphology. **b.** taxonomy. **c.** classification. **d.** phylogeny.

_____ **22.** In the table below, which level of classification is represented by the cell labeled *A*?

a. kingdom **b.** phylum **c.** division **d.** order

_____ **23.** In the table below, which of the following best fits the cell labeled *B*?

a. *sapiens* **b.** *Canis* **c.** *Homo* **d.** *Animalia*

Classification of Three Different Organisms

Organism	Class	A	Family	Genus
Bacterium	Scotobacteria	Spirochaetales	Spirochaetaceae	*Cristispira*
Box elder	Angiospermae	Sapindales	Aceraceae	*Acer*
Human	Mammalis	Primates	Hominidae	B

Name ______________________ Class ____________ Date ____________

SHORT ANSWER **Answer the questions in the space provided.**

24. List the levels of classification developed by Linnaeus, from the broadest category to the most specific.

____

____

____

25. Compare and contrast Aristotle's system of classification with that of Linnaeus.

____

____

____

____

26. The kingdom Protista includes a wide variety of organisms that are more distantly related to each other than plants are to animals. Why are they grouped together in one kingdom?

____

____

27. Describe one way in which the embryos of vertebrates and echinoderms are fundamentally different from the embryos of other orders.

____

____

28. Explain how embryological evidence helps to define phylogeny.

____

____

____

29. Compare and contrast the six-kingdom system of classification with the three-domain system. What evidence prompted the development of the three-domain system?

____

____

____

____

Name ______________________ Class ____________ Date ____________

DRAWING CONCLUSIONS Follow the directions given below.

30. The phylogenetic tree below shows one hypothesis about the relationships among the Galápagos finches that Darwin catalogued. The tree is based on morphological evidence alone. Use the tree to answer the questions below.

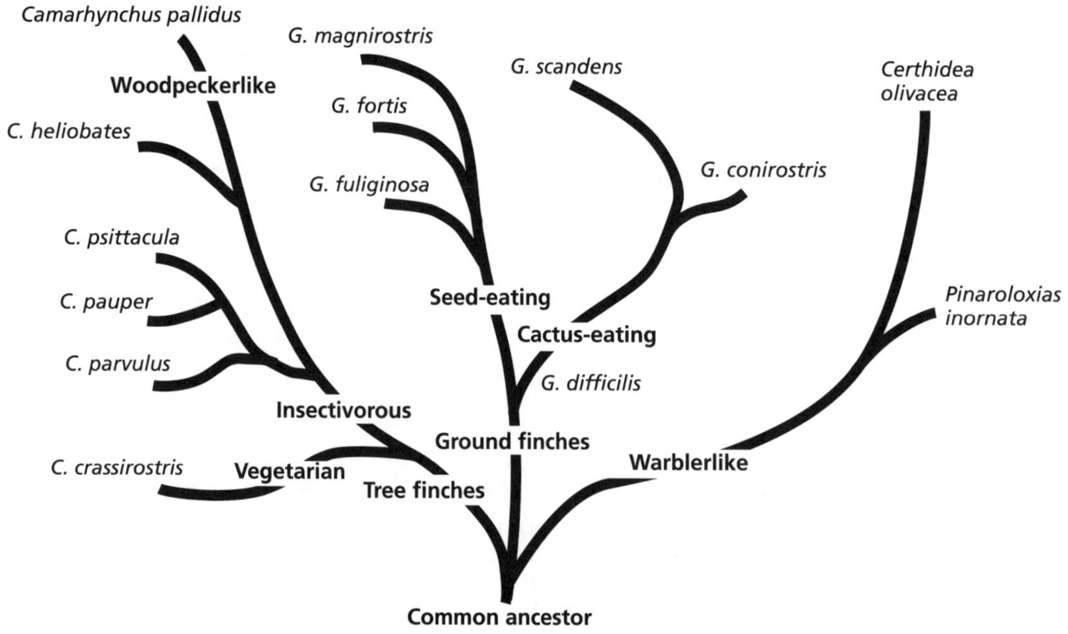

a. Early finches diverged into ground finches and tree finches (which include the warblerlike finches). What environmental pressures might have caused this divergence?

____

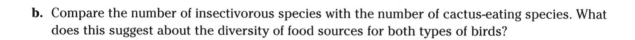

b. Compare the number of insectivorous species with the number of cactus-eating species. What does this suggest about the diversity of food sources for both types of birds?

____

____

c. The finches' environments and food are noted on this tree, but this information did not contribute to shaping the tree. The tree derives from the birds' morphology. What morphological feature might all three seed-eating ground finches have in common?

____

d. What evidence might a cladistic taxonomist use to propose that any two species in this tree share a close evolutionary relationship?

____

e. What kinds of information available to modern taxonomists might cause them to reconsider the branching patterns shown on this tree?

____

____

Name ______________________ Class ____________ Date ____________

CHAPTER 19 TEST

INTRODUCTION TO ECOLOGY

MATCHING **Write the correct letter in the blank before each numbered term.**

_____ **1.** community

_____ **2.** generalist

_____ **3.** ecology

_____ **4.** resources

_____ **5.** habitat

_____ **6.** population

_____ **7.** greenhouse effect

_____ **8.** global warming

a. where an organism lives

b. phenomenon that insulates Earth from the freezing temperature of space

c. members of a single species living in one place at one time

d. organisms interacting in a specific area

e. increase in average global temperature due to trapped excess greenhouse gases

f. a species with a broad niche

g. study of the interactions between organisms and their environment

h. energy and materials needed by a species

TRUE-FALSE **If a statement is true, write *T* in the blank. If a statement is false, write *F* in the blank, and then in the space provided, explain why the statement is false.**

_____ **9.** The world's population tripled from 2 billion to 6 billion people in just 66 years.

____

_____ **10.** The greenhouse effect is a phenomenon caused by excess fossil fuels being burned.

____

_____ **11.** A tolerance curve shows the range of a certain environmental factor that a species can tolerate and the optimal range for that factor.

____

_____ **12.** Regulators change their internal conditions as their environment changes.

____

_____ **13.** The realized niche of a species is the range of resources it actually uses.

____

Name ____________________ Class __________ Date __________

MULTIPLE CHOICE **Write the letter of the most correct answer in the blank.**

A

B

C

D

______ **14.** Which of the figures above depicts a conformer?

a. A　　**b.** B　　**c.** C　　**d.** D

______ **15.** The small percentage of ultraviolet radiation that strikes the Earth from the sun is the cause of

a. climate changes.
b. sunburns and skin cancer.
c. global warming.
d. the greenhouse effect.

______ **16.** The broadest, most inclusive level of organization in ecology is

a. an ecosystem.　　**b.** a community.　　**c.** a population.　　**d.** the biosphere.

______ **17.** When organisms affect and are affected by other organisms in their surroundings and with the nonliving parts of their environment, it is called

a. ecology.
b. disturbances of the ecosystem.
c. interdependence.
d. modeling.

______ **18.** An example of an abiotic factor is

a. tree.　　**b.** sunlight.　　**c.** bird.　　**d.** grass.

______ **19.** Some organisms adjust their tolerance to abiotic factors through

a. adaptation.　　**b.** acclimation.　　**c.** application.　　**d.** resources.

______ **20.** Conformers are organisms that

a. use energy to control internal conditions.
b. change over many generations.
c. do not regulate internal conditions.
d. None of the above

______ **21.** A long term strategy to avoid unfavorable conditions by moving to another, more favorable habitat is called

a. dormancy.　　**b.** migration.　　**c.** hibernation.　　**d.** All of the above

_____ **22.** A species' fundamental niche is

a. the range of resources it can potentially use.
b. the range of conditions it can potentially tolerate.
c. where it probably competes for resources.
d. All of the above

_____ **23.** The range of resources a species actually uses is called

a. an abiotic factor.
b. resource tolerance.
c. a realized niche.
d. a regulator.

SHORT ANSWER **Answer the questions in the space provided.**

24. Briefly explain three environmental problems caused by humans.

____

____

____

25. Explain an advantage to and a limitation of the use of models in ecology.

____

____

____

26. What does it mean when ecologists say that a species has a broad niche?

____

____

27. List the five levels of organization in the environment?

____

____

28. Look at the picture at right, and list the biotic factors you see. Name any abiotic factors that might interact with this environment.

____

____

____

____

____

Name ______________________ Class ____________ Date ____________

29. How are the terms *acclimation, dormancy,* and *migration* related?

____

____

____

____

DRAWING CONCLUSIONS **Follow the directions given below.**

30. Refer to the drawing below as you answer a–c.

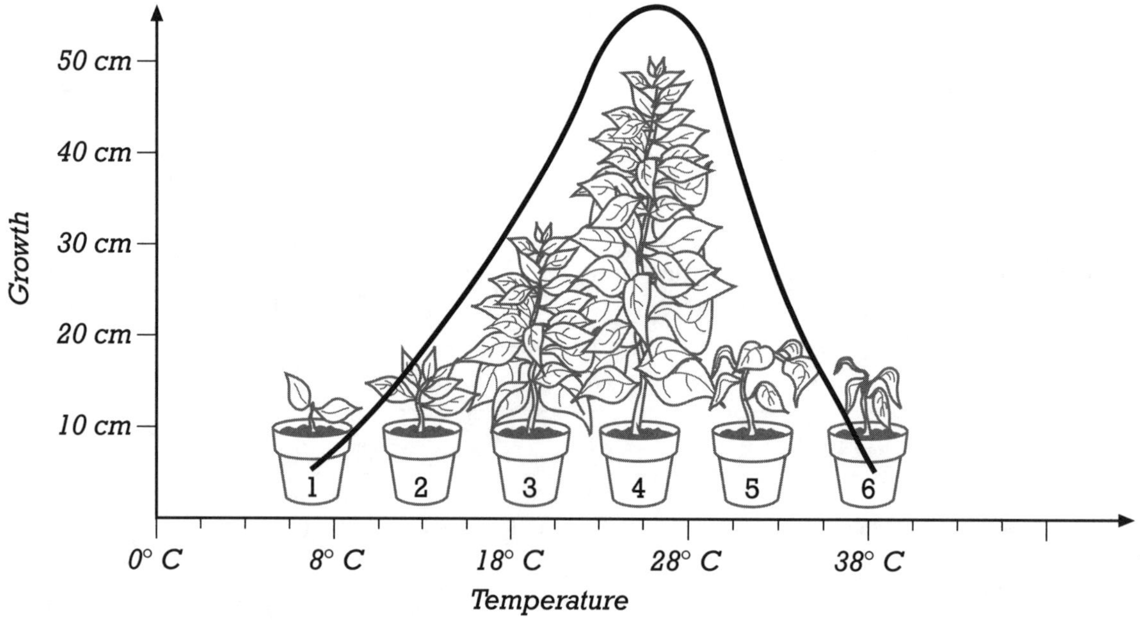

a. What kind of graph is shown above? What does it measure? ____________

____

____

b. If you could give more water and sunlight to plant 1 and plant 6, could you expect a change in their growth as measured by this graph? ____________

____

____

c. Explain what might happen if plant 2 were exposed to 28°C temperature and plant 4 were exposed to 13°C temperature? ____________

____

____

Name ____________ Class ________ Date ________

CHAPTER 20 TEST

POPULATIONS

MATCHING Write the correct letter in the blank before each numbered term.

_____ **1.** S-shaped curve

_____ **2.** clumped distribution

_____ **3.** limiting factor

_____ **4.** carrying capacity

_____ **5.** random distribution

_____ **6.** J-shaped curve

_____ **7.** even distribution

_____ **8.** density-dependent factors

a. exponential growth model

b. individuals spread as far apart as possible

c. food shortages and living space

d. logistic growth model

e. restrains growth of a population

f. individuals dispersed by wind

g. individuals clustered around food resources

h. population size the environment can support for a long time

TRUE-FALSE If a statement is true, write *T* in the blank. If a statement is false, write *F* in the blank, and then in the space provided, explain why the statement is false.

_____ **9.** A country that is densely populated may have areas within it of varying population densities.

____

_____ **10.** The United States has a stable population size because the growth rate is equal to the death rate.

____

_____ **11.** Inbreeding results in decreased genetic variability and reduced ability to adapt to environmental changes.

____

_____ **12.** The control of disease has been an important factor in enabling the global population to grow rapidly since 1650.

____

_____ **13.** Developing countries are characterized as being modern and industrialized and as having high standards of living.

____

Name ______________________ Class ____________ Date ____________

MULTIPLE CHOICE **Write the letter of the most correct answer in the blank.**

______ **14.** Which of the following definitions of a property of populations is incorrect?

a. Population size is the number of individuals in a population.
b. Population density is the number of individuals in a population per unit area or volume.
c. Population dispersion is the distribution of individuals in a population over time.
d. Population dynamics include birth rate, death rate, and life expectancy.

______ **15.** When the birth rate and the death rate of a population are equal,

a. the population is growing in size.
b. the population is remaining constant in size.
c. the population is decreasing in size.
d. the life expectancy of individuals in the population is very great.

______ **16.** Exponential growth of a population may occur

a. in populations of bacteria grown in the laboratory.
b. at some times in a population following the logistic population growth model.
c. in the absence of limiting factors.
d. All of the above

______ **17.** Which of the following is *not* characteristic of the carrying capacity of an environment?

a. It is determined by density-independent factors.
b. It may vary as the environment changes.
c. Population growth ceases because the birth rate equals the death rate.
d. It is the maximum number of individuals the environment can support over a long period of time.

______ **18.** Populations that contain only a few individuals are

a. genetically more diverse than large populations.
b. able to withstand environmental disturbances because they become genetically uniform as a result of inbreeding.
c. susceptible to extinction from habitat destruction, diseases, and other environmental disturbances because they are less able to recover from such changes.
d. never bred in captivity because they fail to thrive when released into the wild.

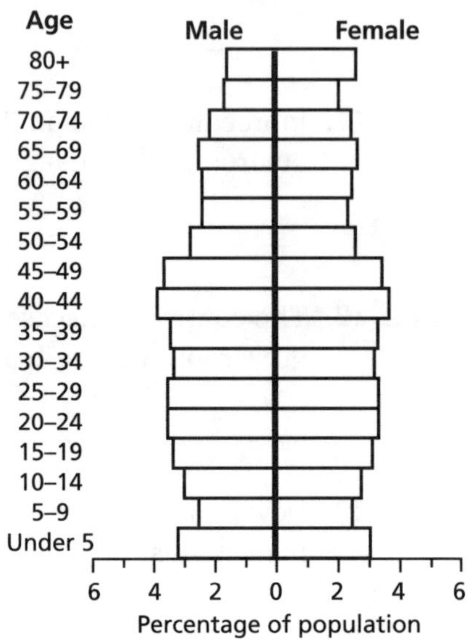

______ **19.** The graph of population age structure shown to the right most likely represents the population of a developed country because

a. there are more females than males in the oldest age class.
b. there are many more people in the pre-reproductive age classes than there are in the post-reproductive age classes.
c. the population has a large potential for rapid growth.
d. the population size is relatively even throughout all the age classes and sexes.

_____ **20.** The graph of the age structure of a population shown on the previous page represents

a. the birth and death rates of the population.
b. the life expectancy of the population.
c. the likelihood of an individual surviving to an old age.
d. the percentage of people in each age class.

_____ **21.** In the exponential model of population growth, the birth rate

a. increases while the death rate remains constant.
b. remains constant while the death rate decreases.
c. and the death rate remain constant.
d. and the death rate increase.

_____ **22.** How did the agricultural revolution promote human population growth?

a. It improved economic conditions for many people.
b. It improved the availability and stability of food supplies.
c. It enabled people to move to new areas and establish new sites for population growth.
d. It increased the general level of health of most people of the world.

_____ **23.** Beginning about 1650, the global human population

a. had a low birth rate and a high death rate.
b. reached the Earth's carrying capacity.
c. began to grow exponentially.
d. had a birth rate equal to the death rate.

SHORT ANSWER Answer the questions in the space provided.

24. How can a population appear to be evenly distributed when it is viewed up close but clumped in its distribution when viewed from far away? ______________________

____

____

25. What is the difference between density-independent limiting factors and density-dependent limiting factors? Provide an example of each. ______________________

____

____

26. The global human population growth rate increased dramatically after World War II. What component of the following equation for determining growth rate changed in order for this to occur?

birth rate – death rate = growth rate ______________________

____

27. Describe some of the characteristics of a country whose population is growing rapidly.

____

____

28. Describe some of the characteristics of a country whose population is growing slowly or is stable.

____

____

29. What type of survivorship curve is characteristic of species in which most individuals live close to the full life expectancy? ______________________

What type of survivorship curve is characteristic of species in which most individuals die at a very young age? ______________________

What type of survivorship curve is characteristic of species in which individuals die at a relatively constant rate throughout their life expectancy? ______________________

DRAWING CONCLUSIONS **Follow the directions given below.**

30. Population size is sometimes estimated by sampling a part of the population. The mark-and-recapture method is widely used in estimating the size of animal populations. In this technique, individuals are removed at random from the population, marked, and returned to the population. After a fixed time, another sample is taken (recaptured). An estimate of the total population is then obtained by calculating the ratio of the total number of marked individuals to the number of unmarked individuals counted in the second sample. Use the equation below to find an estimate of a population size by solving for N, where T = number marked in first capture, t = number of marked animals recaptured, n = total animals recaptured, and N = estimate of the total population.

$$\frac{T}{N} = \frac{t}{n}$$

a. Six ferrets were removed from an abandoned prairie dog town, marked with radio collars, and returned. Two weeks later, 12 ferrets were recaptured. Three wore collars. Estimate the size of the population of ferrets in this area. ______________________

b. In a second recapture, 12 ferrets were recaptured and six had collars. Estimate the size of the population. Compare this with your original estimate. ______________________

____

c. If no ferrets with collars are recaptured, can you estimate the size of the total population? Why or why not? ______________________

____

____

Name ______________________ Class ______________ Date ______________

CHAPTER 21 TEST

COMMUNITY ECOLOGY

MATCHING Write the correct letter in the blank space before each numbered term.

_____ **1.** mutualism

_____ **2.** species richness

_____ **3.** parasitism

_____ **4.** secondary succession

_____ **5.** commensalism

_____ **6.** primary succession

_____ **7.** predation

_____ **8.** species diversity

a. number of species and abundance of each

b. killing and consuming another organism

c. interaction in which both species benefit

d. sequence of species in a disturbed area

e. interaction in which one species benefits and the other is harmed

f. number of species

g. interaction in which one species benefits

h. plants growing where bare rock was

TRUE-FALSE If a statement is true, write *T* in the blank. If a statement is false, write *F* in the blank, and then in the space provided, explain why the statement is false.

_____ **9.** A harmless species that is a mimic of a dangerous species is preyed upon, while the dangerous species is avoided.

____

_____ **10.** Tapeworms are such highly adapted parasites that they do not have a digestive system.

____

_____ **11.** Larger land areas usually include a greater diversity of climates than smaller land areas and can therefore support more species.

____

_____ **12.** If a predatory species were removed from an environment, its prey species could dominate the environment.

____

_____ **13.** Grasses are common pioneer species because they secrete acids that dissolve rock, releasing minerals for plant growth.

____

Name ____________________ Class ____________ Date ____________

MULTIPLE CHOICE **Write the letter of the most correct answer in the blank.**

_____ **14.** Which of the following is an example of mimicry?

a. heat-sensitive pits of rattlesnakes
b. leaflike coloration of a mantis
c. bright coloration of certain frogs
d. colored rings of a coral snake

_____ **15.** Which of the following is *not* an example of a predator's adaptation for finding prey?

a. spiders' webs that trap flying insects
b. stripes on a tiger's coat that blend with the grassland habitat of small animals
c. stripes on a nonpredatory wasp that resemble the stripes of a predatory wasp
d. rattlesnakes' heat-sensitive pits that detect warm-bodied prey

_____ **16.** Which of the pairs of parasites listed below are endoparasites?

a. tapeworms and leeches
b. malaria parasites and tapeworms
c. leeches and fleas
d. ticks and mosquitoes

_____ **17.** Competition is most intense between closely related species that

a. are similar in appearance.
b. have different beak sizes.
c. use the same resources.
d. use different resources.

_____ **18.** Which of the following is *not* a hypothesis that helps to explain the greater species richness that occurs at tropical latitudes than at latitudes farther from the tropics?

a. Plants can photosynthesize all year creating more energy reserves.
b. Tropical habitats are the oldest on Earth and have not been disturbed by the ice ages.
c. Tropical habitats have stable climates, so species have diversified more in these areas.
d. There is less competition for resources among species in the tropics.

_____ **19.** The longest-held hypothesis to explain the relationship between species richness and community stability states that communities with more species

a. contain more links between species and thus can withstand greater disturbance.
b. inhabit large land areas, which are always richer in species than small land areas.
c. recover more quickly from environmental disturbances.
d. can evolve more new species than communities with fewer species.

_____ **20.** Pioneer species

a. disperse many seeds over a large area.
b. are usually small plants.
c. are usually fast-growing.
d. All of the above

_____ **21.** The graph below illustrates

a. commensalism.
b. competitive exclusion.
c. a predator-prey relationship
d. resource partitioning.

***Paramecia* Interactions**

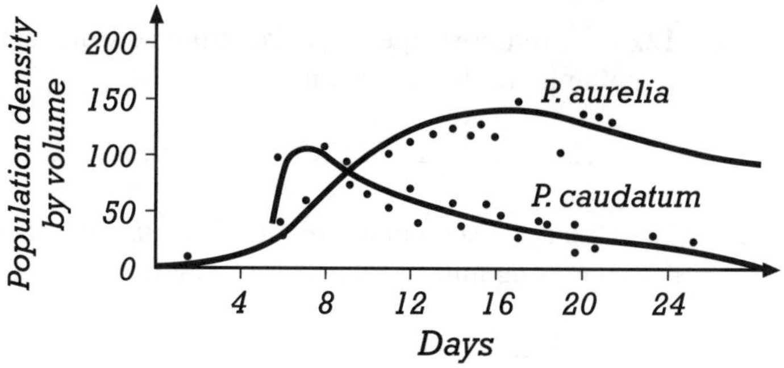

______ **22.** Species richness in grasses was found to improve a community's stability. Which of the following results led to this conclusion?

a. Species-rich grass plots that were subjected to freezing temperatures lost less plant mass and took less time to recover than grass plots with fewer species.
b. Species-rich grass plots that were subjected to drought lost less plant mass and took less time to recover than grass plots with fewer species.
c. Species-rich grass plots that were subjected to human habitat destruction lost fewer plants than grass plots with fewer species.
d. All of the above

______ **23.** In the process of succession,

a. an unchanging climax community is the final stage.
b. organisms change the environment so that it can support the growth of other species.
c. progress toward a climax community cannot be altered by further disturbances.
d. grasses are present in primary succession but absent in secondary succession.

SHORT ANSWER Answer the questions in the space provided.

24. What are the adaptive advantages of thorns, tough leaves, and toxins to plants?

____

____

25. Explain why a species of barnacles, *Semibalanus balanoides*, is dominant in areas that are usually under water and another species of barnacles, *Chthamalus stellatus*, is dominant in areas that have prolonged dry periods. ______________________________

____

____

26. What kind of relationship is illustrated by cattle egrets and Cape buffalo? What kind of relationship is illustrated by certain flowers and nectar-feeding bats?

____

____

27. How are humans causing a decrease in species richness in certain environments?

____

____

28. Describe the environmental conditions present during succession in Glacier Bay, Alaska.

____

____

Name ______________________________ Class ______________ Date ______________

29. The tables below list the tree species and the number of individuals of each species in two plots of land. Which plot has greater species richness? Which plot has greater species diversity?

____

____

PLOT 1

Species	Number
Yellow poplar	102
Sassafras	60
Cucumber magnolia	46
Red maple	42
Red oak	23
Butternut	9
Shagbark hickory	5
American beech	2

PLOT 2

Species	Number
Yellow poplar	99
Cucumber magnolia	143
Red maple	113
Red oak	102
Butternut	97
American beech	75

DRAWING CONCLUSIONS Follow the directions given below.

30. In desert regions of the southwestern United States, some species of ants and rodents eat seeds produced by desert plants. Many seeds are consumed by both animals. An experiment was conducted to determine the effects of ants and rodents on seed numbers in the wild. In this experiment, (1) only ants were removed from some plots of land, (2) only rodents were removed from some plots, (3) both ants and rodents were removed from some plots, or (4) both ants and rodents were allowed to remain on some plots. After a period of time, data were collected from the plots. These data are presented in the table below.

	Only ants removed	Only rodents removed	Ants and rodents removed	Ants and rodents remain
Number of ant colonies	0	547	0	313
Number of rodents	176	0	0	123
Number of seeds per square meter	356	375	1,527	362

a. Which plots were the control plots in this experiment?

____

b. What happened to the seed density in plots in which either ants or rodents were removed?

____

c. What happened to the seed density in plots in which both ants and rodents were removed?

____

Name ______________________ Class ______________ Date ______________

CHAPTER 22 TEST

ECOSYSTEMS AND THE BIOSPHERE

MATCHING **Write the correct letter in the blank space before each numbered term.**

______ **1.** nitrification

______ **2.** decomposers

______ **3.** neritic zone

______ **4.** denitrification

______ **5.** temperate grasslands

______ **6.** carnivores

______ **7.** oceanic zone

______ **8.** savannas

a. area rich in wildlife having two seasons—wet and dry

b. nitrates converted into nitrogen gas

c. deep water in the open ocean

d. eat other consumers

e. ammonia converted into nitrates and nitrites

f. areas with low rainfall, rich soil, and grasses

g. obtain nutrients from dead organisms

h. ocean over a continental shelf

TRUE-FALSE **If a statement is true, write *T* in the space provided. If a statement is false, write *F* in the blank, and then in the space provided, explain why the statement is false.**

______ **9.** Decomposers break down living organisms and thus help prevent population explosions of species.

____

______ **10.** During a biogeochemical cycle, water, minerals, or carbon dioxide moves from the abiotic portion of the environment into living things and back again.

____

______ **11.** Carbon moves from the biotic portion of its cycle into the abiotic portion during photosynthesis.

____

______ **12.** Deserts differ from other biomes in that they have high temperatures all year.

____

______ **13.** Estuaries are areas of shallow water where fresh water flows into the sea.

____

Name ______________________________ Class ______________ Date ______________

MULTIPLE CHOICE **Write the letter of the most correct answer in the blank.**

______ **14.** Organisms that obtain energy by making their own organic molecules are called

a. consumers. **b.** herbivores. **c.** producers. **d.** decomposers.

______ **15.** The highest net primary productivity is found in

a. lakes and temperate grasslands.
b. estuaries and tropical rain forests.
c. savannas.
d. the open ocean.

______ **16.** Food chains differ from food webs in that food chains

a. include more organisms than do food webs.
b. include producers and consumers, while food webs include only consumers.
c. depict only one line of energy transfer, while food webs depict many interrelated food chains.
d. depict only one line of energy transfer to a top consumer, while food webs depict all possible lines of energy transfer to a top consumer.

______ **17.** Which of the following best characterizes the differences between tundra and taiga biomes?

a. Tundra biomes are located at lower latitudes than taiga biomes.
b. Tundra biomes are warmer and have lower average annual precipitation than taiga biomes.
c. Tundra has small, slow-growing plants with root systems limited by a layer of permafrost, while taiga has trees adapted to cold temperatures.
d. Tundra has extremely long and cold winters, and taiga has short and warm winters.

______ **18.** Temperate deciduous forests are characterized by

a. pronounced seasons with high average annual precipitation.
b. the presence of trees that lose their leaves during the winter.
c. mild winters, moderate average annual precipitation, and broad-leaved trees.
d. pronounced seasons, broad-leaved trees, and grasses being the dominant plants.

______ **19.** Which of the following is *not* a water-conservation adaptation found in at least some desert organisms?

a. mechanisms that enable water storage
b. mechanisms that reduce water loss
c. mechanisms that increase activities during the day
d. mechanisms that reduce heat loss during the day

______ **20.** The photic zones of the oceans differ from the aphotic zones in that

a. there are living things in the photic zones but no living things in the aphotic zones.
b. the photic zones are warmer than the aphotic zones.
c. the photic zones are found near the tropics, while the aphotic zones are found far from the tropics.
d. the photic zones receive sunlight, while the aphotic zones do not.

______ **21.** The most productive zone in the oceans is the

a. neritic zone. **b.** intertidal zone. **c.** pelagic zone. **d.** benthic zone.

______ **22.** Omnivores eat

a. only producers.
b. only consumers.
c. producers and consumers.
d. only other omnivores.

______ **23.** Animals that live in savannas

a. must deal with long periods of drought.
b. must be able to survive cold temperatures.
c. are primarily carnivores.
d. are primarily omnivores.

SHORT ANSWER **Answer each question in the space provided.**

24. What is a trophic level, and what determines an organism's trophic level?

____

____

25. Why is so little of the energy from one trophic level transferred up to the next trophic level?

____

____

26. During which process(es) in the carbon cycle is carbon converted from an inorganic form into an organic form? ____

____

____

27. The diagram below illustrates the nitrogen cycle. Label each arrow with the process it represents.

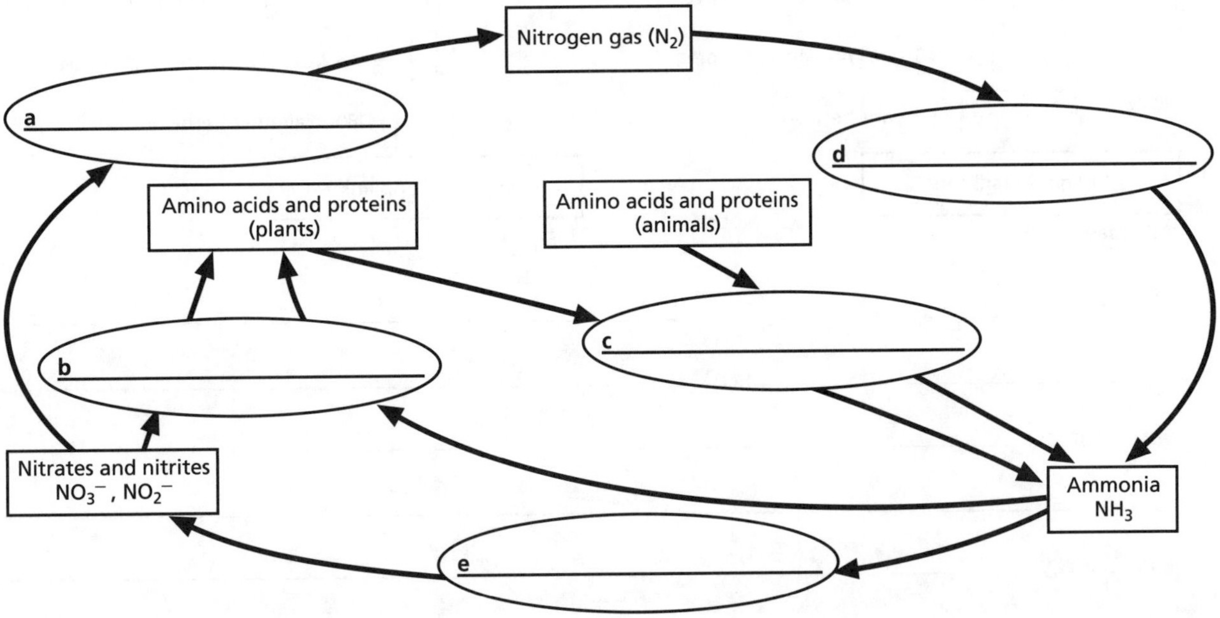

Name ______________________ Class ____________ Date ____________

28. What are the distinguishing characteristics of a tropical rain forest, and how do they differ from those of temperate deciduous forests? ____

____

____

29. Lakes and ponds can be divided into two categories. What are these categories, and how do they differ from each other? ____

____

____

DRAWING CONCLUSIONS

30. The pyramids shown below depict the numbers of organisms, the biomass, and the energy at different trophic levels in an aquatic ecosystem. In the spaces labeled *a–c* below, analyze and describe each pyramid. Explain why each measured parameter results in the same general shape.

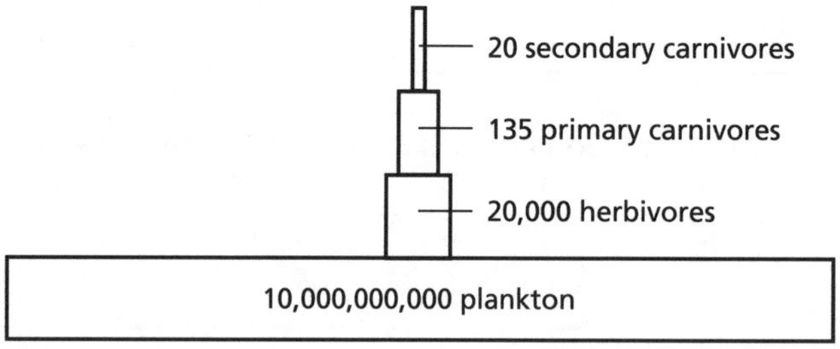

Numbers of organisms

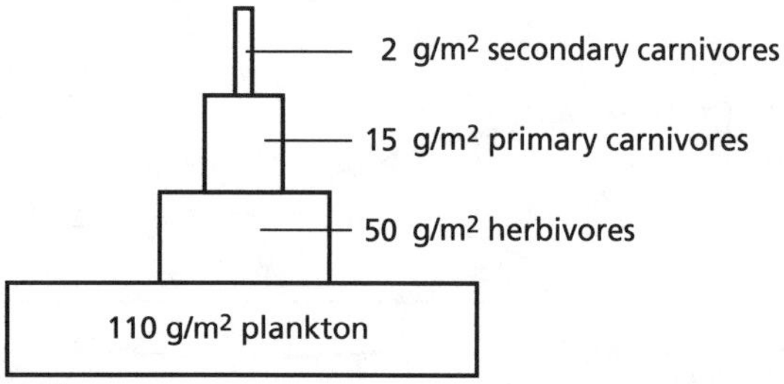

Biomass

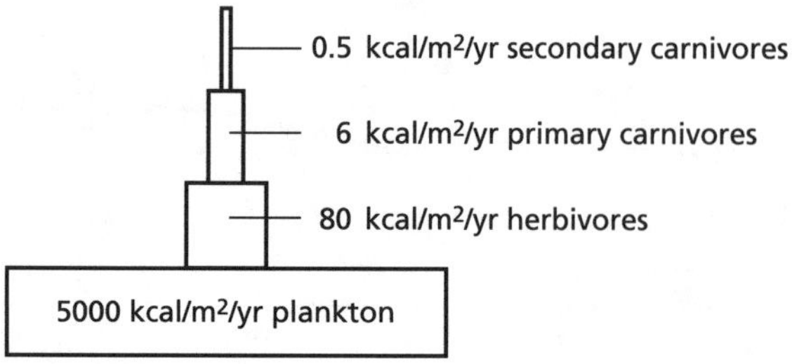

Energy

a. Numbers ____

____

b. Biomass ____

____

c. Energy ____

____

Name ______________________________ Class ______________ Date ______________

CHAPTER 23 TEST

ENVIRONMENTAL SCIENCE

MATCHING Write the correct letter in the blank space before each numbered term.

_____ **1.** chlorofluorocarbon

_____ **2.** biodiversity

_____ **3.** flyways

_____ **4.** genetic diversity

_____ **5.** El Niño

_____ **6.** restoration biology

_____ **7.** conservation biology

_____ **8.** fossil-fuel burning

a. identification and maintenance of natural areas

b. migratory bird routes

c. destroys ozone

d. the variety of organisms at a site

e. the reversal of damage to natural areas

f. increases carbon dioxide levels

g. amount of genetic variation at a site

h. occasional warm-water current in the Pacific

TRUE-FALSE If a statement is true, write *T* in the blank. If a statement is false, write *F* in the blank, and then in the space provided, explain why the statement is false.

_____ **9.** Ozone in the upper atmosphere screens out much of the sun's ultraviolet radiation.

____

_____ **10.** Increased levels of carbon dioxide in the atmosphere have not caused an increase in global temperatures.

____

_____ **11.** Most of the organisms that are alive today have been described and classified.

____

_____ **12.** Mammals make up a small percentage of the total number of species on Earth today.

____

_____ **13.** The common practice of providing food for migratory birds at intervals along their flyways helps to conserve these birds.

____

MULTIPLE CHOICE **Write the letter of the most correct answer in the blank.**

______ **14.** Convection cells

a. cause ozone from the lower atmosphere to move into the upper atmosphere.
b. affect other convection cells around the world and therefore affect climate worldwide.
c. circulate carbon dioxide generated at the surface of the Earth and therefore induce global warming.
d. mix warm air with cool air, thereby stabilizing air temperatures worldwide.

______ **15.** El Niños have resulted in

a. decreased anchovy exports in Peru.
b. reduced grain production in Australia.
c. fewer forest fires in the southeastern United States.
d. All of the above

______ **16.** Many scientists think that humans have caused an increase in the size of the ozone hole by

a. burning large quantities of fossil fuels.
b. generating a lot of carbon dioxide that has resulted in an increase in the atmospheric carbon dioxide level.
c. releasing large quantities of chlorofluorocarbons into the atmosphere.
d. All of the above

______ **17.** Which of the following measures of biodiversity takes into consideration the number of species present at a site as well as the number of individuals of each species?

a. species evenness
b. species richness
c. species diversity
d. all of the above

______ **18.** The graph below depicts changes in global temperature over a period of time. What time period is represented in this graph?

a. the past 500 years
b. the time since the last ice age
c. from 1900 to the present
d. the next 200 years

Global Temperature

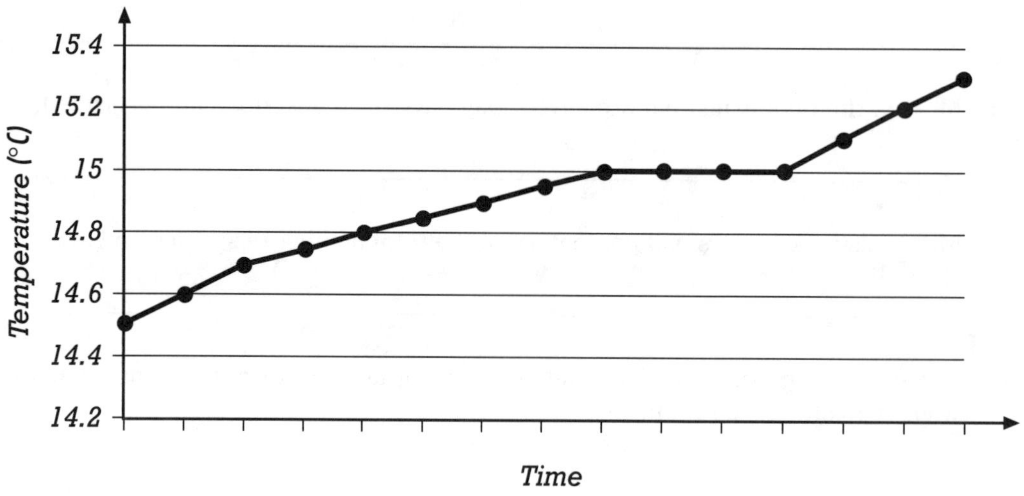

______ **19.** Which of the following has significantly reduced biodiversity on Earth?

a. mining for fossil fuels
b. agriculture
c. air and water pollution
d. wars

______ **20.** Conserving the biodiversity of plants for the possibility of discovering plants with medicinal use involves placing ______ on biodiversity.

a. utilitarian value
b. debt-for-nature swap value
c. nonutilitarian value
d. ecotourism value

______ **21.** Migratory birds are particularly vulnerable to extinction because

a. they are aquatic birds, and water availability in aquatic habitats varies over time.
b. they are prey to many predators along their flyways.
c. they are typically small birds and often don't survive their migrations.
d. they require a critical habitat at intervals along their migratory route as well as at their destinations.

______ **22.** The Florida Everglades is an unusual ecosystem in that

a. a major component of it is a large, slow-moving river that is linked to other water bodies in the region.
b. the inland water systems are composed of salt water.
c. it is home to many species of water birds.
d. it is mainly swampland dominated by grasses.

______ **23.** Which of the following is *not* a part of the plan to restore the Everglades?

a. elimination of some of the drainage canals that were built to drain water from the region
b. removal of melaleuca trees
c. designation of some of the birds as endangered species
d. purchase of additional land for park protection

SHORT ANSWER Answer each question in the space provided.

24. How do convection cells affect climates all over the world? ______________________

____

____

25. What effects might a decrease in the ozone layer have on humans and other organisms?

____

____

26. How are upper atmospheric ozone levels, atmospheric carbon dioxide levels, global temperature, undeveloped land areas, and various natural resources expected to be affected by continued increases in the Earth's human population? ______________________

____

____

27. Which of Earth's biomes has the greatest biodiversity and is therefore most critical to preserve in order to maintain Earth's biodiversity? ______________________

____

____

28. Describe the origins and strategies of debt-for-nature swap and ecotourism.

____

____

29. What are the expected effects of reintroducing the gray wolf to Yellowstone National Park?

____

____

DRAWING CONCLUSIONS

30. Examine the flowchart below that depicts some effects of human intervention on Earth's ecosystems. Complete the flowchart by writing appropriate responses in spaces *a–f*.

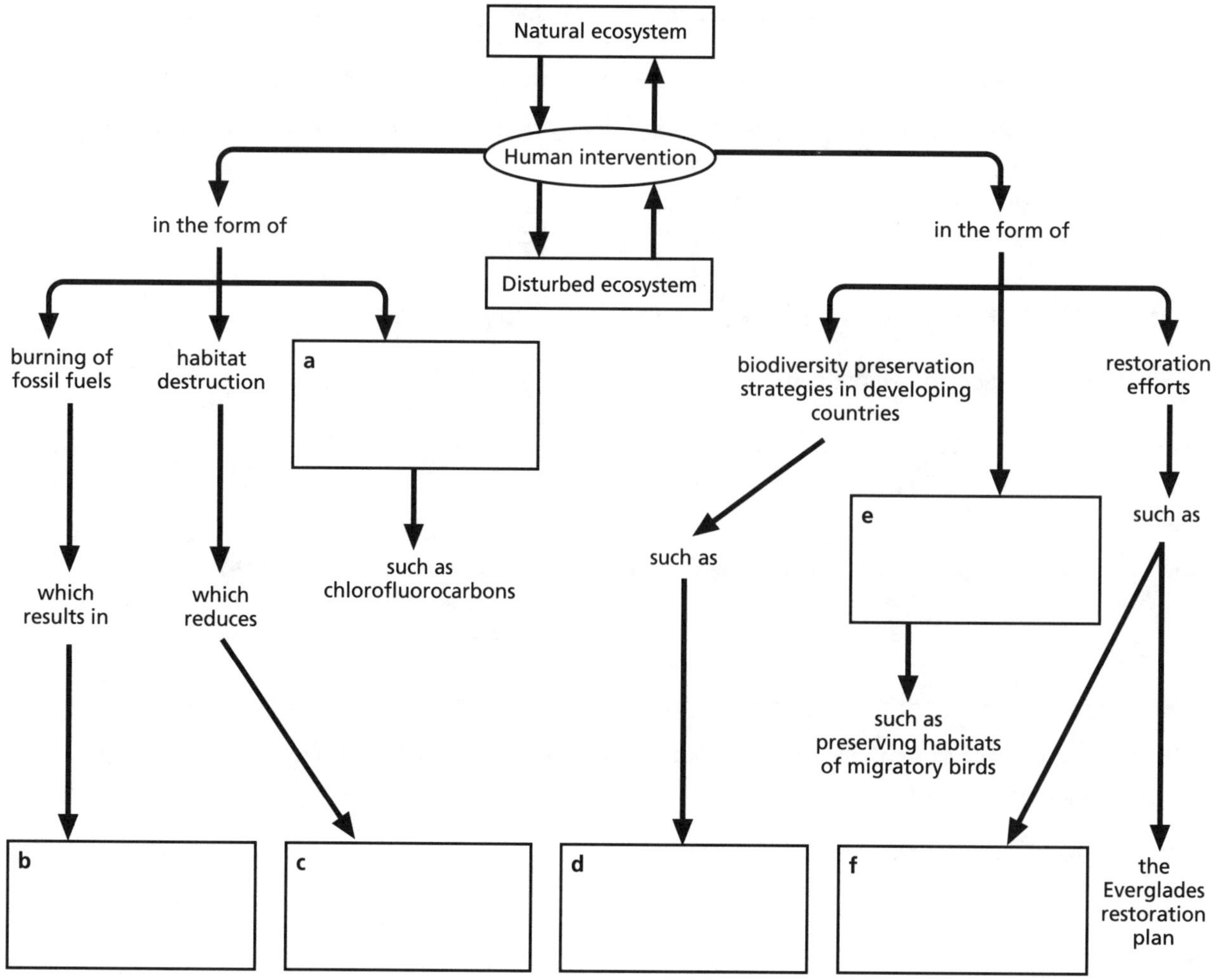

Name ______________________ Class ______________ Date ______________

CHAPTER 24 TEST

BACTERIA

MATCHING **Write the correct letter in the blank before each numbered term.**

_____ 1. *Rhizobium*

_____ 2. photoautotrophic bacteria

_____ 3. eubacteria

_____ 4. chemoautotrophic bacteria

_____ 5. Gram-negative bacteria

_____ 6. actinomycetes

_____ 7. saprophytic bacteria

_____ 8. archaebacteria

a. peptidoglycan is absent in cell walls

b. obtain energy from inorganic substances

c. produce many antibiotics

d. obtain energy from dead organisms

e. peptidoglycan is present in cell walls

f. produce an endotoxin

g. capture energy from sunlight

h. perform nitrogen fixation

TRUE-FALSE **If a statement is true, write *T* in the blank. If a statement is false, write *F* in the blank, and then in the space provided, explain why the statement is false.**

_____ 9. Bacteria that can survive only in the absence of oxygen are called obligate aerobes.

____

_____ 10. Ancient bacteria known as archaebacteria are now extinct.

____

_____ 11. Gram-negative bacteria appear purple when they undergo the Gram-stain procedure.

____

_____ 12. The bacterial cell wall prevents the passage of antibiotics and is the only means by which bacteria can resist antibiotics.

____

_____ 13. The terms *eubacteria* and *archaebacteria* refer to members of a single kingdom.

____

Name ______________________ Class ____________ Date ____________

MULTIPLE CHOICE **Write the letter of the most correct answer in the blank.**

______ **14.** Which of the following associations *incorrectly* describes an archaebacterium and its characteristics?

a. extreme halophile—high salt environments
b. methanogen— aerobic environments
c. thermoacidophile—hot, acidic environments
d. methanogen—human intestinal tract

______ **15.** Gram-positive bacteria differ from Gram-negative bacteria in

a. their response to the Gram stain.
b. the make-up of their cell walls.
c. their susceptibility to antibiotics.
d. All of the above

______ **16.** Which of the following bacteria are thought to be responsible for establishing Earth's oxygen-rich atmosphere?

a. methanogens
b. extreme halophiles
c. cyanobacteria
d. spirochetes

______ **17.** Genetic recombination in bacteria

a. is a form of sexual reproduction.
b. includes transformation and translation.
c. includes transformation and transduction.
d. always requires a conjugation bridge.

______ **18.** Bacterial cells typically lack

a. a cell membrane. **b.** mitochondria. **c.** a cell wall. **d.** a chromosome.

______ **19.** Which of the following is *not* a bacterial structure that provides the type of movement indicated?

a. pilus—crawling motion
b. flagellum—turning and tumbling while moving forward
c. slime layer—gliding
d. spiral shape—corkscrew motion

______ **20.** Genetic recombination in bacteria *always* involves

a. viruses.
b. transfer of DNA through a conjugation bridge.
c. transfer of one or more plasmids.
d. transfer of genes between bacterial cells.

______ **21.** Bacterial diseases of the intestines are usually transmitted by

a. sneezes and coughs.
b. direct contact.
c. contaminated water or food.
d. contaminated wounds.

______ **22.** Which of the following is not a mechanism of action of an antibiotic?

a. inhibiting cell wall synthesis
b. inhibiting conjugation
c. inhibiting protein synthesis
d. inhibiting DNA synthesis

_____ **23.** On what bases have bacteria traditionally been classified?

a. shape
b. response to Gram stain
c. type of respiration
d. All of the above

SHORT ANSWER Answer the questions in the space provided.

24. Identify three ways that bacteria are used to produce substances for human use.

____

____

____

25. Explain how chemoautotrophs differ from photosynthetic autotrophs.

____

____

26. Define the term *genetic recombination* as it applies to bacteria, and list three ways that genetic recombination occurs in bacteria. ____

____

____

____

27. Describe two ways that bacteria cause disease. ____

____

____

28. Explain why antibiotic resistance among bacteria is increasing. ____

____

29. The diagrams below represent three common bacterial shapes. Label each bacterial shape in the space provided.

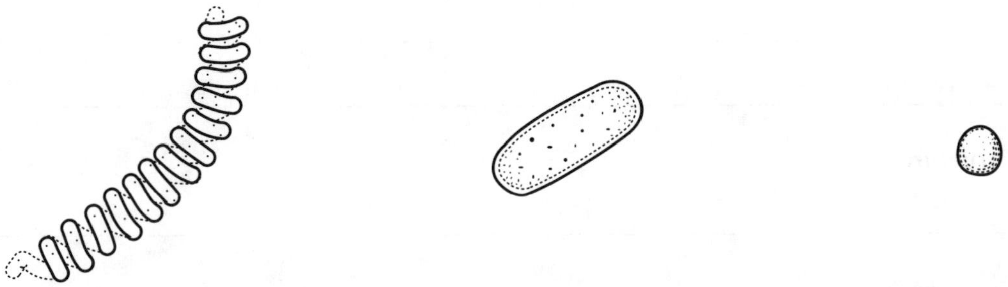

a ____________________ **b** ____________________ **c** ____________________

Name ________________________ Class ____________ Date ____________

DRAWING CONCLUSIONS **Follow the directions given below.**

30. The diagram below represents a bacterial cell. Label each structure indicated in the spaces provided. Then describe the function of the structures listed below the figure.

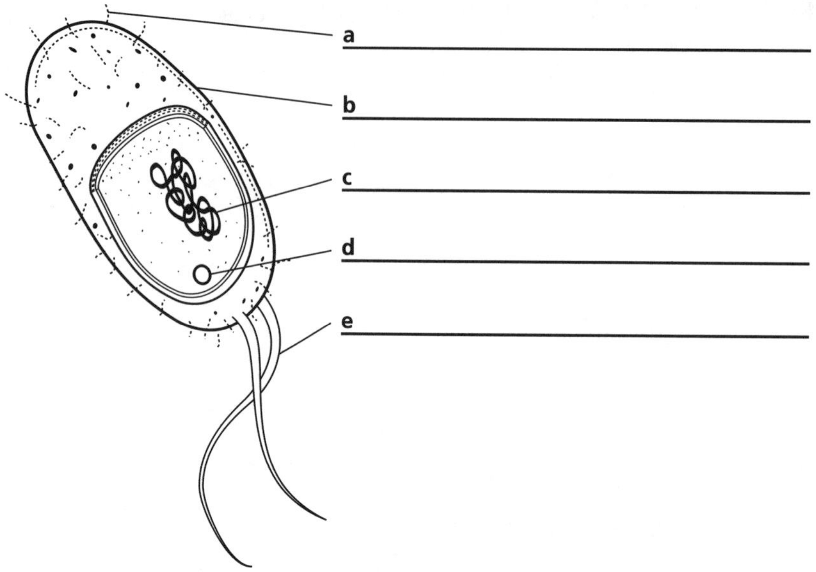

a. Structure *a*

____

____

b. Structure *b*

____

____

c. Structure *c*

____

____

d. Structure *d*

____

____

e. Structure *e*

____

____

Name ______________________ Class ____________ Date ____________

CHAPTER 25 TEST

VIRUSES

MATCHING **Write the correct letter in the blank before each numbered term.**

_____ **1.** reverse transcriptase

_____ **2.** provirus

_____ **3.** envelope

_____ **4.** inactivated virus

_____ **5.** prophage

_____ **6.** attenuated virus

_____ **7.** capsid

_____ **8.** receptor site

a. protein structure in all viruses

b. bacteriophage integrated in host DNA

c. virus that is able to replicate but not cause disease in its host

d. protein in some RNA viruses

e. place where a virus attaches to host cell

f. membrane structure in some viruses

g. HIV integrated in host DNA

h. virus that does not replicate within its host

TRUE-FALSE **If a statement is true, write *T* in the blank. If a statement is false, write *F* in the blank, and then in the space provided, explain why the statement is false.**

_____ **9.** Viruses are grouped according to the type and number of nucleic acid strands they contain, their shape, and whether or not they are enveloped.

____

_____ **10.** New virus particles are made using instructions encoded in host DNA.

____

_____ **11.** Retroviruses have an enzyme that makes DNA from RNA.

____

_____ **12.** In general, viruses are larger than cells.

____

_____ **13.** Viruses have been linked to some forms of cancer.

____

Name ______________________ Class ____________ Date ____________

MULTIPLE CHOICE **Write the letter of the most correct answer in the blank.**

______ **14.** A viral genome consists of

a. either DNA or RNA.
b. either DNA or protein.
c. both RNA and protein.
d. both DNA and RNA.

______ **15.** The lytic cycle differs from the lysogenic cycle in that the

a. lysogenic cycle kills the host cells and the lytic cycle does not kill host cells.
b. lytic cycle occurs immediately following infection and the lysogenic cycle occurs after a period of months or years.
c. lytic cycle kills the host cells and the lysogenic cycle does not kill host cells.
d. lytic cycle is characteristic of bacteriophages and the lysogenic cycle is characteristic of viruses that infect eukaryotic cells.

______ **16.** The viral nucleic acid becomes integrated into the host cell's DNA during a virus's

a. lytic cycle.
b. lysogenic cycle.
c. lytic cycle and lysogenic cycle.
d. None of the above

______ **17.** Which of the following is not effective in viral-disease prevention or treatment?

a. antibiotics
b. vaccines
c. antiviral drugs
d. control of animals that spread viruses

______ **18.** Which of the following associations between a virus and the human disease it causes is *incorrect?*

a. HIV—AIDS
b. chickenpox virus—shingles
c. hepatitis B virus—yellow fever
d. influenza virus—flu

______ **19.** Wendell Stanley is best known for

a. determining the structure of HIV.
b. being first to culture a virus.
c. being the first to crystallize a virus.
d. producing the first vaccine against TMV.

______ **20.** Reverse transcriptase

a. synthesizes RNA using DNA as a template.
b. synthesizes DNA using protein as a template.
c. synthesizes DNA using RNA as a template.
d. All of the above

______ **21.** The diagram at right represents a(n)

a. adenovirus.
b. retrovirus.
c. bacteriophage.
d. AIDS virus.

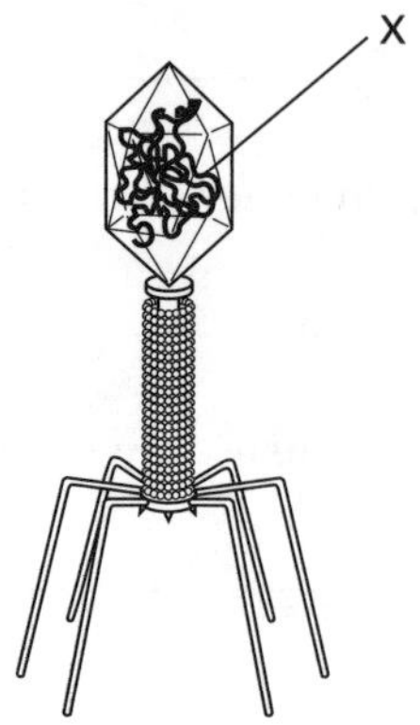

______ **22.** The structure labeled X in the diagram at right is

a. nucleic acid.
b. the collar.
c. the tail.
d. a tail fiber.

______ **23.** What most limits the effectiveness of vaccines in preventing viral diseases?

a. It is difficult to make enough vaccine to protect the entire population.
b. Viruses constantly change, and the vaccine may not recognize a new form of a virus.
c. Occasionally a vaccine can *cause* the disease it is meant to prevent.
d. Some viral diseases are caused by a combination of two or more viruses.

SHORT ANSWER **Answer the questions in the space provided.**

24. Explain why viruses are thought to have evolved from cells. ______________________

____

____

25. Distinguish between a temperate virus and a virulent virus. ______________________

____

____

26. Are viruses considered living organisms? Why or why not? ______________________

____

____

____

27. The diagram below represents an HIV particle. Label each structure indicated in the space provided.

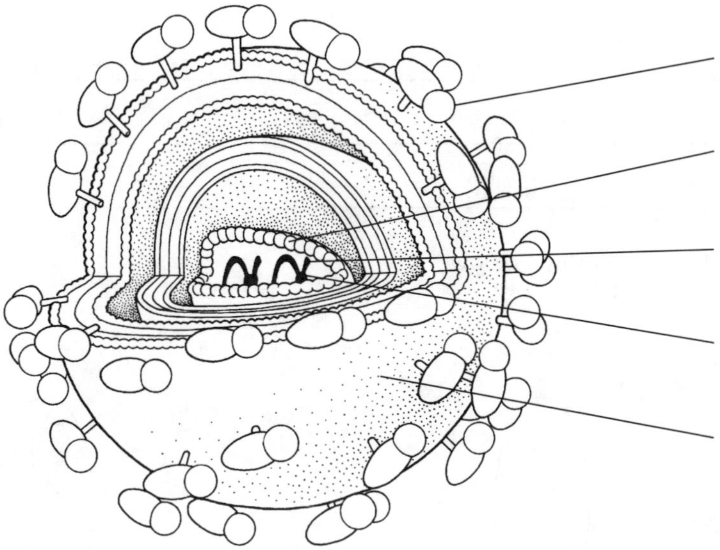

a ______________________

b ______________________

c ______________________

d ______________________

e ______________________

Name ______________________________ Class ______________ Date ______________

28. Compare viroids and prions with viruses. ______________________________

____

____

____

29. Explain how human actions facilitate outbreaks of disease caused by emerging viruses.

____

____

DRAWING CONCLUSIONS Follow the directions given below.

30. In a virology lab, bacterial cells infected with a temperate DNA virus were cultured. After causing the virus to become lytic, the researchers purified the viruses and analyzed their DNA. They found that some of the DNA was not viral DNA. Further analysis showed that the nonviral DNA was from the genome of the infected bacterial cells.

a. Explain how and when the bacterial genes became integrated in the viral genome.

____

____

____

b. List and describe each step of the lysogenic cycle.

____

____

____

____

____

c. Sequence the steps of the lytic cycle shown below.

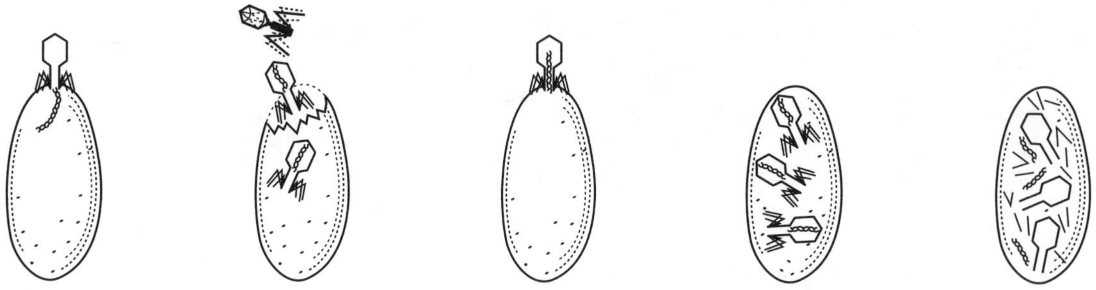

a ______________ b ______________ c ______________ d ______________ e ______________

Name ______________________ Class ____________ Date ____________

CHAPTER 26 TEST

PROTOZOA

MATCHING Write the correct letter in the blank before each numbered term.

_____ 1. *Trypanosoma*

_____ 2. *Paramecium*

_____ 3. *Toxoplasma*

_____ 4. Radiolaria

_____ 5. *Giardia*

_____ 6. *Amoeba*

_____ 7. *Plasmodium*

_____ 8. *Anopheles*

a. moves by pseudopodia

b. causes malaria

c. moves by cilia

d. covered by a protective test

e. transmits malaria to humans

f. found in domestic cats

g. causes Chaga's disease

h. known to contaminate stream water in the United States

TRUE-FALSE If a statement is true, write *T* in the blank. If a statement is false, write *F* in the blank, and then in the space provided, explain why the statement is false.

_____ 9. Conjugation is a process of sexual reproduction in ciliates.

____

_____ 10. Protozoa are thought to have descended from multicellular eukaryotes.

____

_____ 11. All protozoa are parasitic during at least part of their life.

____

_____ 12. The process shown in the diagram at right is called cytoplasmic streaming.

____

____

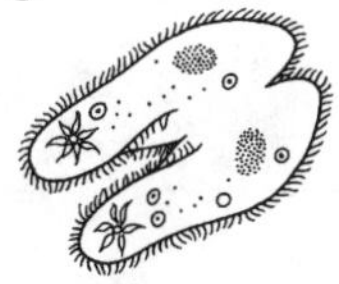

_____ 13. The protozoan that once inhabited the shell at right was probably a foraminiferan.

____

____

Name ________________________________ Class ______________ Date ____________

MULTIPLE CHOICE **Write the letter of the most correct answer in the blank.**

_____ **14.** Protozoan habitats are characterized by the presence of

a. host organisms. **b.** algae. **c.** moisture. **d.** blood.

_____ **15.** Which of the following is an adaptation to extreme environments?

a. cyst formation **b.** food vacuoles **c.** eyespots **d.** multiple fission

_____ **16.** Sarcodines use their pseudopodia for

a. capturing food. **b.** engulfing food. **c.** movement. **d.** All of the above

_____ **17.** Which of the following structures is *not* involved in feeding in ciliates?

a. contractile vacuole
b. cilia
c. oral groove
d. gullet

_____ **18.** Certain sarcodines affect Earth's geology by

a. secreting acids that break down rock into soil.
b. ingesting calcium carbonate and secreting silicon dioxide.
c. having mineralized shells that form sedimentary rock after they die.
d. washing up onto shores when they die, and causing the accumulation of silicon dioxide and calcium carbonate.

_____ **19.** What do trypanosomiasis, Chaga's disease, leishmaniasis, and giardiasis have in common?

a. They are all caused by sporozoans.
b. They are all transmitted by insects.
c. They all affect primarily the heart and the brain.
d. They are all caused by zooflagellates.

_____ **20.** Which of the following is *not* characteristic of the life cycle of *Plasmodium?*

a. The life cycle can be completed solely in the mosquito host, but cannot be completed in the human host.
b. Sexual reproduction occurs in the mosquito host, and asexual reproduction occurs in the human host.
c. The organism forms four different types of cells during its life cycle.
d. Because there are two hosts of the disease organism the disease can be controlled by reducing the population of the nonhuman host.

_____ **21.** Pseudopodia are extensions of a sarcodine's

a. pellicle. **b.** cilia. **c.** flagella. **d.** cytoplasm.

_____ **22.** In *Paramecium,* the macronucleus

a. participates in the exchange of genetic material during conjugation.
b. is also called the micronucleus.
c. contains the micronucleus.
d. contains multiple copies of DNA.

_____ **23.** Which of the following best describes members of the kingdom Protista?

a. They are mutlticellular and eukaryotic.
b. They are mutlticellular and prokaryotic.
c. They are single-celled and eukaryotic.
d. They are single-celled and prokaryotic.

SHORT ANSWER Answer the questions in the space provided.

24. Would a motile protozoan or a nonmotile protozoan be more likely to be free-living? Explain your answer.

____

____

____

25. Explain the role of protozoa in aquatic-ecosystem food chains.

____

____

26. Distinguish between the terms *protist* and *protozoan*.

____

____

____

27. The diagram below represents the life cycle of *Plasmodium.* Label the four stages of the life cycle indicated in the space provided.

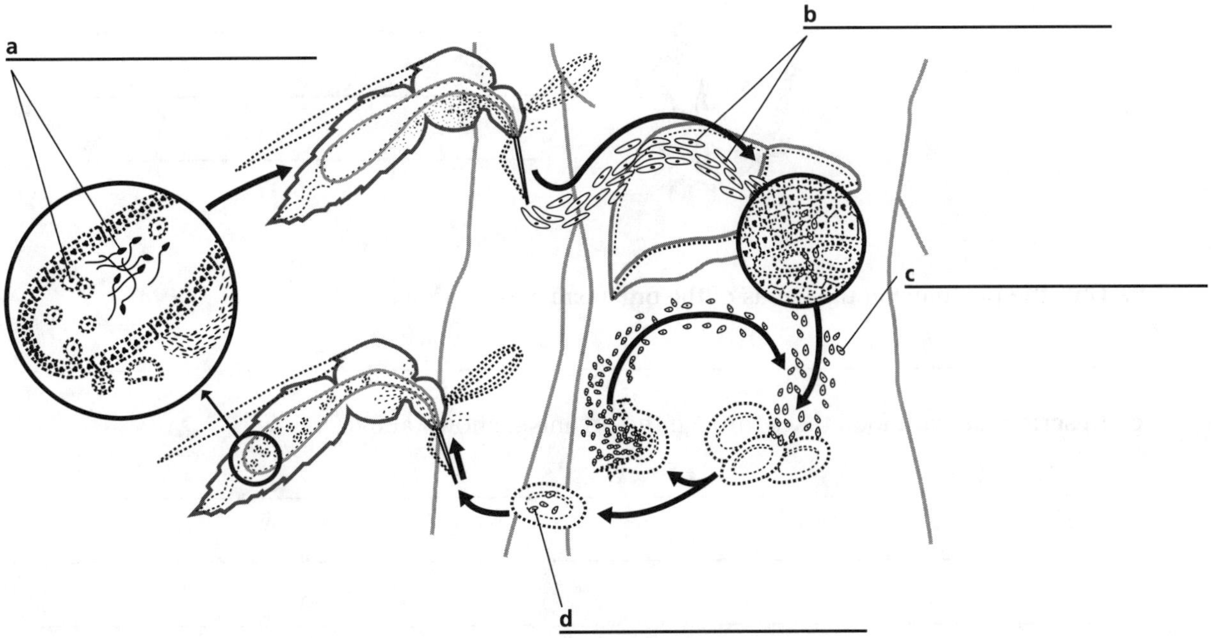

28. Explain how conjugation in protozoa differs from conjugation in bacteria.

______

______

______

29. Describe three means of locomotion among protozoa.

______

______

______

DRAWING CONCLUSIONS Follow the directions given below.

30. The diagram below represents a protozoan.

a. Label each structure in the space indicated.

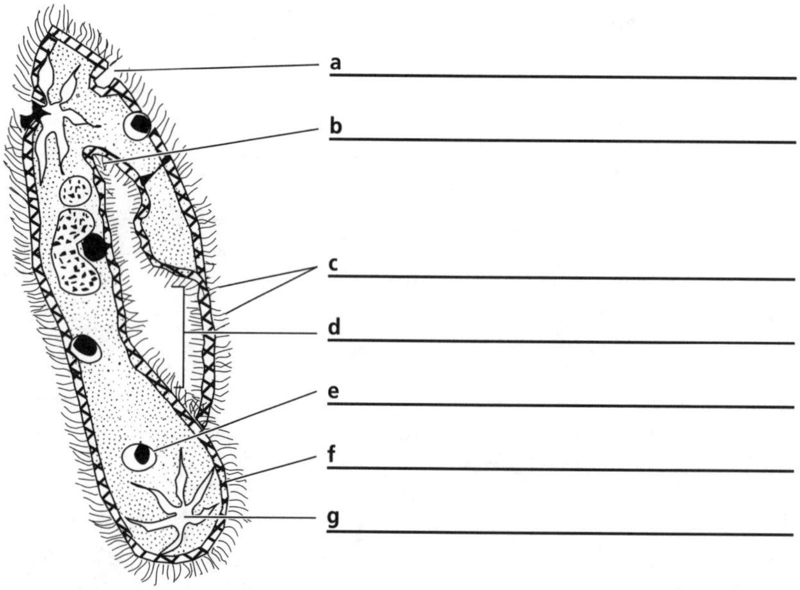

b. Give the phylum and the genus of the organism shown above.

______

c. Describe the path food takes through the organism shown above.

______

______

______

______

Name ______________________ Class ____________ Date ____________

CHAPTER 27 TEST

ALGAE AND FUNGUSLIKE PROTISTS

MATCHING Write the correct letter in the blank space before each numbered term.

_____ **1.** *Macrocystis*

_____ **2.** *Ulva*

_____ **3.** *Euglena*

_____ **4.** Rhodophyta

_____ **5.** Chlorophyta

_____ **6.** *Noctiluca*

_____ **7.** *Volvox*

_____ **8.** plasmodium

a. colonial alga

b. slime-mold feeding form

c. probably the plant ancestral phylum

d. cause of red tides

e. has both plantlike and animal-like characteristics

f. group of red algae

g. may grow to 100 m in length

h. reproduces by alternation of generations

TRUE-FALSE If a statement is true, write *T* in the blank. If a statement is false, write *F* in the blank, and then in the space provided, explain why the statement is false.

_____ **9.** All algae contain the pigment chlorophyll *a*.

_____ **10.** Both algae and plants form gametes in multicellular chambers called gametangia.

_____ **11.** Euglenoids are either autotrophic or heterotrophic, depending on their environment.

_____ **12.** The organism shown at right is a member of the phylum Dinoflagellata.

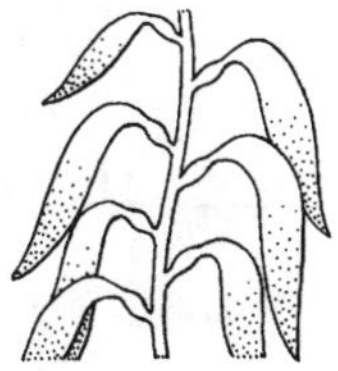

_____ **13.** The organism shown at right is a member of the phylum Bacillariophyta.

MULTIPLE CHOICE **Write the letter of the most correct answer in the blank.**

_____ **14.** Algae differ from most other protists in that they are

a. unicellular and photosynthetic.
b. unicellular or multicellular and photosynthetic.
c. multicellular and photosynthetic.
d. unicellular and photosynthetic or heterotrophic.

_____ **15.** Which of the following is characteristic of all algae?

a. pyrenoids **b.** a conjugation tube **c.** a thallus **d.** a holdfast

_____ **16.** Most algae form gametes that are

a. visibly similar but chemically different.
b. visibly different from each other.
c. visibly and chemically similar to each other.
d. visibly different but chemically similar.

_____ **17.** Which phylum of algae includes the most-diverse organisms in terms of form, habitat, and lifestyle?

a. Rhodophyta **b.** Dinoflagellata **c.** Chlorophyta **d.** Chrysophyta

_____ **18.** Diatoms are unlike other algae in that they

a. are nonmotile.
b. store food in the form of laminarin.
c. surround themselves in boxes made of silicon dioxide.
d. lack cell walls.

_____ **19.** Which of the following best describes euglenoids?

a. They are parasitic.
b. They can form cysts when exposed to environmental stress.
c. They lack contractile vacuoles.
d. They lack cell walls and are highly motile.

_____ **20.** Slime molds typically live

a. in moist environments containing dead plant material.
b. on moist, living plants.
c. in water.
d. inside living animals.

_____ **21.** Which of the following best describes the life cycle of a slime mold?

a. The feeding form is nonmotile, and the fruiting body is motile.
b. The feeding form is motile, and the fruiting body is nonmotile.
c. The feeding form cannot survive in dry environments, and the fruiting body can.
d. The feeding form is unicellular, and the fruiting body is multicellular.

Name ______________________ Class ____________ Date ____________

______ **22.** All water molds can be characterized as

a. living in aquatic environments.
b. saprophytes.
c. parasites.
d. having filamentous bodies.

______ **23.** Algal reproductive structures form gametes

a. in multicellular chambers called gametangia.
b. in unicellular chambers called gametangia.
c. in organelles called pyrenoids.
d. None of the above

SHORT ANSWER **Answer the questions in the space provided.**

24. Compare slime molds with water molds. ______________________

____

____

____

25. List the phyla that contain seaweeds. How do seaweeds compare with other algae?

____

____

____

26. The diagram below represents asexual reproduction and sexual reproduction in *Chlamydomonas*. Label the two types of reproduction in the spaces provided.

______________________ ______________________

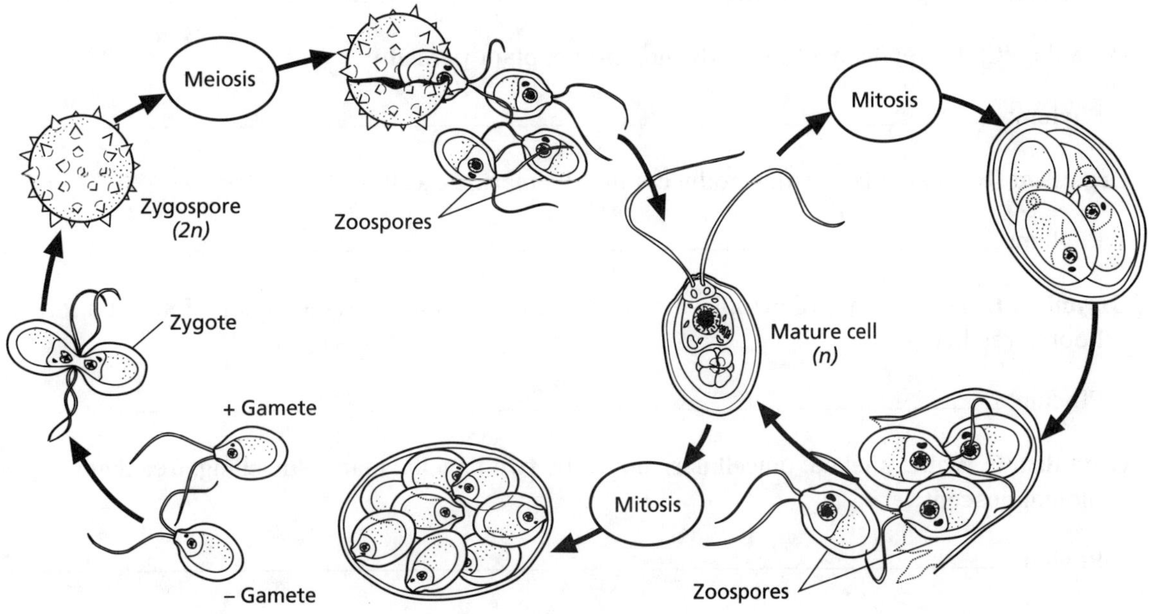

27. Describe sexual reproduction in oomycetes. ______________________

____

____

____

28. Describe the characteristic features of reproduction in *Ulva.* ______________________

____

____

____

29. What kinds of household products contain diatom shells? ______________________

____

____

DRAWING CONCLUSIONS Follow the directions given below.

30. Six protists are described below. In the space after each description, write the name of the phylum to which the organism belongs.

Organism A: Green; unicellular; moves using a flagellum; lives in fresh water; is free-living; lacks cell walls

Phylum: ______________________

Organism B: Brown; 60 m long; nonmotile; has leaflike, stemlike, and rootlike structures; marine-dwelling, free-living

Phylum: ______________________

Organism C: White; filamentous body; nonmotile; plant parasite

Phylum: ______________________

Organism D: Green; filamentous body; nonmotile; marine-dwelling; free-living

Phylum: ______________________

Organism E: Yellow; mass of cytoplasm with many nuclei; ameboid movement; found on forest floors, free-living

Phylum: ______________________

Organism F: White; shelled; unicellular; moves by two flagella; marine-dwelling; free-living; bioluminescent

Phylum: ______________________

Name ______________________ Class ____________ Date ____________

CHAPTER 28 TEST

FUNGI

MATCHING **Write the correct letter in the blank before each numbered term.**

_____ **1.** mold

_____ **2.** *Amanita* sp.

_____ **3.** zygosporangium

_____ **4.** *Agaricus* sp.

_____ **5.** ascocarp

_____ **6.** yeast

_____ **7.** lichen

_____ **8.** mycorrhiza

a. visible, cuplike sexual reproductive structure

b. association between a fungus and plant roots

c. fused gametangia

d. tangled mass of hyphae

e. edible mushroom

f. poisonous mushroom

g. association between a fungus and a green alga

h. unicellular fungi that resemble bacteria

TRUE-FALSE **If a statement is true, write *T* in the blank. If a statement is false, write *F* in the blank, and then in the space provided, explain why the statement is false.**

_____ **9.** The cell walls of fungi are composed of cellulose.

____

_____ **10.** All fungi reproduce asexually and sexually.

____

_____ **11.** Mycorrhizae and lichens are associations in which the fungus benefits and the other organism is harmed.

____

_____ **12.** Fungi imperfecti reproduce only sexually.

____

_____ **13.** Fungi evolved from prokaryotes through endosymbiosis.

____

Name ______________________ Class ____________ Date ____________

MULTIPLE CHOICE **Write the letter of the most correct answer in the blank.**

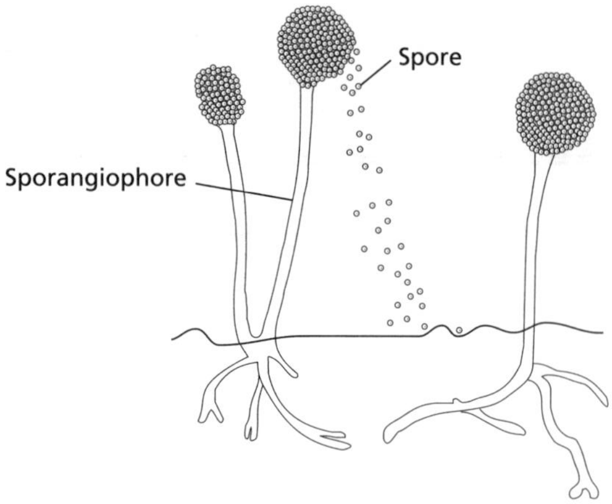

______ **14.** The fungus represented at right is a(n)

a. zygomycete.
b. basidiomycete.
c. ascomycete.
d. oomycete.

______ **15.** The type of reproduction represented in the diagram at right is called

a. sexual reproduction.
b. asexual reproduction.
c. alternation of generations.
d. meiosis.

______ **16.** A mycelium is an interwoven mat of

a. spores. **b.** septa. **c.** hyphae. **d.** conidia.

______ **17.** All asexual reproductive spores in fungi are

a. diploid.
b. composed of only one cell.
c. produced on stalklike structures.
d. produced on either "plus" or "minus" hyphae.

______ **18.** Which of the following is *not* a means by which humans use fungi to make food?

a. cooking fungal structures
b. genetically engineering fungi
c. alcohol production
d. bread production

______ **19.** Which of the following is *not* a medically useful substance produced by a fungus?

a. penicillin
b. hepatitis B vaccine
c. cortisone
d. aflatoxin

______ **20.** Fungi cause disease in humans through

a. infection only.
b. allergies only.
c. infection and allergies.
d. infection, poisoning, and allergies.

______ **21.** Unlike animals, fungi

a. ingest their food before digesting it.
b. photosynthesize their food before digesting it.
c. photosynthesize their food before ingesting it.
d. digest their food before ingesting it.

______ **22.** The structure labeled X in the diagram at right is called a(n)

a. coenocytic hypha.
b. mycelium.
c. septum.
d. conidia.

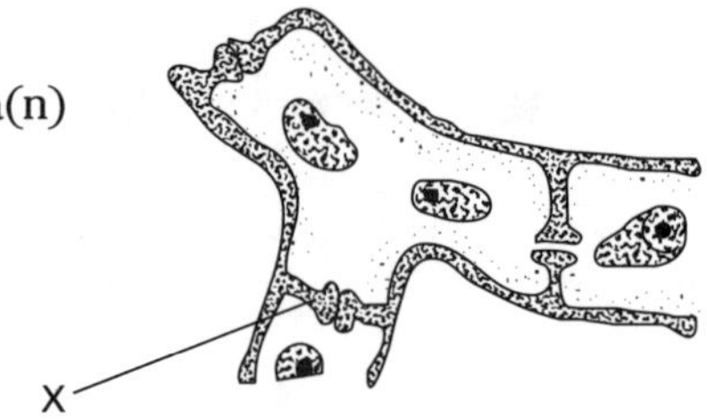

______ **23.** The fungus represented at right is a(n)

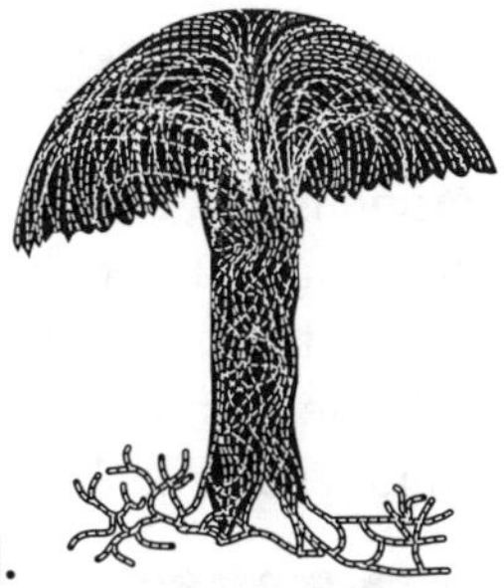

a. zygomycete.
b. basidiomycete.
c. ascomycete.
d. deuteromycete.

SHORT ANSWER Answer the questions in the space provided.

24. List three different kinds of asexual spores formed by fungi, and describe how they are produced.

____

____

____

25. How does a gametangium differ from a zygosporangium? ______________________

____

____

26. What are mycorrhizae, and what is their ecological role? ______________________

____

____

27. Identify one way in which fungi differ from organisms in each of the other kingdoms of eukaryotic organisms. ______________________

____

____

28. Explain why being able to reproduce both sexually and asexually is an adaptive advantage.

____

____

____

29. Compare an ascocarp with a basidiocarp. ______________________

____

____

DRAWING CONCLUSIONS Follow the directions given below.

30. An experiment was conducted in which a lichen, the lichen's component fungus, and the lichen's component alga all were grown in three different locations. In each location, 10 1-cm diameter disks each of the lichen, the fungus, and the alga were set on the ground, watered, and allowed to grow for three months. The data in the table below show the average size of the disks of lichen, fungus, and alga in each of the three locations after three months.

Comparison of the Growth of Lichen, Fungus, and Alga

	Average disk diameter (cm)		
Organism	**Location 1**	**Location 2**	**Location 3**
Lichen	4	5	5.5
Fungus alone	1.5	0	5
Alga alone	1	0	4.5

a. What hypothesis were the experimenters testing? ______________________

____

____

b. What were the independent and dependent variables in this experiment?

____

____

c. What are your interpretations of the results obtained in each of the three locations?

____

____

____

d. What conclusions can you make about the hypothesis? ______________________

____

____

____

e. If location 2 is bare rock how might lichen contribute to ecological succession?

____

____

Name ______________________ Class ____________ Date ____________

CHAPTER 29 TEST

THE IMPORTANCE OF PLANTS

MATCHING **Write the correct letter in the blank before each numbered term.**

_____ **1.** cereals

_____ **2.** hay fever

_____ **3.** legumes

_____ **4.** nitrogen fixation in roots

_____ **5.** fruits

_____ **6.** mycorrhize

_____ **7.** root crops

_____ **8.** vegetables

a. leaf, stem, root, and seed foods

b. beneficial plant-fungus interaction

c. foods of the pea family

d. allergic response to plant pollen

e. dry fruits of grain plants

f. roots or underground stems

g. beneficial plant-bacteria interaction

h. foods usually containing seeds

TRUE-FALSE **If a statement is true, write *T* in the blank. If a statement is false, write *F* in the blank and then, in the space provided, explain why the statement is false.**

_____ **9.** Essential amino acids that are missing in cereals can be obtained from legumes.

____

_____ **10.** The aesthetic value of plants is unimportant compared with their food value.

____

_____ **11.** Aspirin, digitalis, cortisone, and quinine are plant products used as medicines.

____

_____ **12.** Plant ecology is the study of the interactions among plants.

____

_____ **13.** The introduction of microorganisms, animals, and other plants can adversely affect native and crop plants.

____

MULTIPLE CHOICE **Write the letter of the most correct answer in the blank.**

_____ **14.** Ninety percent of our food supply comes from _____ species of plants.

a. 10
b. 20
c. 100
d. 2000

_____ **15.** Most of the world's cultivated land is used to grow

a. cereals.
b. root crops.
c. legumes.
d. vegetables.

_____ **16.** Legumes can be grown without the use of

a. irrigation.
b. pesticides.
c. farm machinery.
d. nitrogen fertilizer.

_____ **17.** Which of the following is a root crop?

a. soybean
b. peanuts
c. cassava
d. sorghum

_____ **18.** Which of the following is scientifically classified as a fruit but commonly referred to as a vegetable?

a. broccoli
b. cabbage
c. green beans
d. asparagus

_____ **19.** Which of the following is *not* currently used to increase food production?

a. carbon dioxide sprays on fields
b. pesticides
c. fertilizers
d. improved cultivars

_____ **20.** Wheat is

a. one of the oldest agricultural crops.
b. one of the crops produced in the largest amounts worldwide.
c. a crop that has been modified by humans over time.
d. All of the above

_____ **21.** Fungi can

a. cause disease in plants.
b. increase plant uptake of water and inorganic nutrients.
c. change the structure of plant roots.
d. All of the above

_____ **22.** Which of the following is *not* a poisonous plant?

a. holly **b.** mistletoe **c.** giant ragweed **d.** tobacco

_____ **23.** Which two cereal grains are grown in greatest quantity?

a. corn and wheat
b. rice and wheat
c. sorghum and corn
d. rice and barley

Name ______________________ Class ____________ Date ____________

SHORT ANSWER **Answer the questions in the space provided.**

24. Identify three nondietary uses of plants. ______________________

____

____

____

25. Identify three ways that humans have increased food production.

____

____

____

26. Where do scientists hope to find new sources of medicines? ______________________

____

____

27. How does the overgrowth of water hyacinth on lakes and rivers negatively affect the environment?

____

____

28. In the space below each illustration, describe what effect the insect may have on the plant and what might happen if an insecticide were used on the plant.

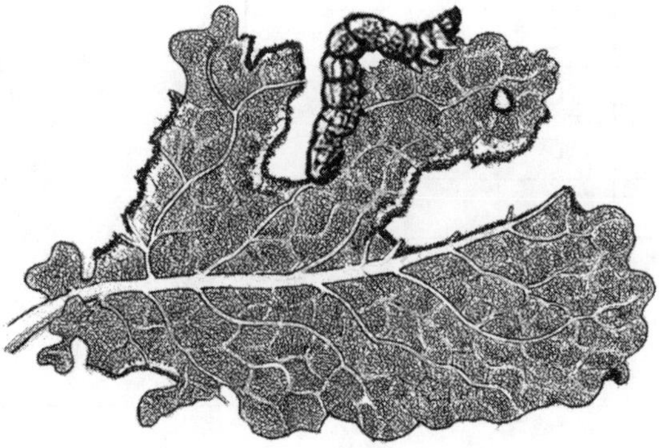

______________________ ______________________

______________________ ______________________

______________________ ______________________

______________________ ______________________

29. Identify three substances used by plants that are also needed by humans. ____________

____

____

DRAWING CONCLUSIONS Follow the directions given below.

30. Refer to the tables below to answer the following questions. In the tables below, some legumes and grains are rated according to how much of each of four amino acids they contain. A rating of *D* indicates that the food contains a tiny amount of an amino acid. A rating of *A* indicates that the food contains a day's allowance of an amino acid.

Table A Legumes

Legume	Amino acids			
1/4–1/3 cup, dry	tryptophan	isoleucine	lysine	cysteine and methionine
Kidney beans	C	B	A+	D
Lima beans	C	B	A+	C
Tofu	A	B	A	C
Lentils	C	B	A+	D
Navy beans	C	B	A+	D

Table B Grains

Grain	Amino acids			
1/4–1/3 cup, dry	tryptophan	isoleucine	lysine	cysteine and methionine
Wheat	B	C	C	B
Rye	C	C	C	B
Barley	A	C	C	B
Millet	A+	C	C	B
Oatmeal	B	C	C	B

a. According to Table A, which legume is the best source of all of the amino acids rated?

____

b. According to Table B, which grain is the best source of all of the amino acids rated?

____

c. Compare the ratings of the legumes with those of the grains. Are legumes and grains high in the same amino acids? Explain your answer. ____________

____

____

Name ______________________ Class ____________ Date ____________

CHAPTER 30 TEST

PLANT EVOLUTION AND CLASSIFICATION

MATCHING Write the correct letter in the blank before each numbered term.

_____ **1.** gametophyte

_____ **2.** xylem

_____ **3.** dicot

_____ **4.** phloem

_____ **5.** ginkgo

_____ **6.** cuticle

_____ **7.** sporophyte

_____ **8.** monocot

a. waxy covering on plant surfaces

b. nonphotosynthetic moss phase

c. transports organic compounds

d. parallel leaf venation

e. photosynthetic moss phase

f. transports water

g. fleshy seeds

h. net leaf venation

TRUE-FALSE If a statement is true, write *T* in the blank. If a statement is false, write *F* in the blank and then, in the space provided, explain why the statement is false.

_____ **9.** The cuticle of a plant allows the uptake of carbon dioxide and loss of oxygen.

____

_____ **10.** Vascular tissue allows plants to grow tall because it transports water to the top of the plant and carbohydrates to the roots.

____

_____ **11.** The plant material in peat bogs decomposes quickly because the bogs are very alkaline.

____

_____ **12.** Gymnosperms produce "naked" seeds, while angiosperms produce seeds protected inside a fruit.

____

_____ **13.** The only plant phyla that produce seeds are Coniferophyta and Anthophyta.

____

Name ______________________ Class ____________ Date ____________

MULTIPLE CHOICE **Write the letter of the most correct answer in the blank.**

______ **14.** Sphagnum is often used

a. for medicinal purposes.
b. as a food.
c. to enrich soil and help it retain water.
d. as a combustible fuel.

______ **15.** Nonvascular plants are distinguished by the

a. absence of xylem and phloem.
b. presence of rhizomes.
c. absence of cuticle.
d. presence of spores.

______ **16.** A seed is

a. a modified spore.
b. produced on the gametophyte.
c. a plant embryo inside a protective coat.
d. All of the above

______ **17.** Which of the following is *not* an ecological role of mosses?

a. on rock, accumulating inorganic and organic matter that other plants can grow in
b. preventing soil erosion from rainfall by covering the soil's surface
c. growing in areas where vegetation has been destroyed by fire
d. growing faster than undesirable plants

______ **18.** Bryophytes are

a. nonvascular plants that produce roots but not stems and leaves.
b. low-growing plants that live in moist environments.
c. completely terrestrial because they do not require water in order to reproduce sexually.
d. All of the above

______ **19.** All vascular plants

a. have conducting tissues and alternation of generations.
b. are large, have conducting tissues, and produce spores.
c. have conducting tissues and produce seeds.
d. have conducting tissues and produces spores, seeds, and flowers.

______ **20.** True roots, stems, and leaves are characteristics of

a. all plants. **b.** all vascular plants. **c.** all seed plants. **d.** all angiosperms.

______ **21.** Which of the following phyla of plants produces seeds?

a. Lycophyta **b.** Sphenophyta **c.** Pterophyta **d.** Coniferophyta

______ **22.** The plant structure shown at right is part of a

a. nonvascular, flowering plant.
b. vascular, seeded gymnosperm.
c. vascular, seeded angiosperm.
d. nonvascular liverwort.

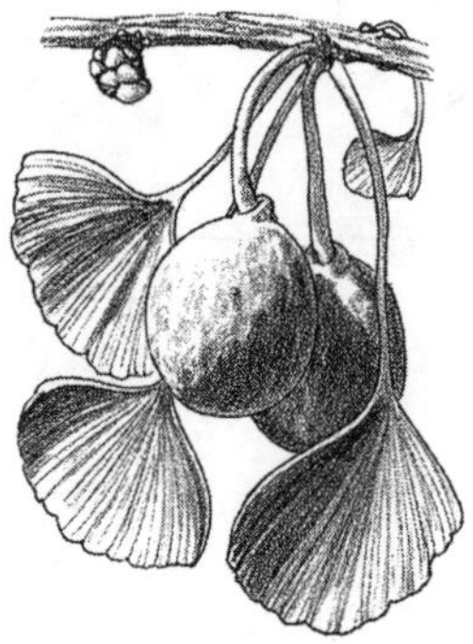

______ **23.** The plant structure shown at right is part of a

a. nonvascular, seedless fern.
b. vascular, seedless cycad.
c. vascular, seeded angiosperm.
d. nonvascular, seedless gymnosperm.

SHORT ANSWER **Answer the questions in the space provided.**

24. What are the primary functions of spores and seeds? ______

25. In what ways do green algae differ from plants? ______

26. Why do nonvascular plants have to live in moist environments? ______

27. Name three bryophytes, and identify their common characteristics. ______

28. Which plant phylum contains the tallest and most massive plants? Is this a phylum of nonvascular, seedless vascular, or seed plants? ______

29. Conifers are often found living at high elevations in locations with cold, dry winters. What characteristic enables them to retain their leaves in these conditions? ______

Name ______________________ Class ____________ Date ____________

DRAWING CONCLUSIONS **Follow the directions given below.**

30. Examine the diagram of a generalized life cycle of land plants below as you answer questions a–e.

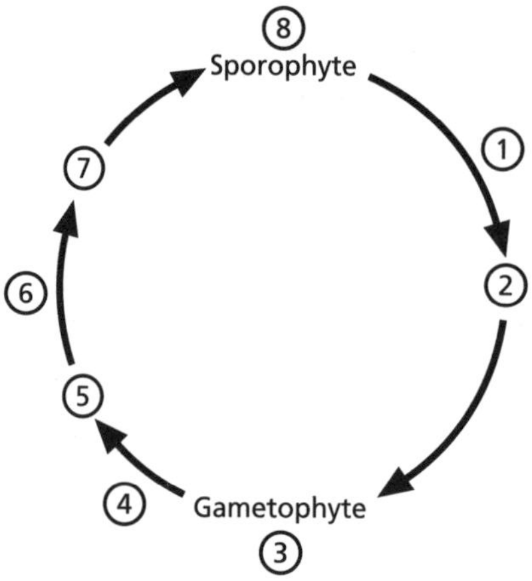

a. What type of cell reproduction occurs during stage *1?* ______________________

____

____

b. What is the name of the structures produced during stage *2?* Are these haploid or diploid?

What type of cell reproduction occurs during stage *4?* ______________________

____

____

c. What is/are the name(s) of the structures produced during stage *5?* Are these haploid or diploid?

____

____

d. What process occurs during stage *6?* ______________________

____

____

e. What is the name of the structures produced during stage *7?* What structure is produced between stages *7* and *8* in gymnosperms and angiosperms? ______________________

____

____

____

____

Name ______________________ Class ____________ Date ____________

CHAPTER 31 TEST

PLANT STRUCTURE AND FUNCTION

MATCHING **Write the correct letter in the blank before each numbered term.**

_____ **1.** collenchyma

_____ **2.** lateral root

_____ **3.** intercalary meristem

_____ **4.** fibrous root system

_____ **5.** sclerenchyma

_____ **6.** taproot system

_____ **7.** parenchyma

_____ **8.** vascular cambium

a. even, thick-walled, rigid cells

b. meristem between xylem and phloem

c. root branching off of a primary root

d. irregular, thick-walled cells

e. root system with an enlarged primary root

f. meristem found only in monocots

g. root system with many branch roots

h. thin-walled cells that can be cube-shaped or elongated

TRUE-FALSE **If a statement is true, write *T* in the blank. If a statement is false, write *F* in the blank and then, in the space provided, explain why the statement is false.**

_____ **9.** In monocots and dicots, primary growth occurs in the apical meristems and intercalary meristems.

____

_____ **10.** Primary growth results in the lengthening of plant structures, and secondary growth results in the widening of plant structures.

____

_____ **11.** Plant roots are always found below ground level.

____

_____ **12.** Macronutrients are elements that are required for plant growth, while micronutrients are elements that are not required for plant growth.

____

_____ **13.** Dicot stems contain vascular cambium, which may produce secondary growth, while monocot stems lack vascular cambium and therefore cannot produce secondary growth.

____

Name ______________________________ Class ____________ Date ____________

MULTIPLE CHOICE **Write the letter of the most-correct answer in the blank.**

_____ **14.** Which type of plant cell functions in metabolic activities such as photosynthesis, storage, and healing?

a. collenchyma **b.** parenchyma **c.** sclerenchyma **d.** All of the above

_____ **15.** Which of the following associations between a plant tissue system and its function(s) is *incorrect?*

a. dermal tissue system—absorption, gas exchange, protection
b. ground tissue system—support, storage, photosynthesis
c. vascular tissue system—support, transport
d. All of the above are correct.

_____ **16.** Primary growth in roots results in _____ and secondary growth results in _____

a. lengthening of roots; thickening of roots.
b. lengthening of roots; branching of roots.
c. germination of roots; lengthening of roots.
d. production of the apical meristem; division of cells in the apical meristem.

_____ **17.** The function of the endodermis in roots is to

a. absorb water and minerals from the soil.
b. produce branch roots.
c. store water and/or carbohydrates.
d. regulate the movement of substances into the vascular tissue of the root.

_____ **18.** Which of the following associations between a root structure and its function(s) is incorrect?

a. epidermis—absorption of water and minerals
b. cortex—storage of water and/or starch
c. endodermis—structural support and anchorage of the plant
d. vascular cylinder—transport of water, minerals, and carbohydrates

_____ **19.** Which of the following may be found in stems but not in roots?

a. apical meristems **b.** nodes **c.** vascular tissue **d.** secondary growth

_____ **20.** Lateral roots form from _____, while lateral stems form from _____

a. the pericycle inside the root; buds on the surface of the stem.
b. the pericycle on the surface of the root; buds inside the stem.
c. the endodermis inside the root; buds on the surface of the stem.
d. meristematic tissue throughout the root; meristematic tissue in nodes of the stem.

_____ **21.** Annual rings in woody plants form as a result of

a. the production of secondary phloem, which contains cells of different sizes that were produced during different times of the growing season.
b. the production of alternating rings of secondary xylem and secondary phloem.
c. the production of secondary xylem, separated by bands of vascular cambium.
d. the production of secondary xylem, which contains cells of different sizes that were produced during different times of the growing season.

Name ______________________ Class ____________ Date ____________

______ **22.** Which of the following associations between a leaf adaptation and its function is incorrect?

a. tendrils—support of a climbing vine
b. tubular leaves—trapping insects
c. spines—increasing the photosynthetic surface area
d. dense coating of hairs—reducing light absorption

______ **23.** Water is transported from the roots to the leaves of a plant by the process of

a. expiration.
b. transpiration.
c. primary growth.
d. absorption.

SHORT ANSWER Answer the questions in the space provided.

24. What is the function of tracheids? ______________________

____

____

25. What are the lateral meristems of plants, and what is their function?

____

____

26. What adaptations of roots maximize water and mineral absorption?

____

____

27. Identify the structures that a water molecule would move through on its way from the soil into the xylem of a plant root. ______________________

____

____

28. Identify the cells depicted in the illustration, describe how they function, and describe their role in the activities conducted by leaves.

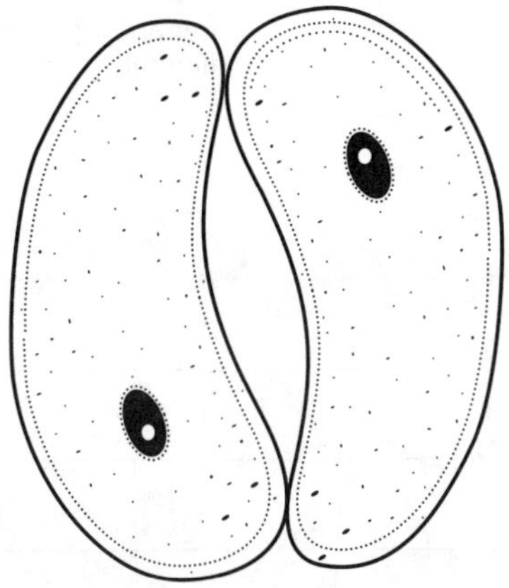

____

____

____

____

____

____

29. How are carbohydrates transported throughout a plant? ______________________________

____

____

DRAWING CONCLUSIONS Follow the directions given below.

30. The diagram depicts several processes that occur in plants. For each of the lettered processes, identify the activity occurring and the specific structure and location where the process occurs. Refer to the diagram as you write your answers on lines a–e below.

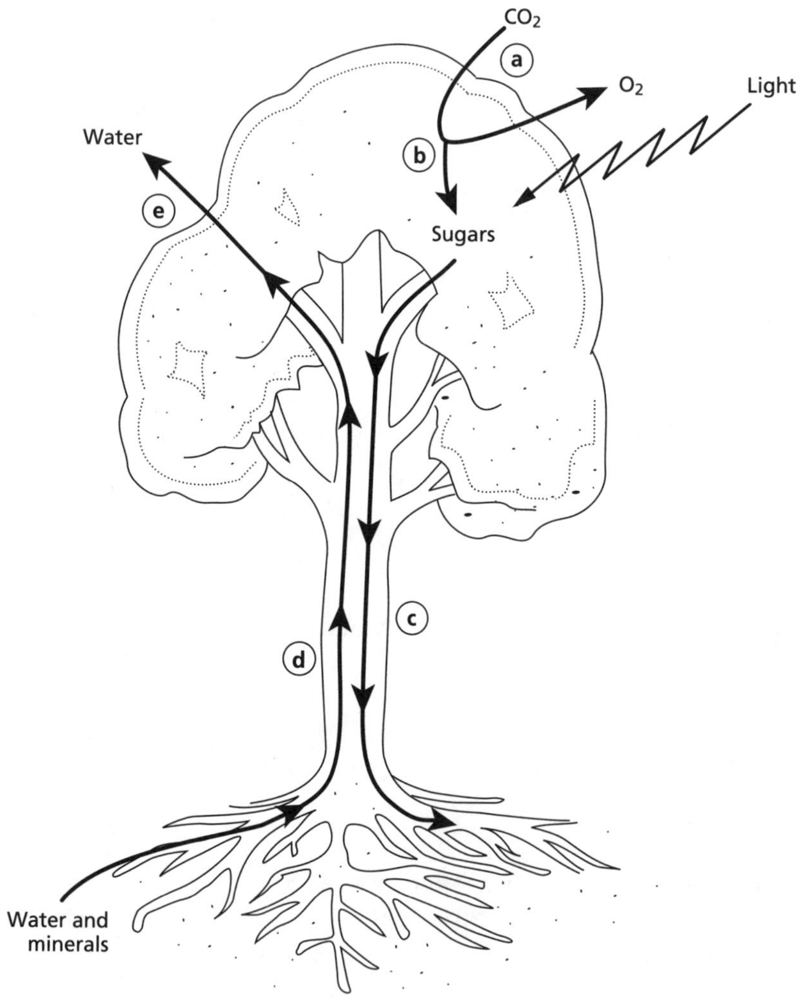

a. ____

b. ____

c. ____

d. ____

e. ____

Name ____________________ Class __________ Date __________

CHAPTER 32 TEST

PLANT REPRODUCTION

MATCHING **Write the correct letter in the blank below each numbered term.**

_____ 1. stamen

_____ 2. heterospory

_____ 3. embryo sac

_____ 4. fleshy simple fruits

_____ 5. dry simple fruits

_____ 6. pistil

_____ 7. pollen grain

_____ 8. homospory

a. male gametophyte
b. stigma, style, and ovary
c. producing only one type of spore
d. legumes, grains, nuts, and achenes
e. anther and filament
f. female gametophyte
g. producing two types of spores
h. berries, pomes, drupes, and pepos

TRUE-FALSE **If a statement is true, write *T* in the blank. If a statement is false, write *F* in the blank and then, in the space provided, explain why the statement is false.**

_____ 9. The sporophyte of mosses differs from that of ferns and conifers in that it is not photosynthetic.

____

_____ 10. Moss plants are heterosporous, while fern and conifer plants are homosporous.

____

_____ 11. Angiosperms and gymnosperms both have pollen grains that form pollen tubes, but the pollen tubes of angiosperms grow much faster than those of gymnosperms.

____

_____ 12. Double fertilization occurs in all seed plants.

____

_____ 13. The cotyledons of dicots usually remain below the soil surface following seed germination, while the cotyledons of monocots usually emerge above the soil surface.

____

Name ______________________ Class ____________ Date ____________

MULTIPLE CHOICE **Write the letter of the most-correct answer in the blank.**

______ **14.** A dominant gametophyte, homospory, archegonia and antheridia, eggs and flagellated sperm, and zygotes developing in the archegonium characterize the life cycle of

a. ferns. **b.** mosses. **c.** conifers. **d.** flowering plants.

______ **15.** Which of the following is characteristic of conifers but *not* of mosses or ferns?

a. a dominant sporophyte
b. antheridia and archegonia
c. nonmotile sperm cells
d. homospory

______ **16.** In the life cycle of a fern,

a. archegonia and antheridia are produced on the same gametophyte.
b. antheridia produce egg cells and archegonia produce sperm cells.
c. megaspores and microspores are produced.
d. pollen grains transport nonmotile sperm cells to egg cells.

______ **17.** Which of the following statements about a floral part and its function is incorrect?

a. The stamen produces microspores that develop into pollen grains.
b. The pistil produces megaspores that develop into embryo sacs.
c. Sepals protect the other parts of a developing flower.
d. Petals provide nourishment for a developing embryo.

______ **18.** During fertilization in flowering plants, one sperm cell fuses with an egg cell to form a zygote and a second sperm cell fuses with two polar nuclei to form

a. a single polar nucleus.
b. endosperm.
c. a second zygote.
d. an ovum.

______ **19.** Large, showy flowers tend to be ____, while small, inconspicuous flowers tend to be ____.

a. wind-pollinated; animal-pollinated
b. cross-pollinated; self-pollinated
c. animal-pollinated; wind-pollinated
d. bird- or mammal-pollinated; insect-pollinated

______ **20.** In monocot seeds, food is stored in the ____, while in dicot seeds, it is stored in the ____.

a. plumule; seed coat
b. cotyledons; endosperm
c. endosperm; cotyledons
d. plumule; endosperm

______ **21.** The diagrams below show different structures in the life cycle of flowering plants. Which sequence of letters corresponds to the following sequence of structures: male gametophyte, female gametophyte, product of fertilization?

a. *A, B, C* **b.** *B, C, A* **c.** *C, A, B* **d.** *C, B, A*

A
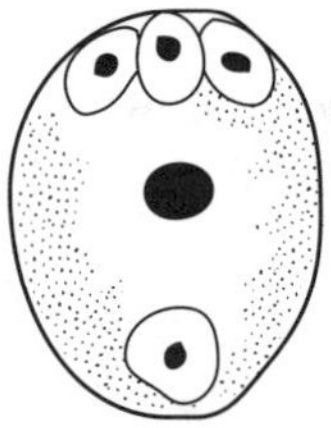
B
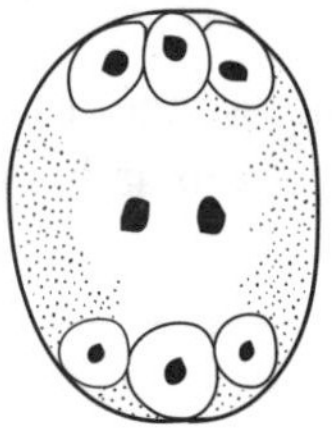
C

Name ______________________ Class ______________ Date ______________

______ **22.** Which of the following produces an aggregate fruit formed from several pistils of a single flower?

a. milkweed plant **b.** apple plant **c.** sunflower plant **d.** strawberry plant

______ **23.** Adaptations that aid fruit and seed dispersal include

a. bright fruit coloration.
b. winglike extensions of seed coats.
c. very small seeds.
d. All of the above

SHORT ANSWER **Answer the questions in the space provided.**

24. Write the following structures in their proper order of production in the life cycle of a fern plant: antheridium and archegonium, egg and sperm cells, mature gametophyte, mature sporophyte, sporangium, spores, and zygote. ______________________

25. What are the products of meiosis in megaspore mother cells, and what happens to these products?

____

26. What are the products of meiosis in microspore mother cells, and what happens to these products?

____

27. How do the vegetative propagation methods of layering, grafting, tissue culturing and making cuttings differ from each other? ______________________

28. What factors may be required to break dormancy of a seed, and what is an adaptive advantage of seed dormancy? ______________________

29. What is required for almost all seeds to germinate? ______________________

Name ______________________ Class ____________ Date ____________

DRAWING CONCLUSIONS Follow the directions given below.

30. Use the diagram below of an incomplete, generalized life cycle of a plant to answer questions a–e.

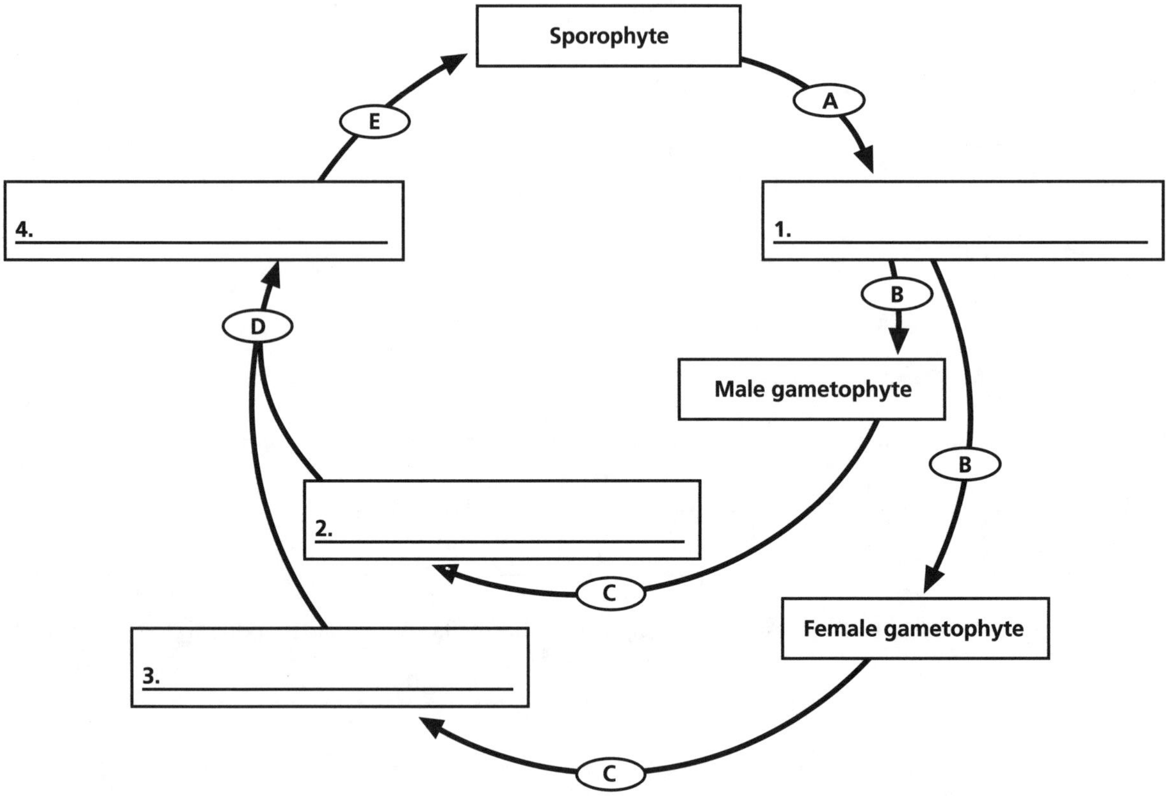

a. Label the structures indicated by the numbered spaces in the diagram.

b. At which stage(s) in the diagram, A, B, C, D, and/or E, does mitosis occur?

____

c. At which stage(s) in the diagram, A, B, C, D, and/or E, does meiosis occur?

____

d. At which stage(s) in the diagram, A, B, C, D, and/or E, does fertilization occur?

____

e. Which structures in the completed diagram are haploid?

____

Name ______________________ Class ____________ Date ____________

CHAPTER 33 TEST

PLANT RESPONSES

MATCHING **Write the correct letter in the blank before each numbered term.**

_____ **1.** thigmonasty

_____ **2.** auxin

_____ **3.** ethylene

_____ **4.** phytochrome

_____ **5.** abscisic acid

_____ **6.** cytokinin

_____ **7.** nyctinasty

_____ **8.** gibberellin

a. promotes cell division, promotes lateral buds

b. closes stomata, promotes dormancy

c. movement response to cycle of light and darkness

d. promotes cell growth, inhibits lateral buds

e. movement response to touch

f. promotes growth by elongation and seed germination

g. pigment involved in photoperiodism

h. promotes fruit ripening and abscission

TRUE-FALSE **If a statement is true, write *T* in the blank. If a statement is false, write *F* in the blank and then, in the space provided, explain why the statement is false.**

_____ **9.** Commercial uses of gibberellins include promoting seed germination, increasing fruit number, and inducing the development of desirable fruit colors.

____

_____ **10.** In plants, tropisms are slow responses and nastic movements are rapid responses.

____

_____ **11.** In most plants, phototropism is thought to occur because auxin moves to the shaded side of a shoot and causes cells on this side to elongate.

____

_____ **12.** Application of gibberellins can sometimes substitute for cold temperatures in plants that have a vernalization requirement.

____

_____ **13.** Fall coloration occurs when chlorophyll absorbs different wavelengths of light as day lengths shorten.

____

Name ______________________________ Class ______________ Date ____________

MULTIPLE CHOICE **Write the letter of the most correct answer in the blank.**

______ **14.** Which of the following is *not* a function of auxins?

a. promoting apical dominance
b. increasing fruit number
c. promoting seed dormancy
d. preventing fruit drop

______ **15.** In many plants, the branches near the shoot tip are shorter than branches near the base. This is referred to as

a. chemotropism. **b.** nyctinasty. **c.** thigmonasty. **d.** apical dominance.

______ **16.** Which of the following is *not* a commercial use of auxins?

a. the promotion of root formation on leaf and stem cuttings
b. the prevention of fruit drop before maturity
c. the increase in the number of fruits produced per plant
d. the induction of stomatal closure

______ **17.** Cytokinins and auxins are used commercially to promote

a. seed dormancy.
b. root and shoot formation in tissue cultures.
c. fruit ripening.
d. fruit drop so that remaining fruits become larger.

______ **18.** Which of the following associations between a tropism and the environmental stimulus to which it responds is *incorrect?*

a. chemotropism—chemicals produced in a particular part of the plant
b. gravitropism—the force of gravity
c. phototropism—the duration of daylight
d. thigmotropism— contact with a solid object

______ **19.** Which of the following is *not* a function of nastic movements?

a. discouraging insect feeding
b. reducing water loss
c. capturing insect prey
d. growing toward a light source

______ **20.** Which of the following is the cause of the plant responses depicted in the illustration below?

a. auxin produced at the shoot tip
b. gain and loss of turgor pressure in cells
c. contact with an animal
d. gravity

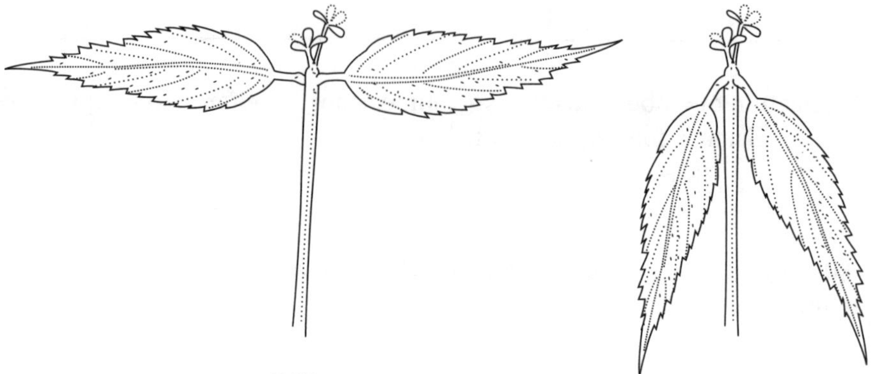

DAY NIGHT

______ **21.** The critical night length for a plant is the number of hours of darkness required to

a. induce flowering.
b. prevent flowering.
c. convert P_{fr} to P_r.
d. convert P_r to P_{fr}.

______ **22.** Vernalization requires exposure to

a. a critical night length to induce flowering.
b. a critical night length to prevent flowering.
c. cold temperatures to induce flowering.
d. cold temperatures to prevent flowering.

______ **23.** Cell elongation on the shaded side of a plant is part of the phenomenon called

a. gravitropism. **b.** phototropism. **c.** thigmotropism. **d.** chemotropism.

SHORT ANSWER Answer the questions in the space provided.

24. The expression "one bad apple spoils the barrel" refers to the effects of which type of plant hormone? Explain the meaning of the expression. ______________________________

25. Why is leaf abscission an adaptive advantage? ______________________________

26. What is the currently accepted explanation for the mechanism of gravitropism?

27. What is the fastest type of plant movement, and how fast does it occur?

28. Under what conditions, natural or artificial, will a long-day plant flower?

29. When do most biennial plants flower? ______________________________

DRAWING CONCLUSIONS **Follow the directions given below.**

30. The illustrations below depict experiments conducted by Fritz Went in the 1920s to determine the mechanism of phototropism. Refer to the illustrations as you answer questions a–e.

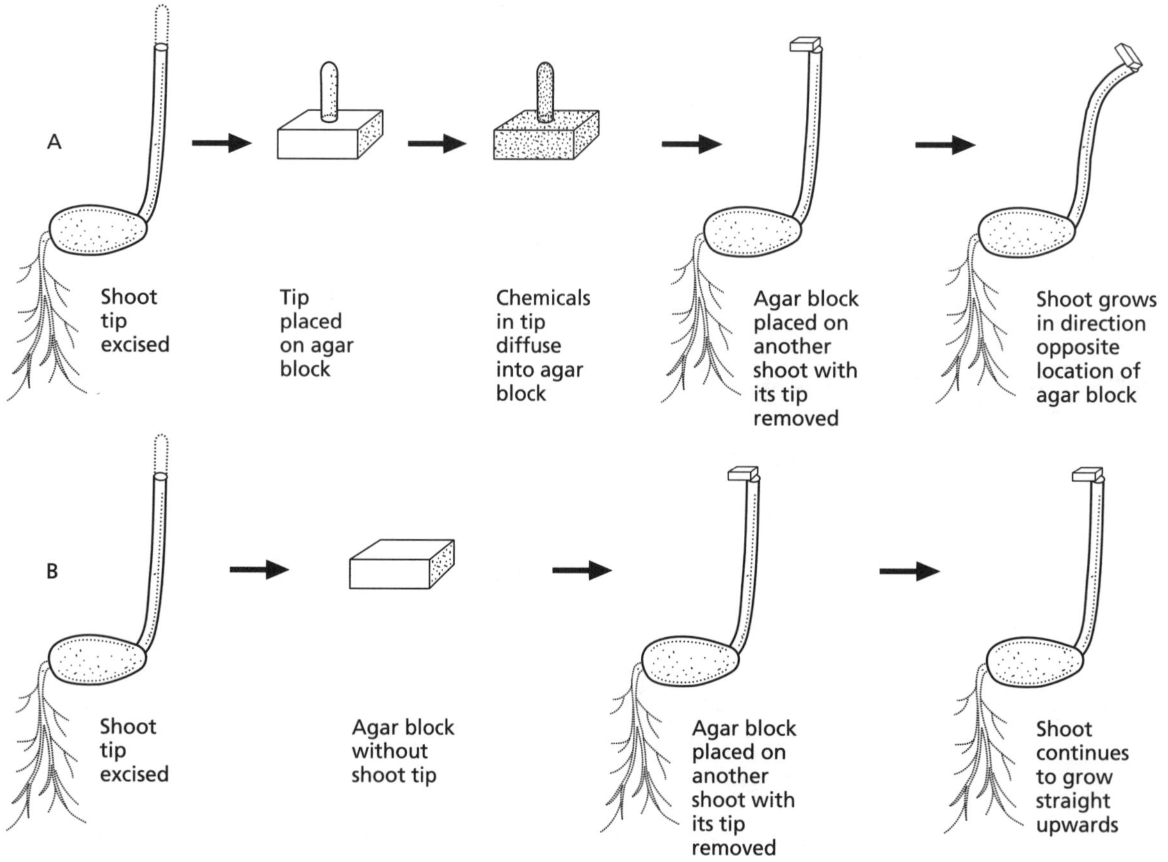

a. Based on your study of plant hormones, what kind of plant hormone is likely to have caused the shoot tip in part *A* of the experiment to bend as it grew?

____

b. Which step, *A* or *B* above, served as a control in this experiment? Explain your answer.

____

____

____

c. How could you test whether your answer to item *a* is correct? ______________________

____

____

____

Name ______________________ Class ____________ Date ____________

CHAPTER 34 TEST

INTRODUCTION TO ANIMALS

MATCHING **Write the correct letter in the blank before each numbered term.**

______ **1.** Annelida

______ **2.** Chordata

______ **3.** Mollusca

______ **4.** Echinodermata

______ **5.** Cnidaria

______ **6.** Protista

______ **7.** Arthropoda

______ **8.** Rotifera

a. sea star
b. hydra
c. lobster
d. amoeba
e. clam
f. earthworm
g. rotifer
h. frog

TRUE-FALSE **If a statement is true, write *T* in the blank. If a statement is false, write *F* in the blank, and in the space provided, explain why the statement is false.**

______ **9.** Every member of the phylum Chordata has a backbone.

____

______ **10.** Flatworms have three germ layers but do not have a coelom.

____

______ **11.** Humans are more closely related to mollusks than to echinoderms.

____

______ **12.** Gas exchange in gills and lungs occurs across moist membranes.

____

______ **13.** During development, a blastula is formed before a gastrula.

____

Name ______________________ Class ______________ Date ______________

MULTIPLE CHOICE **Write the letter of the most correct answer in the blank.**

______ **14.** Which two types of tissue are found only in animals?

a. reproductive and circulatory
b. plasma membrane and cellulose
c. photosynthetic and autotrophic
d. nervous and muscular

______ **15.** In multicellular organisms, different kinds of cells perform different tasks. What is the adaptation of a cell for a particular function called?

a. differentiation **b.** specialization **c.** development **d.** segmentation

______ **16.** What is a germ layer?

a. the outer covering of cells in the digestive system
b. a fundamental tissue type found in animal embryos
c. a part of the body to which muscles are attached
d. a part of the body where ingested bacteria multiply

______ **17.** What is the trait common to all invertebrates?

a. no backbone
b. bilateral symmetry
c. indirect development
d. exoskeleton

______ **18.** What internal structure is a functional part of an open circulatory system, which is found in arthropods and some mollusks?

a. lungs **b.** kidneys **c.** integument **d.** coelom

______ **19.** Many characteristics of vertebrates are adaptations to life on land and fall into two broad categories. What are these categories?

a. internal fertilization and heterotrophy
b. protection from extreme heat and cold
c. body support and water conservation
d. cephalization and bilateral symmetry

______ **20.** From what germ layer do the skeleton, muscles, and blood of an animal arise?

a. ectoderm **b.** mesoderm **c.** endoderm **d.** blastoderm

______ **21.** In protostomes, the blastopore develops into the

a. mesoderm. **b.** archenteron. **c.** mouth. **d.** anus.

______ **22.** What characteristic is displayed by the animal in the diagram?

a. cephalization
b. lack of symmetry
c. radial symmetry
d. three germ layers

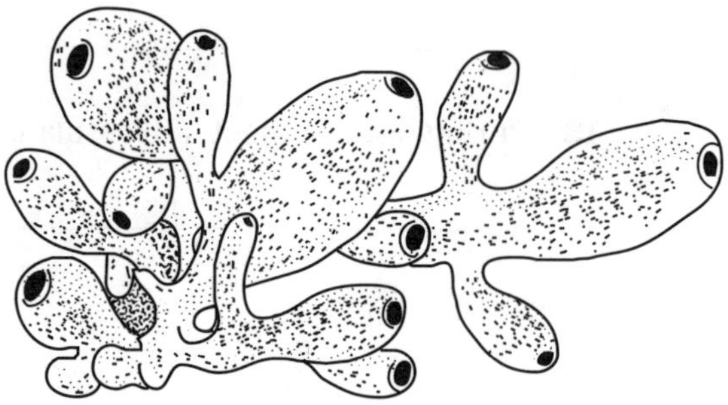

______ **23.** What would happen to the cells of a grasshopper zygote if they were separated at the four-celled stage of development?

a. The cells would develop into four separate but complete grasshoppers.
b. The cells would undergo an indirect larval stage of development.
c. The cells would merge together again and form one individual.
d. The cells would not develop and therefore would die.

SHORT ANSWER Answer the questions in the space provided.

24. As inferred by scientists, what were the steps involved in the evolution of multicellular animals?

____

____

____

25. What two characteristics of sponges are unique in the kingdom Animalia?

____

____

26. What is segmentation, and is it found in all animals?

____

____

27. There are many differences between the development of protostomes and the development of deuterostomes. What are two *similarities* in the way the coelom is formed in these animals?

____

____

____

28. Label the diagrams below with the type of mesoderm formation shown, and on each diagram, label the blastocoel, the coelom, and the archenteron.

a ____________________

b ____________________

c ____________________

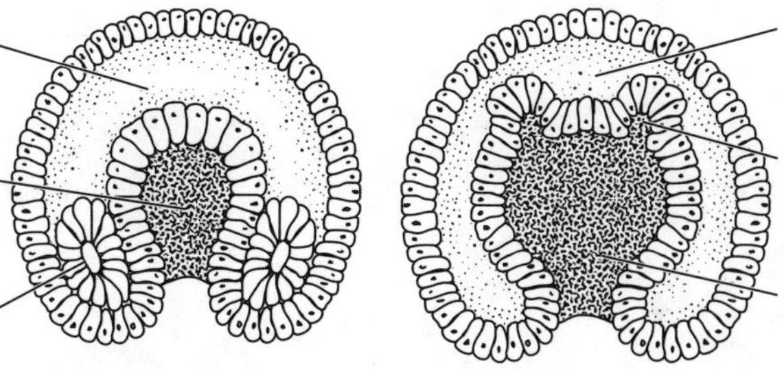

e ____________________

f ____________________

g ____________________

d ____________________ h ____________________

29. List four characteristics of the development of a human embryo that differ from the development of a clam embryo.

____

____

____

____

DRAWING CONCLUSIONS Follow the directions given below.

30. The following characteristics are normally seen in vertebrates only, invertebrates only, or both. In the space provided, indicate which group or groups of organisms show the traits listed:

a. two germ layers ________________

b. three germ layers ________________

c. radial symmetry ________________

d. bilateral symmetry ________________

e. cephalization ________________

f. exoskeleton ________________

g. endoskeleton ________________

h. segmentation ________________

i. backbone ________________

j. sexual reproduction ________________

k. external fertilization ________________

l. open circulatory system ________________

m. closed circulatory system ________________

n. gills ________________

o. lungs ________________

Name ______________________ Class ____________ Date ____________

CHAPTER 35 TEST

SPONGES, CNIDARIANS, AND CTENOPHORES

MATCHING Write the correct letter in the blank before each numbered term.

______ **1.** mesoglea

______ **2.** Anthozoa

______ **3.** gemmule

______ **4.** spicule

______ **5.** polyp

______ **6.** cnidocyte

______ **7.** spongin

______ **8.** Hydrozoa

a. stage of cnidarian life cycle

b. jellylike material

c. contains a nematocyst

d. the coral class

e. *Obelia* is in this class

f. skeleton protein

g. food-filled ball of amebocytes

h. particle of calcium carbonate or silicon dioxide

TRUE-FALSE If a statement is true, write *T* in the blank. If a statement is false, write *F* in the blank, and in the space provided, explain why the statement is false.

______ **9.** All sponges have a skeleton composed of spongin.

____

______ **10.** Sponges can reproduce sexually.

____

______ **11.** Sponges have no larval stage.

____

______ **12.** All cnidarians have a medusa stage and a polyp stage.

____

______ **13.** All hydrozoans live in marine habitats.

____

Name ______________________ Class ____________ Date ____________

MULTIPLE CHOICE Write the letter of the most correct answer in the blank.

______ **14.** The type of cell that draws water into a sponge is called

a. an osculum. **b.** a collar cell. **c.** a cnidocyte. **d.** an amebocyte.

______ **15.** Water leaves the interior of a sponge through

a. the osculum.
b. an incurrent siphon.
c. an ostia.
d. an amebocyte.

______ **16.** Sponges reproduce asexually by producing

a. cysticercae. **b.** spores. **c.** hydatid cysts. **d.** gemmules.

______ **17.** In jellyfish (Scyphozoa), sexual reproduction occurs during the

a. gastraea stage.
b. neurula stage.
c. medusa stage.
d. polyp stage.

______ **18.** How many germ layers do cnidarians have?

a. zero **b.** one **c.** two **d.** three

______ **19.** The Portuguese man-of-war is a member of the

a. phylum Cubozoa.
b. class Hydrozoa.
c. phylum Anthozoa.
d. class Scyphozoa.

______ **20.** A distinguishing defensive structure of cnidarians is the

a. collostyle.
b. osculum.
c. hypostyle.
d. nematocyst.

______ **21.** A distinguishing feature of the phylum Ctenophora is the

a. colloblast.
b. osculum.
c. hypoblast.
d. nematocyst.

______ **22.** Ctenophores have a sensory structure for orientation called the

a. statoblast.
b. semicircular canal.
c. otoblast.
d. apical organ.

______ **23.** Sponges and cnidarian polyps are similar in that they both

a. are bioluminescent.
b. are sessile.
c. have no true tissues.
d. display radial symmetry.

Name ______________________ Class __________ Date __________

SHORT ANSWER **Answer the questions in the space provided.**

24. Trace the path of a food particle that is swept into the body of a sponge from ingestion to removal of wastes.

____

____

25. Describe the various modes of reproduction used by sponges.

____

____

____

26. Compare the bodies of sponges and cnidarians. How many cell layers are found in each organism? How many openings does the central body cavity of each organism have? Which phylum has mesoglea?

____

____

27. What body type is found in the dominant form of a typical scyphozoan? How does that differ from the body type of an anthozoan?

____

____

28. What symbiotic organisms are found within coral cells? Why are corals largely restricted to shallow depths near the equator?

____

____

29. The figures below show two cnidarian forms. In the blank below each figure, label the form of the animal shown. On each figure, label the epidermis, gastrovascular cavity, and mouth.

a ______________

b ______________

c ______________

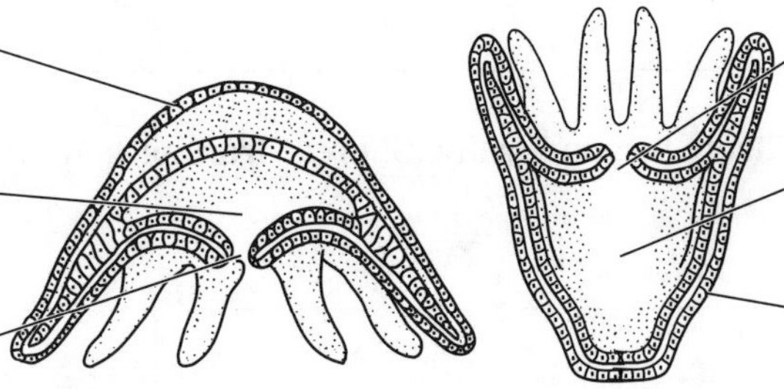

e ______________

f ______________

g ______________

d ______________ h ______________

Name ______________________ Class ______________ Date ______________

DRAWING CONCLUSIONS **Follow the directions given below.**

30. The diagram below shows the life cycle of the common jellyfish *Aurelia.* Answer the questions below based on the diagram.

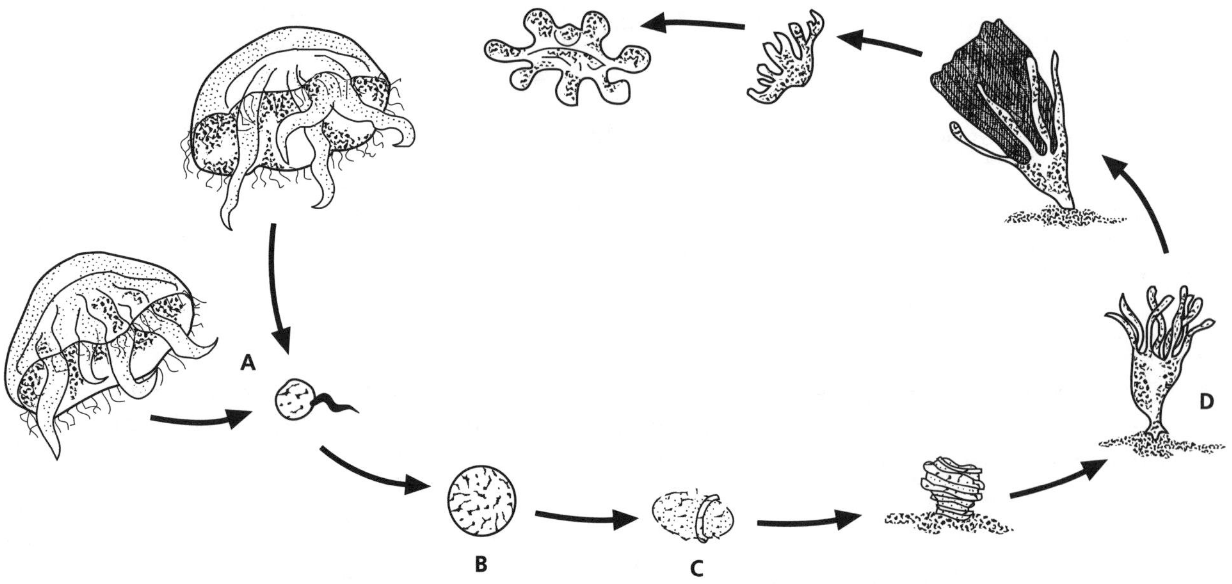

a. What type of fertilization, internal or external, is occurring in *A?*

____

b. What is the structure indicated by *B* called?

____

c. What is the larval structure indicated by *C* called? What happens to this larva?

____

____

____

d. How are offspring produced by the structure indicated by *D?*

____

____

e. Would these offspring likely be genetically different from or genetically similar to each other? Explain your answer.

____

____

____

Name ______________________ Class ______________ Date ______________

CHAPTER 36 TEST

FLATWORMS, ROUNDWORMS, AND ROTIFERS

MATCHING Write the correct letter in the blank before each numbered term.

_____ 1. elephantiasis

_____ 2. rotifer

_____ 3. gastrovascular cavity

_____ 4. trichinosis

_____ 5. hookworm

_____ 6. mastax

_____ 7. flame cell

_____ 8. cloaca

a. caused by a filarial worm

b. collects excess water

c. associated with cysts

d. always parasitic

e. planarian digestive system

f. typically free-living

g. rotifer excretory chamber

h. breaks food into pieces

TRUE-FALSE If a statement is true, write *T* in the blank. If a statement is false, write *F* in the blank, and in the space provided, explain why the statement is false.

_____ 9. Excessive uptake of water by freshwater planarians occurs by osmosis.

____

_____ 10. All flukes live inside the body of the host.

____

_____ 11. The intermediate host of *Schistosoma* is a cow.

____

_____ 12. Tapeworms do not have a mouth.

____

_____ 13. Larvae of some filarial worms are transmitted by mosquito bites.

____

Name ________________ Class ________ Date ________

MULTIPLE CHOICE **Write the letter of the most correct answer in the blank.**

______ **14.** The lack of a respiratory system in flatworms is compensated for by their

a. flat shape.
b. bilateral symmetry.
c. gastrovascular cavity.
d. parasitic lifestyle.

______ **15.** Planarians move over solid surfaces with the aid of

a. pseudopodia.
b. parapodia.
c. cilia and mucus.
d. retractile hooks.

______ **16.** Animals that are typically hermaphroditic include

a. hookworms. **b.** *Ascaris.* **c.** rotifers. **d.** flatworms.

______ **17.** Flukes are protected against the host's immune system by

a. flame cells.
b. a layer of cilia.
c. an endoskeleton.
d. the tegument.

______ **18.** The anterior, knob-shaped portion of a tapeworm is called the

a. strobila. **b.** scolex. **c.** proglottid **d.** opistohaptor.

______ **19.** Animals that lack digestive systems include

a. rotifers. **b.** tapeworms. **c.** hookworms. **d.** flukes.

______ **20.** The life cycle of a beef tapeworm has

a. one type of host.
b. two types of hosts.
c. three types of hosts.
d. at least two but sometimes three types of hosts.

______ **21.** The most common roundworm human parasite in the United States is

a. the hookworm. **b.** *Ascaris.* **c.** the pinworm. **d.** *Trichinella.*

______ **22.** Rotifers respond to dry conditions by

a. dying.
b. migrating toward water.
c. drying up until wet conditions return.
d. reproducing rapidly by binary fission.

______ **23.** Platyhelminthes have

a. three germs layers and a coelom.
b. three germs layers and a pseudocoelom.
c. three germs layers and no body cavity.
d. two germ layers and no body cavity.

Name ______________________ Class ____________ Date ____________

SHORT ANSWER Answer the questions in the space provided.

24. Describe the life cycle of *Schistosoma.*

____

____

____

25. Describe three methods used to prevent trichinosis infection.

____

____

26. How does a flatworm tegument differ from a roundworm cuticle?

____

____

27. How does an acoelomate differ from a pseudocoelomate? Name a phylum of acoelomates with three germ layers.

____

____

____

28. Compare a planarian's movement through water with its movement over a surface.

____

____

____

29. In the diagram below of *Dugesia*, label the pharynx, the excretory tubule, a nerve, and the eyespots.

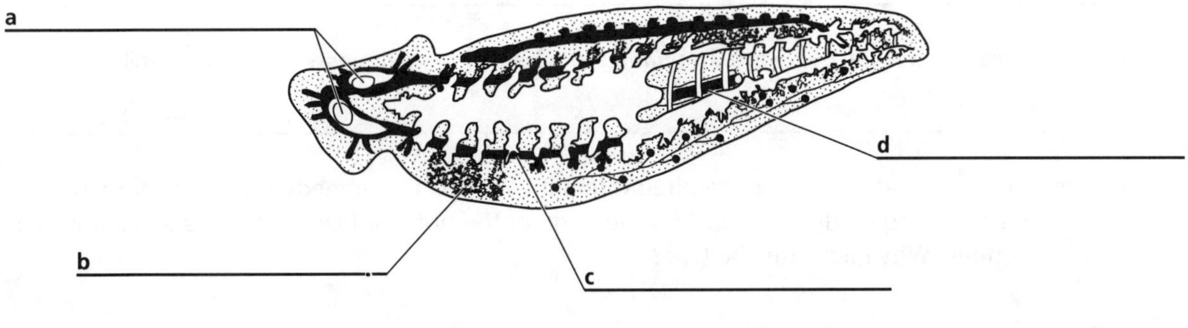

Name ______________________ Class __________ Date __________

DRAWING CONCLUSIONS **Follow the directions given below.**

30. Recently in Europe, multiple cases of trichinosis were tracked down to a single restaurant where diners ate uncooked horse meat. The restaurant owner claims that no one contracted trichinosis from his horse meat. The diagram below shows an example of the life cycle of *Trichinella* in the wild. Refer to the diagram as you answer questions *a–e*.

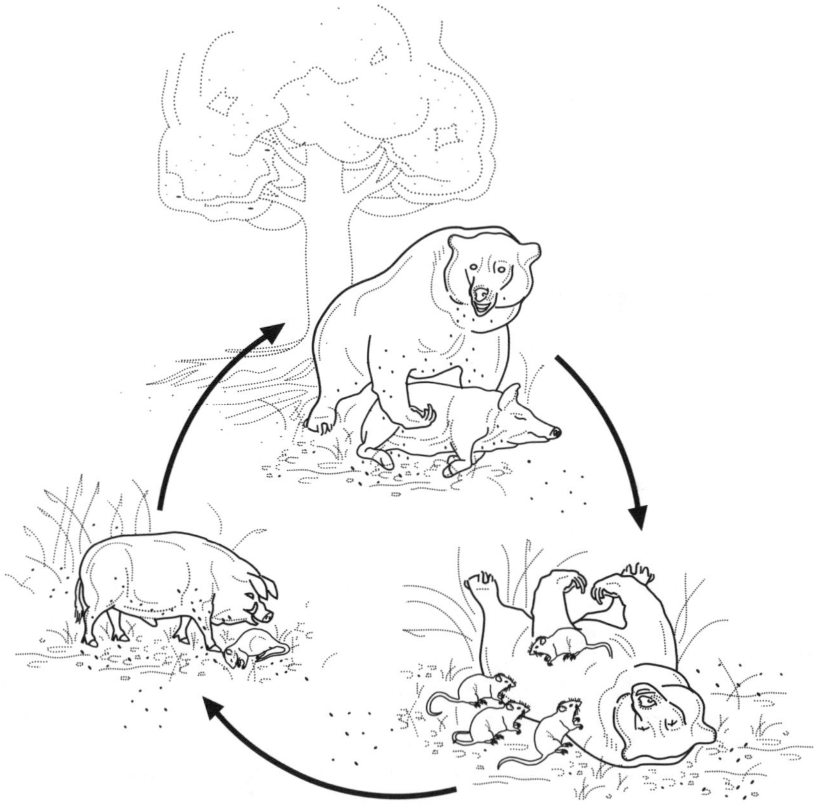

a. Are horses a likely host of *Trichinella*? Why or why not?

____

b. Where would a human most likely be placed in this diagram of the life cycle of *Trichinella*?

____

c. How can a person who eats meat avoid being infected by *Trichinella?*

____

d. What part of their life cycle are *Trichinella* in when they are ingested by a new host?

____

e. Infections by parasitic worms are often difficult to control. The medicines given for worm infections are frequently very hard on the body of the host, unlike antibiotics given for bacterial infections. Why might this be true?

____

____

Name ____________________ Class __________ Date __________

CHAPTER 37 TEST

MOLLUSKS AND ANNELIDS

MATCHING Write the correct letter in the blank beside each numbered term.

_____ **1.** Polychaeta

_____ **2.** cephalopod

_____ **3.** siphon

_____ **4.** nephridium

_____ **5.** Oligochaeta

_____ **6.** nautilus

_____ **7.** torsion

_____ **8.** Hirudinea

a. functions in excretion

b. twisting of visceral mass

c. class of annelids with antennae

d. carries water currents

e. has foot concentrated near head

f. class of annelids with suckers

g. cephalopod with an exterior shell

h. class of earthworms

TRUE-FALSE If a statement is true, write *T* in the blank. If a statement is false, write *F* in the blank, and then in the space provided, explain why the statement is false.

_____ **9.** A coelom does not aid in the transport of blood.

____

_____ **10.** Swimming trochophores are propelled by cilia.

____

_____ **11.** Earthworms do not have a digestive tract.

____

_____ **12.** Polychaetes are the only annelids that have a trochophore stage.

____

_____ **13.** Earthworms require a mate in order to reproduce.

____

Name ______________________ Class ____________ Date ____________

MULTIPLE CHOICE Write the most correct answer in the blank.

______ **14.** A coelom differs from a pseudocoelom in that in a coelom

a. the cavity does not contain fluid.
b. the body-wall muscles are separated from the gut.
c. the circulatory system is surrounded by endoderm.
d. the cavity is filled with endoderm.

______ **15.** A feature shared by many mollusks and annelids is

a. an open circulatory system.
b. complete body segmentation.
c. a trochophore larva.
d. a pseudocoelom.

______ **16.** A feature of some mollusks but not of annelids is

a. setae.
b. complete segmentation.
c. a trochophore larva.
d. a radula.

______ **17.** The primary function of the radula is to

a. aid in feeding.
b. process nerve signals.
c. aid in excretion.
d. aid in dispersal.

______ **18.** The radula is

a. a smooth layer beneath the cuticle.
b. a flexible, tonguelike strip with teeth.
c. a type of ganglion.
d. a rough layer just outside the cuticle.

______ **19.** The circulatory system of a gastropod

a. is closed.
b. is open.
c. lacks a heart.
d. lacks a hemocoel.

______ **20.** Land snails differ from aquatic snails in that land snails

a. are hermaphrodites.
b. have separate sexes.
c. typically have gills.
d. do not have tentacles.

______ **21.** One advantage of a segmented body is

a. the presence of both a pseudocoelom and a coelom.
b. the duplication of major organ systems.
c. radial symmetry.
d. the ability to function even when some segments are damaged.

______ **22.** To move, earthworms use

a. circular muscles only.
b. both radial muscles and circular muscles.
c. longitudinal muscles only.
d. both circular muscles and longitudinal muscles.

______ **23.** Leeches differ from oligochaetes and polychaetes in that leeches

a. have tentacles.
b. never live on land.
c. have numerous setae.
d. lack setae.

Name ______________________ Class ______________ Date ______________

SHORT ANSWER **Answer each question in the space provided.**

24. What feature of mollusks and annelids suggests that they share a common ancestor? Name a feature that mollusks and annelids do not share.

____

____

____

25. Do annelids have a structure comparable to the molluscan mantle? Explain your answer in terms of the mantle's function.

____

____

____

26. What is the advantage of a closed circulatory system? Name one class of mollusk that has such a system.

____

____

____

27. How does an earthworm obtain oxygen from the environment? How does this limit the earthworm's potential habitats?

____

____

____

28. Describe three differences between polychaetes and annelids.

____

____

____

29. How do the various annelid classes differ with regard to their natural habitats?

____

____

____

Name ______________________ Class ______________ Date ______________

DRAWING CONCLUSIONS Follow the directions given below.

30. The diagram below is of a typical mollusk. Refer to the diagram as you answer items *a–c*.

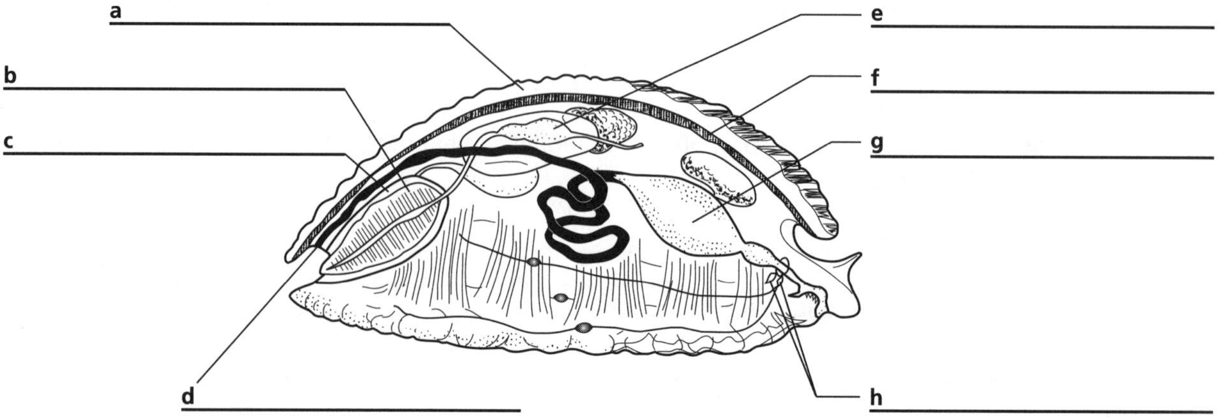

a. Label structures *a–h* in the figure above.

b. How does the mantle help protect a mollusk?

____

____

____

c. How is the surface area for gas exchange optimized in the mollusk?

____

____

____

Name ______________________ Class ____________ Date ____________

CHAPTER 38 TEST

ARTHROPODS

MATCHING Write the correct letter in the blank beside each numbered term.

_____ 1. tagma

_____ 2. antenna

_____ 3. epidermis

_____ 4. chelicera

_____ 5. molting

_____ 6. appendages

_____ 7. spinneret

_____ 8. millipede

a. synthesizes the exoskeleton

b. set of fused segments

c. necessary for growth

d. legs and antennae

e. web-weaving organ

f. feeler

g. two leg pairs per segment

h. pincerlike mouthpart

TRUE-FALSE If a statement is true, write *T* in the blank. If a statement is false, write *F* in the blank, and then in the space provided, explain why the statement is false.

_____ 9. The arthropod exoskeleton provides protection and support.

____

_____ 10. Crayfish use lungs for respiration.

____

_____ 11. Spiders have more walking legs than crayfishes have.

____

_____ 12. The body of a mite displays greater fusion of segments than the bodies of spiders and scorpions.

____

_____ 13. Centipedes have mandibles and maxillae.

____

Name ______________________ Class ____________ Date ____________

MULTIPLE CHOICE **Write the letter of the most correct answer in the blank.**

______ **14.** Muscles that move the segments of arthropods are attached to which layer of the exoskeleton?

a. the outer layer
b. the middle layer
c. the inner layer
d. None of the above

______ **15.** During its lifetime, a typical arthropod will molt

a. at most once, although some arthropods never molt.
b. once.
c. twice.
d. many times.

______ **16.** All arthropods have

a. a pseudocoelom and an endoskeleton.
b. a true coelom and an endoskeleton.
c. a true coelom and an exoskeleton.
d. jointed appendages and an endoskeleton.

______ **17.** One difference between trilobites and crustaceans is the

a. great variation among the various limbs of a trilobite.
b. presence of both mandibles and chelicerae in trilobites.
c. fact that trilobites are extinct.
d. fact that crustaceans are extinct.

______ **18.** A protective feature of the crustacean exoskeleton is the

a. absence of calcium carbonate.
b. presence of cellulose.
c. absence of chitin.
d. presence of calcium carbonate.

______ **19.** Of the following, the diet of an isopod is most similar to that of a

a. centipede. **b.** crayfish. **c.** millipede. **d.** spider.

______ **20.** Food-handling appendages of a typical arachnid include

a. mandibles and chelicerae.
b. chelicerae and maxillae.
c. maxillae and maxillipeds.
d. chelicerae and pedipalps.

______ **21.** One of the differences between spiders and crustaceans is the

a. presence of book lungs in spiders.
b. closed circulatory system of spiders.
c. dorsal nerve cord of crustaceans.
d. presence of green glands in spiders.

______ **22.** Myriapods include

a. crustaceans. **b.** spiders. **c.** centipedes. **d.** trilobites.

______ **23.** Imagine an arthropod consisting of 40 segments. The greatest number of legs is expected if that arthropod is a

a. spider. **b.** millipede. **c.** centipede. **d.** scorpion.

Name ______________________ Class ____________ Date ____________

SHORT ANSWER **Answer each question in the space provided.**

24. What features of an arthropod's body provide evidence of cephalization? Give at least two examples.

____

____

____

25. Describe the arthropod molting process.

____

____

____

26. List all of the arthropod subphyla, and provide one example of a familiar animal for each subphylum.

____

____

____

27. Describe the structures of the crayfish that are involved with the tail flip.

____

____

____

28. What appendages do spiders use to inject venom into their prey? Where in the spider's body is venom produced?

____

____

____

29. How do centipedes capture, kill, and tear apart their prey? In your explanation, emphasize the role of each relevant appendage type.

____

____

____

____

Name ______________________ Class ____________ Date ____________

DRAWING CONCLUSIONS **Follow the directions given below.**

30. The diagram below is of a typical spider. Use the diagram to answer items *a–c*.

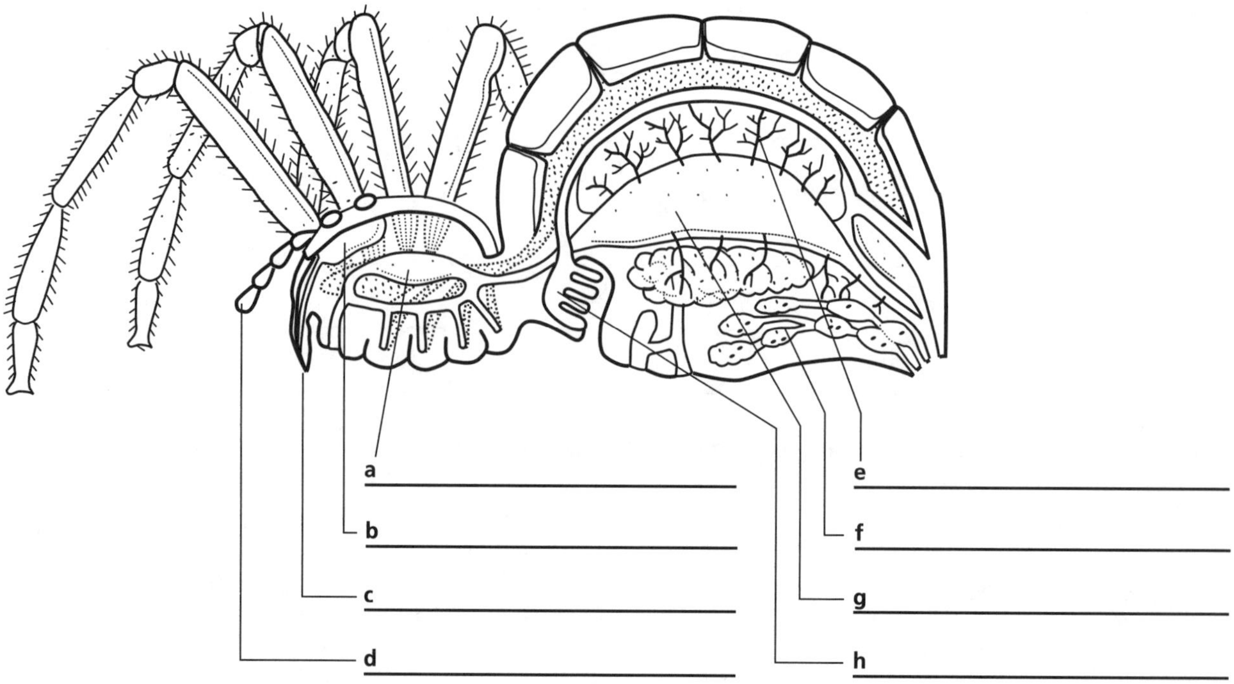

a. Label structures *a–h* in the figure above.

b. Describe how the excretory system of spiders is adapted for life on land.

____

____

____

c. What are the disadvantages of molting?

____

____

____

Name ______________________ Class ____________ Date ____________

CHAPTER 39 TEST

INSECTS

MATCHING Write the correct letter in the blank before each numbered item.

_____ **1.** tympanum

_____ **2.** nymph

_____ **3.** Müllerian mimicry

_____ **4.** Batesian mimicry

_____ **5.** kin selection

_____ **6.** barbed stinger

_____ **7.** round dance

_____ **8.** waggle dance

a. might explain honeybee altruism

b. indicates a distant food source

c. an immature form in some insects

d. indicates a nearby food source

e. both species are harmful

f. vibrating membrane in some sound-producing insects

g. one of two species is harmful

h. modified ovipositor

TRUE-FALSE If a statement is true, write *T* in the blank. If a statement is false, write *F* in the blank, and then in the space provided, explain why the statement is false.

_____ **9.** The insect exoskeleton is covered by a waxy cuticle.

____

_____ **10.** Queen factor is a pheromone.

____

_____ **11.** The insect circulatory system transports oxygen to the tissues.

____

_____ **12.** Royal jelly is especially rich in carbohydrates.

____

_____ **13.** Pheromones are chemicals secreted by insects to protect them from predators.

____

Name ______________________ Class ____________ Date ____________

MULTIPLE CHOICE **Write the letter of the most correct answer in the blank.**

_____ **14.** Unlike other arthropods, insects have

a. Malpighian tubules.
b. a segmented body.
c. a set of jointed appendages.
d. an exoskeleton.

_____ **15.** In winged insects, the wings are found on the

a. head. **b.** thorax. **c.** abdomen. **d.** labrum.

_____ **16.** An insect order that does not have wings is

a. Coleoptera. **b.** Hymenoptera. **c.** Thysanura. **d.** Hemiptera.

_____ **17.** The study of insects is called

a. entomology. **b.** ecology. **c.** enterology. **d.** entelechy.

_____ **18.** Male mosquitoes are attracted to female mosquitoes by

a. the buzzing of wings.
b. the color pattern of the hind wings.
c. a humming sound produced by the mouthparts.
d. a pheromone secreted from the thorax.

_____ **19.** Biological control of cabbage worms and tomato worms is achieved with

a. a predatory mite.
b. the ladybird beetle.
c. sterile male flies.
d. a bacterium.

_____ **20.** Commercially valuable products produced by insects do not include

a. silk. **b.** wax. **c.** atropine. **d.** shellac.

_____ **21.** Increasing the propagation of one's own genes by helping a closely related individual is called

a. innate behavior.
b. kin selection.
c. natural selection.
d. Batesian mimicry.

_____ **22.** When the honeybee hive becomes overcrowded,

a. queen factor production is dramatically increased.
b. the queen leaves, followed by about half of the workers.
c. most of the workers leave, but the queen stays behind.
d. the colony dies off.

_____ **23.** Queen factor is a

a. high-protein substance fed to the larvae.
b. pheromone that attracts male bees to the queen.
c. pheromone that prevents female larvae from developing into queens.
d. component of honey.

Name ______________________ Class ____________ Date ____________

SHORT ANSWER **Answer the questions in the space provided.**

24. Describe the defensive behavior of the bombardier beetle.

____

____

____

25. How do the roles of pheromones differ in ants and moths?

____

____

____

26. How do the mouthparts of drone bees differ from those of workers, and why might this difference be expected?

____

____

____

27. Describe the eyes of the grasshopper, focusing on the types of eyes, the number of each type, and the function of each type.

____

____

____

28. Insects are eaten by humans in many parts of the world. The table below includes one representative from each of three different insect orders. The table shows the percentage of the daily nutritional requirements of humans that 100 g of each type of insect provides. Overall, which order appears to be most nutritious for humans? What is the common name of insects in this order?

Nutritional Value of Insects in Three Orders

Nutrient	Isoptera	Lepidoptera	Coleoptera
Energy	21.5%	13%	19.7%
Magnesium	104%	13.5%	7.5%
Copper	680%	70%	70%
Calcium	4%	36%	19%
Zinc	unknown	unknown	158%

____

Name ______________________ Class __________ Date __________

29. The stingers of wasps differ from those of honeybees. Which insect displays altruistic behavior, and how is this related to the difference in the stingers?

____

____

____

____

DRAWING CONCLUSIONS Follow the directions given below.

30. In the diagrams below, label each stage of metamorphosis and the type of metamorphosis illustrated, then answer the questions that follow.

Incomplete Metamorphosis

a ____________ b ____________ c ____________

Complete Metamorphosis

d ____________ e ____________ f ____________ g ____________

h. What is the adaptive advantage of complete metamorphosis in terms of competition for resources?

____

____

____

i. What is the adaptive advantage of complete metamorphosis in terms of survival in harsh conditions?

____

____

____

Name ______________________ Class ____________ Date ____________

CHAPTER 40 TEST

Echinoderms and Invertebrate Chordates

MATCHING Write the correct letter in the blank before each numbered item.

_____ 1. basket star

_____ 2. tunicate

_____ 3. test

_____ 4. atriopore

_____ 5. ampulla

_____ 6. nerve ring

_____ 7. sea lily

_____ 8. chordate nerve cord

a. component of sea-star nervous system

b. a hollow dorsal tube

c. endoskeleton of sea urchins and sand dollars

d. member of the class Ophiuroidea

e. member of the class Crinoidea

f. lancelet water elimination structure

g. a type of urochordate

h. part of a tube foot

TRUE-FALSE If a statement is true, write *T* in the blank. If a statement is false, write *F* in the blank, and then in the space provided, explain why the statement is false.

_____ 9. All chordates live in the ocean.

____

_____ 10. All echinoderms live in the ocean.

____

_____ 11. Adult cephalochordates are typically sessile.

____

_____ 12. Adult echinoderms are typically sessile.

____

_____ 13. The stone canal is part of the water vascular system.

____

Name ______________________________ Class ______________ Date ______________

MULTIPLE CHOICE **Write the letter of the most correct answer in the blank.**

______ **14.** The age of echinoderms has been estimated as

a. more than 500 million years.
b. less than that of vertebrates.
c. approximately 100 million years.
d. at least one billion years.

______ **15.** Sea cucumbers compose

a. the class Asteroidea.
b. the phylum Asteroidea.
c. the phylum Holothuroidea.
d. the class Holothuroidea.

______ **16.** Sea stars move about with the aid of

a. cilia.
b. tube feet and water pressure.
c. aboral ambulacral plates.
d. pedicellariae.

______ **17.** Sea stars are

a. hermaphroditic and have internal fertilization.
b. hermaphroditic and have external fertilization.
c. separate sexes and have external fertilization.
d. separate sexes and have internal fertilization.

______ **18.** Two similarities between chordates and annelids are

a. a ventral nerve cord and segmentation.
b. bilateral symmetry and segmentation.
c. bilateral symmetry and a backbone.
d. bilateral symmetry and a sessile existence.

______ **19.** Most chordate subphyla

a. are terrestrial.
b. spend part of their lives on land and part in the water.
c. live in the ocean.
d. live in fresh water.

______ **20.** The small pincers that surround the spines on the surface of a sea star are called

a. madreporites. **b.** pedicellariae. **c.** ampullae. **d.** crinoids.

______ **21.** In the diagram of an echinoderm at right, the surface shown is the

a. ventral surface.
b. dorsal surface.
c. aboral surface.
d. oral surface.

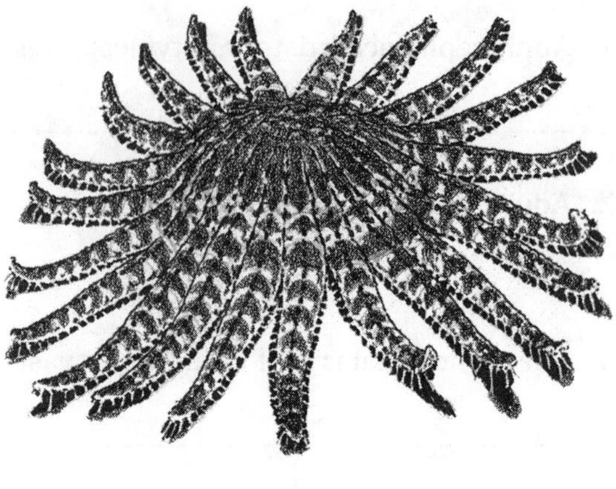

______ **22.** Chordates and echinoderms are both

a. protostomes.
b. deuterostomes.
c. pseudocoelomates.
d. acoelomates.

______ **23.** The jaws, inner ear, and tonsils of terrestrial chordates derive from

a. the coelom.
b. the ventral nerve cord.
c. the muscle segments of the nerve cord.
d. the pharyngeal pouches.

SHORT ANSWER Answer the questions in the space provided.

24. Describe the fates of the notochord among the chordate subphyla Vertebrata, Cephalochordata, and Urochordata.

____

____

____

25. Name four chordate features that are not found in echinoderms.

____

____

26. Describe the differences in morphology between young tunicates and adult tunicates.

____

____

____

27. Describe the importance of the regeneration of body parts to sea-star defense and reproduction.

____

____

28. Describe sexual reproduction among the tunicates. Are there separate sexes? If so, how are they distinguished?

____

____

____

29. What is "Aristotle's lantern"?

____

CRITICAL THINKING Follow the directions given below.

30. Animals of the three phyla of chordates share four distinctive morphological traits at some time during their development: a notochord, a dorsal nerve cord, pharyngeal pouches, and a postanal tail. The table below shows the fate of each trait in an adult animal. Use the table to answer the following questions.

Fates of Chordate Features in Three Subphyla

Feature	Vertebrata	Cephalochordata	Urochordata
Notochord	becomes backbone	retained	lost
Dorsal nerve cord	becomes spinal cord	retained	lost
Pharyngeal pouches	becomes structures in throat and ear	retained	retained
Postanal tail	retained in most species	retained	lost

a. Animals of which subphylum most closely resemble an idealized chordate?

____

b. Which of the three subphyla has lost a structure important to movement, particularly swimming?

____

c. In which subphylum are most of the embryological features retained, but in a modified form?

____

d. Two of the three chordate subphyla contain only marine animals; which two are they? If you knew nothing about a particular animal except that it is sessile, would you think that the animal lives in the water or on land? Explain your answer.

____

____

____

____

e. Name a representative animal from each of the three chordate orders.

____

____

____

Name ______________________ Class ______________ Date ______________

CHAPTER 41 TEST

FISHES

MATCHING **Write the correct letter in the space beside each numbered item.**

_____ **1.** gill

_____ **2.** kidney

_____ **3.** operculum

_____ **4.** olfactory lobe

_____ **5.** lateral line

_____ **6.** swim bladder

_____ **7.** rectal gland

_____ **8.** sinus venosus

a. covers and protects the gills

b. controls buoyancy

c. remove excess Na^+ and $C1^-$ ions

d. allows gas exchange

e. detects chemicals in water

f. collects deoxygenated blood

g. filters wastes from blood

h. detects vibrations in water

TRUE-FALSE **If a statement is true, write *T* in the blank. If a statement is false, write *F* in the blank, and then in the space provided, explain why the statement is false.**

_____ **9.** The oldest known vertebrate fossils are those of jawless fishes that lacked paired fins.

____

_____ **10.** Jaws are thought to have evolved from the first pair of ribs of early fishes.

____

_____ **11.** Most saltwater fishes contain lower concentrations of solutes than the surrounding water does, so they tend to gain water and lose ions.

____

_____ **12.** The limbs of terrestrial vertebrates probably evolved from the lobed fins of a bony fish.

____

_____ **13.** Lampreys are the only surviving jawless fishes.

____

Name ______________________ Class ______________ Date ______________

MULTIPLE CHOICE **Write the letter of the most correct answer in the blank.**

_____ **14.** Which of the following is *not* a characteristic shared by all vertebrates?

a. vertebrae **b.** scales **c.** cranium **d.** endoskeleton

_____ **15.** The major function of the gills is to

a. exchange gases.
b. sense chemicals.
c. regulate buoyancy.
d. detect vibrations.

_____ **16.** Which of the following is a characteristic shared by all members of the class Chondrichthyes?

a. skeleton made of bone
b. herbivory
c. placoid scales
d. freshwater habitat

_____ **17.** Which of the following is an example of a lobe-finned fish?

a. perch **b.** trout **c.** salmon **d.** lungfish

_____ **18.** The balance between salt and water in the body of a fish is maintained by the kidneys and what other organ?

a. gills **b.** heart **c.** liver **d.** swim bladder

_____ **19.** In bony fishes, the main pumping chamber of the heart is the

a. atrium. **b.** ventricle. **c.** sinus venosus. **d.** conus arteriosus.

_____ **20.** A cartilaginous skeleton, placoid scales, and paired fins are characteristic of class

a. Agnatha. **b.** Chondrichthyes. **c.** Osteichthyes. **d.** Amphibia.

_____ **21.** The structure represented by X in the diagram below is the

a. dorsal fin. **b.** pelvic fin. **c.** pectoral fin. **d.** caudal fin.

_____ **22.** The structure represented by Y in the diagram below is the

a. operculum. **b.** gill filament. **c.** pectoral fin. **d.** ventricle.

_____ **23.** The animal shown in the diagram at right belongs to the class

a. Vertebrata.
b. Osteichthyes.
c. Chondrichthyes.
d. Agnatha.

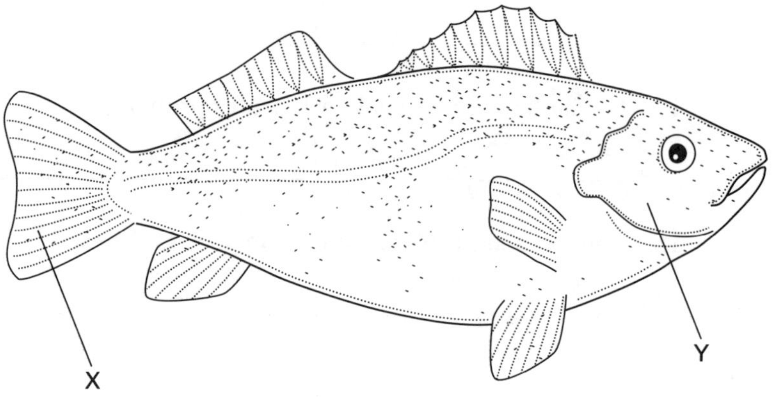

Name ______________________ Class ____________ Date ____________

SHORT ANSWER **Answer each question in the space provided.**

24. Describe the lateral-line system.

____

____

____

25. Briefly describe the type of fertilization found in each of the following classes: Chondrichthyes, Osteichthyes, and Agnatha.

____

____

____

26. Name the senses a shark uses to detect prey.

____

____

____

27. Trace the flow of blood through the fish heart.

____

____

____

28. How did the evolution of jaws and paired fins benefit fish?

____

____

____

29. The tissues in a fish's body are denser than water, so the tendency to sink is a problem. Describe how this problem is resolved in cartilaginous fishes and bony fishes.

____

____

____

____

DRAWING CONCLUSIONS Follow the directions given below.

30. Use the table below to answer questions a–e. Note that characteristics listed apply to the majority of species in each group.

Skeletal Characteristics of Vertebrates

Group	Class	Presence of vertebrae	Composition of skeleton	Presence of scales or feathers
Lampreys and hagfishes	3. ________	yes	cartilage	no
Sharks, rays, and skates	Chondrichthyes	yes	5. ________	yes
1. ________	Osteichthyes	yes	bone	6. ________
Amphibians	Amphibia	yes	bone	no
Reptiles	Reptilia	yes	bone	yes
Birds	4. ________	yes	bone	yes
2. ________	Mammalia	yes	bone	no

a. Complete the table by filling in the blanks.

b. Which groups listed in the table possess a cranium?

____

____

c. To which subphylum do the groups listed in the table belong?

____

d. Are there more aquatic classes or terrestrial classes of animals shown in the table?

____

e. What is a skeletal characteristic found only in aquatic vertebrates?

____

____

Name ______________________ Class ______________ Date ______________

CHAPTER 42 TEST

AMPHIBIANS

MATCHING **Write the correct letter in the blank beside each numbered term.**

______ **1.** cerebellum

______ **2.** medulla oblongata

______ **3.** kidney

______ **4.** amplexus

______ **5.** vent

______ **6.** mesentery

______ **7.** cerebrum

______ **8.** ileum

a. filters nitrogenous waste

b. integrates behavior

c. regulates muscular coordination

d. frog mating embrace

e. membrane holding small intestine in place

f. controls heart rate and respiration rate

g. coiled middle portion of small intestine

h. opening for exiting waste materials

TRUE-FALSE **If a statement is true, write *T* in the blank. If a statement is false, write *F* in the blank, and then in the space provided, explain why the statement is false.**

______ **9.** Amphibians have a four-chambered heart.

____

______ **10.** The tympanic membrane protects and moistens the eye.

____

______ **11.** Caecilians are wormlike creatures that have very small eyes and are often blind.

____

______ **12.** In nearly all species of frogs and toads, eggs are fertilized internally.

____

______ **13.** The systemic circuit of the amphibian circulatory system carries deoxygenated blood from the heart to the lungs and then returns oxygenated blood to the heart.

____

Name ______________________ Class ____________ Date ____________

MULTIPLE CHOICE **Write the letter of the most correct answer in the blank.**

______ **14.** Which of the following is *not* a characteristic of Ichthyostega?

a. four strong limbs
b. large tail fin
c. five toes on each hind foot
d. large, sharp teeth

______ **15.** The hormone thyroxine circulates in a frog's bloodstream and stimulates

a. amplexus.
b. digestion.
c. fertilization.
d. metamorphosis.

______ **16.** Which of the following is a member of the order Urodela?

a. salamander **b.** caecilian **c.** toad **d.** frog

______ **17.** In amphibians, the main pumping chamber of the heart is the

a. sinus venosus. **b.** right atrium. **c.** ventricle. **d.** left atrium.

______ **18.** What structure transmits sounds between the eardrum and the inner ear?

a. columella
b. nictitating membrane
c. tympanic membrane
d. cerebellum

______ **19.** The process by which a frog develops from an egg to an adult form is called

a. amplexus. **b.** metamorphosis. **c.** spawning. **d.** reproduction.

______ **20.** To aid in the process of respiration, most adult amphibians make use of their lungs as well as their

a. skin. **b.** gills. **c.** cloaca. **d.** cerebrum.

______ **21.** An important similarity between amphibians and lobe-finned fishes is

a. the bones of the fish fin and the bones of the amphibian limb.
b. both must return to the water to breed.
c. both have a cartilaginous skeleton.
d. they evolved at the same time in the sea.

______ **22.** In the diagram shown at right, the structure labeled *X* is a

a. kidney.
b. liver.
c. pancreas.
d. lung.

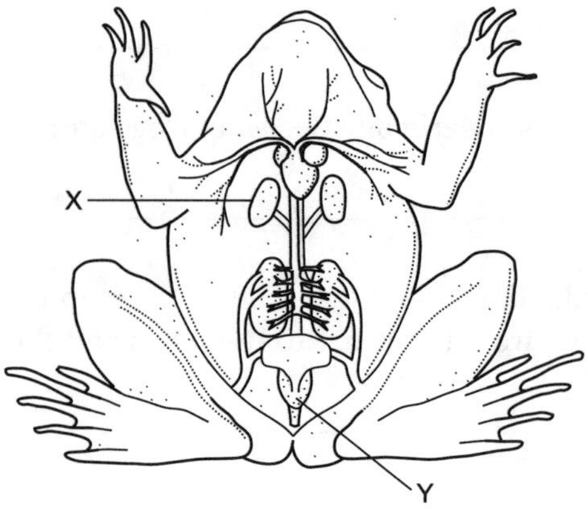

______ **23.** In the diagram shown at right, the structure labeled *Y* is the

a. ileum.
b. duodenum.
c. cloaca.
d. columella.

Name ______________________ Class ____________ Date ____________

SHORT ANSWER Answer each question in the space provided.

24. Describe how a frog breathes. ______________________

____

____

25. List four major characteristics of living amphibians. ______________________

____

____

____

26. How does the skin of amphibians relate to the types of habitats in which an amphibian can survive? ______________________

____

____

____

____

27. Identify three features of the frog skeleton that are adaptations for life on land.

____

____

____

28. Describe the changes that occur during frog metamorphosis. ______________________

____

____

____

____

29. Describe two examples of parental care in amphibians. ______________________

____

____

____

Name ______ Class ______ Date ______

DRAWING CONCLUSIONS **Follow the directions given below.**

30. The diagrams below represent different stages in the life cycle of a frog. In the blank below each diagram, number the stages 2–6. Note that the first stage (d) has been labeled for you. In the blank lines below each diagram, describe what the diagram illustrates.

a ______

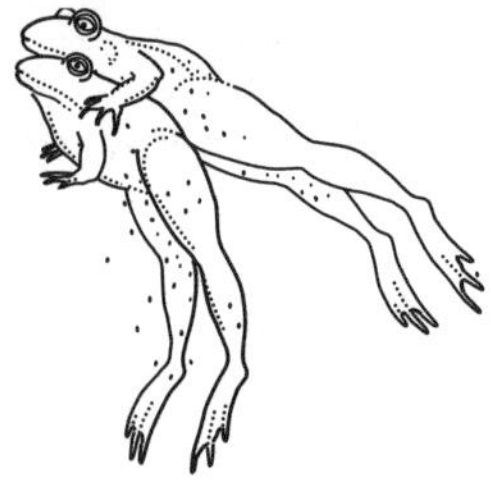

d 1

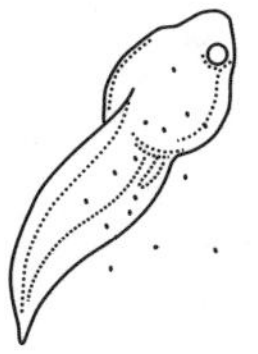

b ______

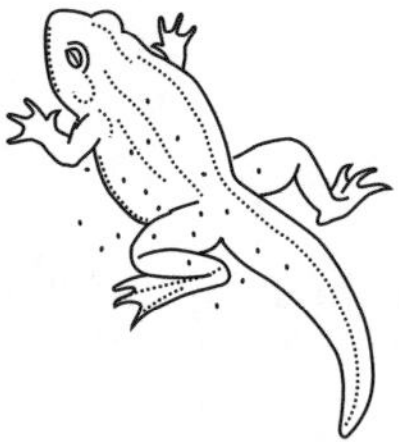

e ______

c ______

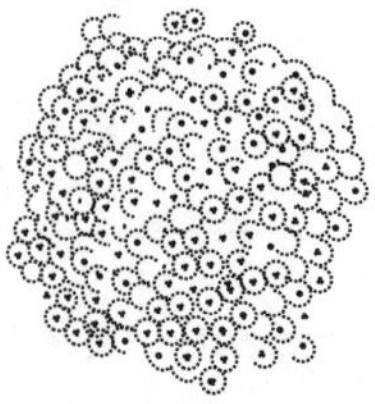

f ______

Name ______________________ Class ____________ Date ____________

CHAPTER 43 TEST

REPTILES

MATCHING **Write the correct letter in the blank beside each numbered item.**

_____ **1.** elapid

_____ **2.** pterosaur

_____ **3.** Crocodilia

_____ **4.** Squamata

_____ **5.** Chelonia

_____ **6.** dinosaur

_____ **7.** plesiosaur

_____ **8.** Rhynchocephalia

a. gavial
b. ancient aquatic reptile
c. ancient terrestrial reptile
d. tuatara
e. chameleon
f. venomous snake
g. ancient flying reptile
h. turtles and tortoises

TRUE-FALSE **If a statement is true, write *T* in the blank. If a statement is false, write *F* in the blank, and then in the space provided, explain why the statement is false.**

_____ **9.** The body temperature of ectotherms is determined primarily by the environment.

____

_____ **10.** Autotomy is illustrated by a lizard's ability to detach its tail and later grow a new one.

____

_____ **11.** The gavial is named for the spiny crest that runs down its back. It feeds on insects, worms, and other small animals at night.

____

_____ **12.** Dinosaurs became extinct 65 thousand years ago, at the end of the Cretaceous period.

____

_____ **13.** Marine turtles must return to land in order to lay eggs.

____

Name ______________________ Class ____________ Date ____________

MULTIPLE CHOICE **Write the letter of the most correct answer in the blank.**

______ **14.** The span of time often called the Age of Reptiles is the

a. Permian period.
b. Mesozoic era.
c. Cretaceous period.
d. Carboniferous period.

______ **15.** The lining of most reptile's lungs might be divided into numerous small sacs called

a. amnions. **b.** bronchi. **c.** arteries. **d.** alveoli.

______ **16.** A snake is most likely to use Jacobson's organ to

a. locate prey. **b.** inject venom. **c.** reproduce. **d.** detect heat.

______ **17.** Which of the following is an advantage of ectothermy?

a. provides enough energy for sustained exertion
b. enables reptiles to live in cold climates
c. requires little energy
d. results in high metabolism

______ **18.** The pattern of reproduction among some reptiles in which the egg is retained within the female's body until shortly before or after hatching is called

a. viviparity. **b.** ectothermy. **c.** ovoviviparity. **d.** endothermy.

______ **19.** Which of the following is a venomous lizard?

a. Komodo dragon **b.** Gila monster **c.** copperhead **d.** chameleon

______ **20.** Which snakes kill prey by injecting venom through large, mobile fangs at the front of the mouth?

a. constrictors **b.** elapids **c.** vipers **d.** monitors

______ **21.** In the diagram below, what structure, labeled *X,* is responsible for the exchange of oxygen and carbon dioxide with the environment?

a. allantois
b. embryo
c. chorion
d. amnion

______ **22.** In the diagram at right, the membrane labeled *Y* represents what part of the amniotic egg?

a. allantois
b. amnion
c. chorion
d. yolk sac

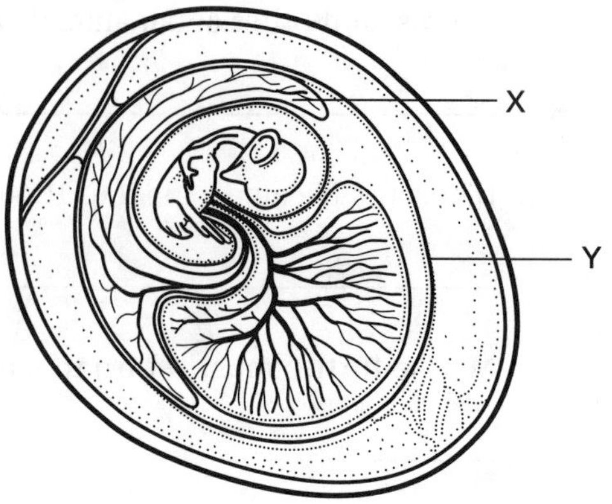

______ **23.** Unlike the skin of amphibians, the skin of reptiles

- **a.** has bony scales like those of fishes.
- **b.** is moist, thin, and watertight.
- **c.** is thick, scaly, and not watertight.
- **d.** is thick, scaly, and watertight.

SHORT ANSWER Answer each question in the space provided.

24. Describe the asteroid-impact hypothesis to explain the extinction of the dinosaurs 65 million years ago.

25. Describe three characteristics of turtles not shared with other reptiles.

26. Explain how a snake is able to swallow something larger than its head.

27. Describe how crocodiles capture their prey.

28. Identify and describe three groups of reptiles that lived during the Mesozoic era.

29. Describe the position and function of the amnion in the reptilian egg.

DRAWING CONCLUSIONS **Follow the directions given below.**

30. Use the simplified schematic diagram of the reptilian circulatory system below to answer items a–e.

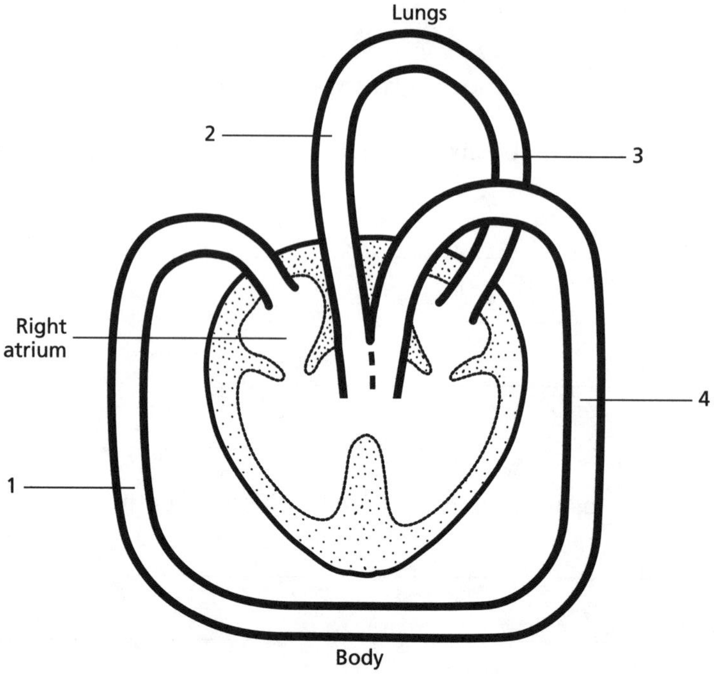

a. On the above diagram, draw arrows to show the path of blood flow through the reptilian circulatory system.

b. For each numbered point in the diagram, indicate in the corresponding blank below whether the blood is oxygenated, deoxygenated, or mixed when the reptile is at rest.

1. ______________________ 3. ______________________

2. ______________________ 4. ______________________

c. If the ventricles were completely separated at the dotted line, would the blood at each labeled point be oxygenated, deoxygenated, or mixed?

1. ______________________ 3. ______________________

2. ______________________ 4. ______________________

d. In which order of reptiles are the ventricles completely separated?

____

e. Under what conditions would diverting blood from the lungs be advantageous to a reptile?

____

____

Name ______________________ Class ____________ Date ____________

CHAPTER 44 TEST

BIRDS

MATCHING **Write the correct letter in the blank beside each numbered item.**

_____ **1.** Anseriformes

_____ **2.** Passeriformes

_____ **3.** Columbiformes

_____ **4.** Struthioniformes

_____ **5.** Falconiformes

_____ **6.** Psittaciformes

_____ **7.** Galliformes

_____ **8.** Strigiformes

a. parrots

b. owls

c. perching songbirds

d. ostriches

e. swans, geese and ducks

f. turkeys, chickens, and quails

g. pigeons and doves

h. raptors

TRUE-FALSE **If a statement is true, write *T* in the blank. If a statement is false, write *F* in the blank, and then in the space provided, explain why the statement is false.**

_____ **9.** The scientific term for the fused collarbones of modern birds is the *syrinx*.

____

_____ **10.** Contour feathers cover the body of nestlings and provide an insulating undercoat in adults.

____

_____ **11.** Because birds are ectothermic, they conserve body heat by fluffing their feathers.

____

_____ **12.** Birds have a heart with two separate ventricles, which prevents the mixing of oxygenated and deoxygenated blood.

____

_____ **13.** A bird has oxygenated air in its lungs during both inhalation and exhalation.

____

Name ______________________ Class ____________ Date ____________

MULTIPLE CHOICE **Write the letter of the most-correct answer in the blank.**

______ **14.** Which of the following is *not* a characteristic of *Archaeopteryx*?

a. shortened, fused tail
b. hollow bones
c. feathers
d. teeth

______ **15.** Which of the following characteristics is shared by dinosaurs and modern birds?

a. teeth **b.** furcula **c.** claws on forelimbs **d.** hollow bones

______ **16.** Hooked structures that project from the barb of a feather are

a. follicles. **b.** shafts. **c.** barbules. **d.** vanes.

______ **17.** Birds in temperate climates usually molt in

a. early spring. **b.** early winter. **c.** late summer. **d.** late spring.

______ **18.** The pygostyle is part of a bird's

a. pectoral girdle. **b.** beak. **c.** flight muscles. **d.** spine.

______ **19.** A scientist who studies birds is called a(n)

a. entomologist. **b.** ornithologist. **c.** anthropologist. **d.** botanist.

______ **20.** In the diagram below, which part of a bird's digestive system is responsible for kneading and crushing food?

a. 1 **b.** 2 **c.** 3 **d.** 4

______ **21.** In the diagram below, what is the name of the organ labeled *1?*

a. proventriculus **b.** liver **c.** gizzard **d.** crop

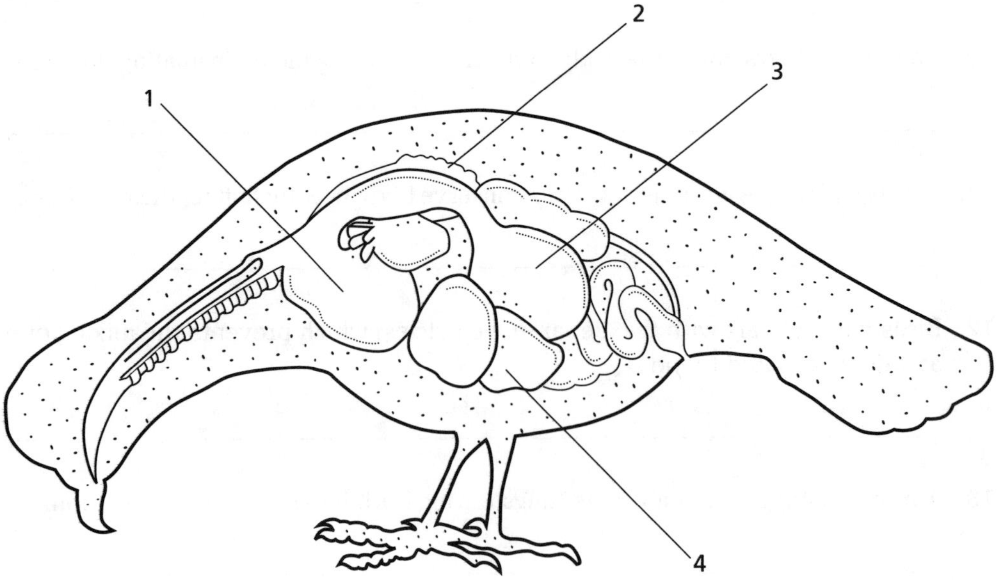

______ **22.** The vocalizations of songbirds are produced by a structure at the base of the trachea called a

a. syrinx. **b.** pygostyle. **c.** crop. **d.** vane.

______ **23.** Two characteristics of the bird skeleton that are adaptations to flight are

a. hollow bones, keeled sternum
b. non-fused bone, flexible skeleton
c. dense strong bones, keeled sternum
d. absence of bones in wings, presence of furcula

SHORT ANSWER **Answer each question in the space provided.**

24. Explain the functions of posterior and anterior air sacs in the respiratory system of a bird.

____

____

25. Compare the terms *altricial* and *precocial* as they pertain to bird reproduction and parental care.

____

____

____

26. List three cues birds may use when navigating during migration. ______________

____

____

____

27. How are birds from the orders Strigiformes and Falconiformes similar? How are they different?

____

____

____

28. List four important characteristics of birds. ______________

____

____

29. Summarize one hypothesis for the evolution of flight. ______________

____

____

____

Name ______________________ Class ____________ Date ____________

DRAWING CONCLUSIONS **Follow the directions given below.**

30. Refer to the diagram below to answer items a–e.

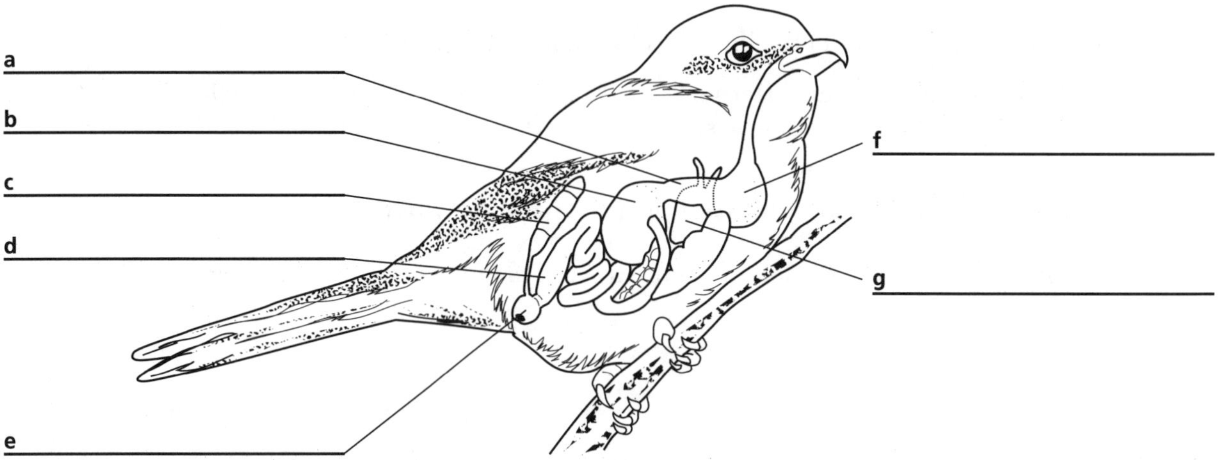

a. Identify each labeled structure in the diagram.

b. Which organ systems are shown in the diagram? ______________________

____

c. Describe two ways that the organ systems shown are adapted for flight.

____

____

____

d. In what way does the gizzard compensate for the lack of teeth? ______________________

____

e. What function does the crop serve? ______________________

____

____

____

Name ______________________ Class ____________ Date ____________

CHAPTER 45 TEST

MAMMALS

MATCHING **Write the correct letter in the blank beside each numbered item.**

_____ **1.** Lagomorpha

_____ **2.** Rodentia

_____ **3.** Monotremata

_____ **4.** Carnivora

_____ **5.** Marsupalia

_____ **6.** Artiodactyla

_____ **7.** Cetacea

_____ **8.** Chiroptera

a. flying mammals

b. cats, bears, and pinnipeds

c. rabbits, hares, and pikas

d. largest mammalian order

e. exclusively aquatic mammals

f. egg-laying mammals

g. hoofed mammals with an even number of toes

h. born at an early stage of development

TRUE-FALSE **If a statement is true, write *T* in the blank. If a statement is false, write *F* in the blank, and then in the space provided, explain why the statement is false.**

_____ **9.** Monotremes are similar to reptiles in that they are viviparous.

____

_____ **10.** Members of the orders Chiroptera and Edentata use echolocation to navigate and find food.

____

_____ **11.** The unusually complete and abundant fossil record of synapsids aids scientists in following anatomical changes that occurred throughout mammalian evolution.

____

_____ **12.** Endothermy allows mammals to live and be active in cold climates and perform strenuous activities for long periods of time.

____

_____ **13.** The opossum is the only marsupial found in the United States.

____

Name ______________________ Class __________ Date __________

MULTIPLE CHOICE **Write the letter of the most correct answer in the blank.**

______ **14.** Which of the following characteristics is shared by all mammals?

a. presence of a cecum
b. lactation in females
c. presence of a rumen
d. viviparous reproduction

______ **15.** Which of the following features is associated with endothermy?

a. specialized teeth
b. single lower jawbone
c. two-chambered heart
d. diaphragm

______ **16.** Mammals that give birth to live young are described as

a. viviparous. **b.** oviparous. **c.** terrestrial. **d.** omnivorous.

______ **17.** The long, pointed nose and sharp teeth of shrews are adaptations for a diet that is

a. herbivorous. **b.** carnivorous. **c.** insectivorous. **d.** oviparous.

______ **18.** The adaptation that allows perissodactyls to digest the cellulose of plant material is called

a. an appendix. **b.** a cecum. **c.** a rumen. **d.** an intestine.

______ **19.** Which specialized mammalian teeth, responsible for gripping, puncturing, and tearing, are especially long in carnivores?

a. incisors **b.** canines **c.** premolars **d.** molars

______ **20.** Two aquatic orders of mammals include

a. Proboscidea and Sirenia.
b. Primates and Lagomorpha.
c. Edentata and Proboscidea.
d. Sirenia and Cetacea.

______ **21.** Which mammal pictured at right belongs to the order Marsupalia?

a. Armadillo
b. Monkey
c. Opossum
d. Platypus

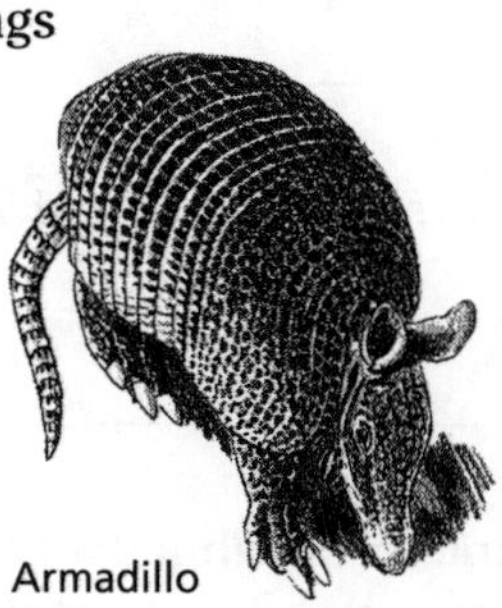
Armadillo

Monkey

______ **22.** Which mammal pictured at right is oviparous?

a. Armadillo
b. Monkey
c. Bat
d. Platypus

Bat

______ **23.** Which mammal pictured at right is able to use echolocation to find food?

a. Armadillo
b. Monkey
c. Bat
d. Opossum

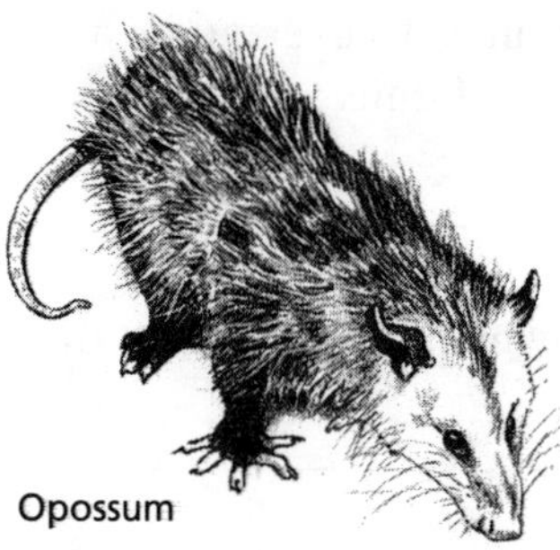
Opossum

Platypus

Name ______________________ Class ______________ Date ______________

SHORT ANSWER **Answer each question in the space provided.**

24. How did the extinction of dinosaurs affect mammalian evolution? ______________

25. Describe one similarity and two differences between the orders Artiodactyla and Perissodactyla.

26. How do the adaptations of mammalian circulatory and respiratory systems contribute to endothermy? ______________

27. Describe the adaptive features for locomotion that characterize the water-dwelling cetaceans, sirenians, and pinnipeds. Include examples from each of the three orders in your answer.

28. Describe one similarity and one difference in the reproduction of monotremes, marsupials, and placental mammals. ______________

29. List the six important characteristics of mammals. ______________

DRAWING CONCLUSIONS Follow the directions given below.

30. Use the diagrams of three mammalian skulls below to answer items a–e.

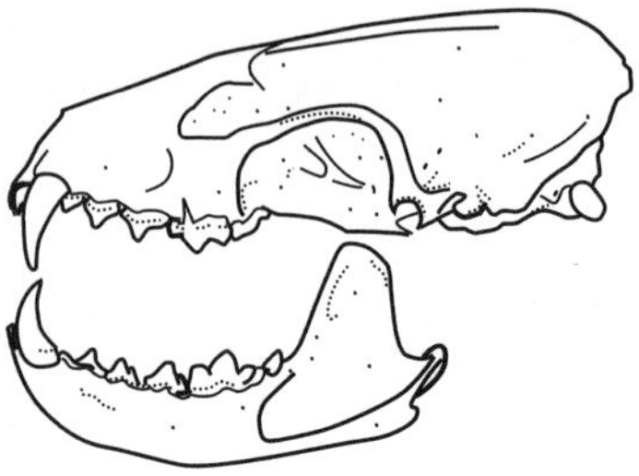

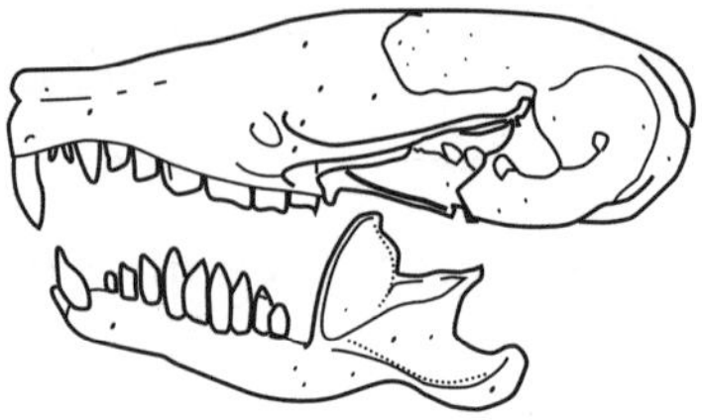

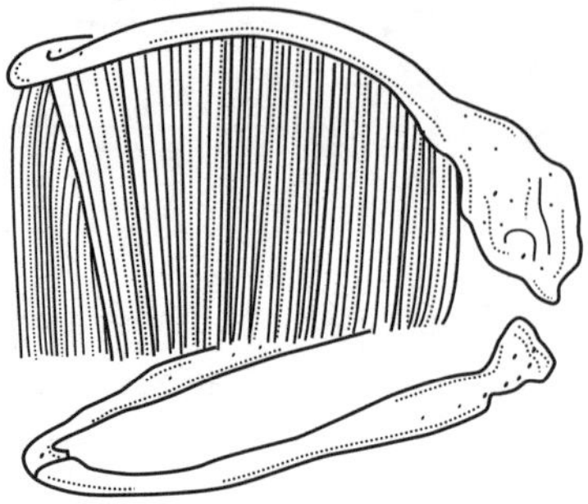

a ______________________ b ______________________ c ______________________

a. Label each of the above skulls with the name of the order to which it belongs: Cetacea, Carnivora, or Insectivora.

b. Explain how the features of skull *a* and skull *c* are related to each organism's diet.

____

____

____

____

c. Which skull is most like that of a mole? Explain your answer.

____

____

d. What is the large comblike structure in skull *c* called? How is it used?

____

____

e. The brain of a mammal is about 15 times heavier than a similarly sized fish, amphibian, or reptile. What part of the brain accounts for most of this size difference?

____

Name ______________________ Class ____________ Date ____________

CHAPTER 46 TEST

SKELETAL, MUSCULAR, AND INTEGUMENTARY SYSTEMS

MATCHING Write the correct letter in the blank before each numbered term.

_____ **1.** cardiac muscle

_____ **2.** ligament

_____ **3.** extensor

_____ **4.** appendicular skeleton

_____ **5.** periosteum

_____ **6.** epithelial tissue

_____ **7.** tendon

_____ **8.** flexor

a. tough membrane covering bone

b. bends a joint

c. cell layers covering body surfaces

d. attaches muscle to bone

e. straightens a joint

f. pumps blood through the body

g. includes bones in arms and legs

h. holds the bones of a joint in place

TRUE-FALSE If a statement is true, write *T* in the blank. If a statement is false, write *F* in the blank, and then in the space provided, explain why the statement is false.

_____ **9.** The thoracic cavity surrounds the spinal cord.

____

_____ **10.** The four types of tissues that make up the human body are muscle tissue, cardiac tissue, nervous tissue, and epithelial tissue.

____

_____ **11.** Bones grow longer as new bone cells replace cartilage.

____

_____ **12.** Muscle contraction is an all-or-nothing response.

____

_____ **13.** Hair color and skin color are determined by keratin.

____

Name ______________________________ Class ______________ Date ______________

MULTIPLE CHOICE **Write the letter of the most correct answer in the blank.**

______ **14.** The skeletal system

a. protects from infection and disease.
b. provides structure, support, and protection for internal organs.
c. maintains water balance and chemical balance and eliminates waste products.
d. regulates body temperature and protects the body from pathogens.

______ **15.** The reproductive organs are located within the

a. cranial cavity.
b. spinal cavity.
c. thoracic cavity.
d. abdominal cavity.

______ **16.** What type of tissue consists of cells that transmit electrical impulses?

a. connective tissue
b. epithelial tissue
c. nervous tissue
d. muscle tissue

______ **17.** Blood cells are produced in the

a. periosteum.
b. bone marrow.
c. epiphyseal plate.
d. synovial fluid.

______ **18.** Muscles move bones by

a. pulling them.
b. pushing them.
c. stretching back and forth.
d. relaxing.

______ **19.** An example of a semimoveable joint is a

a. pivot joint.
b. saddle joint.
c. hinge joint.
d. None of the above

______ **20.** Which type of joint allows the shoulder to make circular motions?

a. pivot joint
b. angular joint
c. gliding joint
d. ball-and-socket joint

______ **21.** Which of the following occurs when a skeletal muscle contracts?

a. The myosin heads remain attached to actin filaments.
b. The myosin filaments overlap.
c. The myosin heads bend outward.
d. The sarcomeres shorten.

______ **22.** The epidermis contains

a. glands.
b. keratin.
c. sensory neurons.
d. muscle tissue.

______ **23.** The axial skeleton includes bones of the

a. arms and legs.
b. skull and spine.
c. shoulder.
d. hips.

Name ____________________ Class ____________ Date ____________

SHORT ANSWER **Answer the questions in the space provided.**

24. Briefly describe how a muscle contracts. ____________________

25. What are the four primary functions of the skin? ____________________

26. Explain the difference between tissues and organs. ____________________

27. Distinguish the epidermis from the dermis. ____________________

28. Name the two types of bone marrow, and briefly describe the function of each.

29. Label the three types of joints shown in the diagrams below.

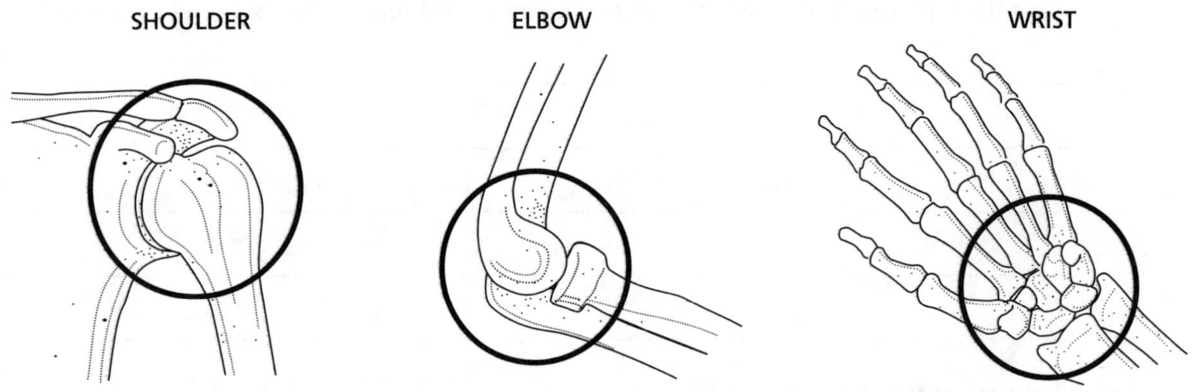

a ____________ **b** ____________ **c** ____________

Name ______________________ Class ____________ Date ____________

DRAWING CONCLUSIONS **Follow the directions given below.**

30. Refer to the figure of the human arm below as you answer *a–e*. Label each part of the figure in the spaces provided.

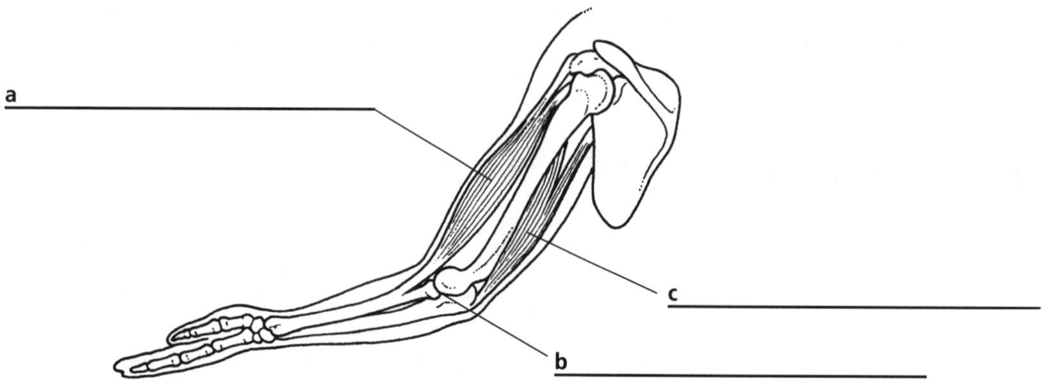

a. Is the muscle labeled *a* a flexor or an extensor? ______________________

____

b. Is the muscle labeled *c* a flexor or an extensor? ______________________

____

c. Define the term *insertion.* Where is the insertion of *a* located? Where is the insertion of *c* located?

____

____

____

____

____

d. Define the term *origin.* Where is the origin of *a* located? Where is the origin of *c* located?

____

____

____

____

____

e. What type of moveable joint is *b?* ______________________

____

Name ______________________________ Class ______________ Date ____________

CHAPTER 47 TEST

CIRCULATORY AND RESPIRATORY SYSTEMS

MATCHING **Write the correct letter in the blank before each numbered term.**

_____ **1.** left ventricle

_____ **2.** arteriole

_____ **3.** atrioventricular node

_____ **4.** lymph node

_____ **5.** hemoglobin

_____ **6.** phagocyte

_____ **7.** larynx

_____ **8.** trachea

a. carries oxygen in blood

b. pumps blood into the systemic circulation

c. produces sounds for communication

d. engulfs microorganisms

e. is an air passageway

f. conducts blood into capillaries

g. filters components of lymph

h. relays electrical impulses

TRUE-FALSE **If a statement is true, write *T* in the blank. If a statement if false, write *F* in the blank, and then in the space provided, explain why the statement is false.**

_____ **9.** Veins that conduct blood to the right atrium carry oxygenated blood.

____

_____ **10.** Plasma nourishes blood cells.

____

_____ **11.** Leukocytes help defend the body from disease.

____

_____ **12.** Expiration must occur at the same time as systole.

____

_____ **13.** Pulmonary circulation is the movement of blood throughout the body.

____

MULTIPLE CHOICE Write the letter of the most correct answer in the blank.

_____ **14.** Which compartment of the heart would receive blood flowing in the wrong direction through a defective mitral valve?

a. right atrium
b. left atrium
c. right ventricle
d. left ventricle

_____ **15.** Which of the following is found in veins but not in arteries?

a. smooth muscle cells
b. endothelial cells
c. connective tissue
d. valves

_____ **16.** Arteries that carry blood with a high concentration of carbon dioxide are part of

a. the cardiovascular system.
b. the circulatory system.
c. pulmonary circulation.
d. All of the above

_____ **17.** The lymphatic system

a. transports blood back to the heart.
b. has veins.
c. connects with systemic circulation.
d. All of the above

_____ **18.** Which of the following is *not* a component of blood?

a. platelets
b. leukocytes
c. alveolar cells
d. red blood cells

_____ **19.** Which type of cell contains proteins that are important for oxygen transport?

a. erythrocytes
b. leukocytes with nuclei
c. platelets
d. alveolar cells

_____ **20.** Platelets are required for the formation of

a. lymph.
b. blood clots.
c. red blood cells.
d. antibodies.

_____ **21.** Immediately before entering alveoli, inspired air passes through

a. veins.
b. the trachea.
c. bronchioles.
d. bronchi.

_____ **22.** What determines whether carbon dioxide is absorbed or released by blood?

a. air pressure within alveoli
b. concentration gradients
c. phagocytes
d. relative amounts of hemoglobin

_____ **23.** The diaphragm

a. divides the heart into a right and left side.
b. covers the aortic valve when it is closed.
c. is important for breathing.
d. None of the above

SHORT ANSWER Answer the questions in the space provided.

24. Is it important to know the blood type of a blood donor if only the donor's plasma will be used?

Explain your answer. ____

25. What prevents backflow of blood as it returns to the heart? ____

26. What is systemic circulation? ____

27. Why is mucus important to the normal functioning of the respiratory system? ____

28. Briefly describe how air is inspired. ____

29. Identify the labeled structures of the human heart in the diagram below.

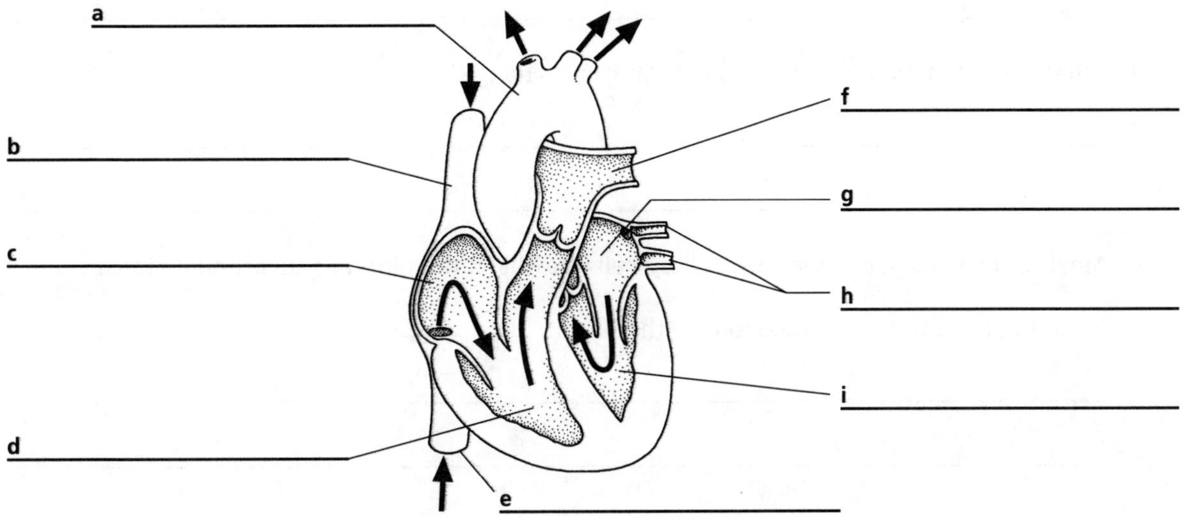

Name ______________________ Class ____________ Date ____________

DRAWING CONCLUSIONS Follow the directions given below.

30. Use the diagram of gas exchange in the lungs below to answer *a–e*.

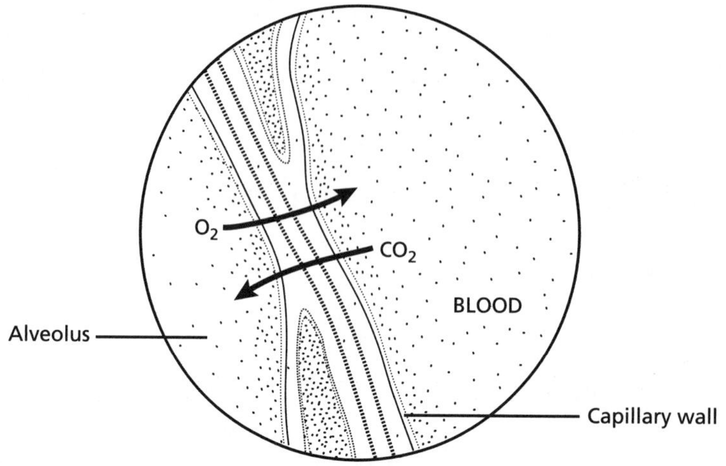

a. In the lungs, what determines the direction of the diffusion of oxygen and carbon dioxide between the blood and alveoli? ______________________

____

____

b. In the lungs, is carbon dioxide more concentrated in the alveoli or in the blood? ____________

____

c. How does holding your breath affect the concentrations of oxygen and carbon dioxide in your lungs? Does holding your breath affect the exchange of oxygen and carbon dioxide? Explain your answer. ______________________

____

____

d. What is the function of red blood cells in gas exchange? ______________________

____

____

e. Most of the carbon dioxide released by cells travels in the blood as bicarbonate ions. What happens to bicarbonate ions in the lungs? ______________________

____

____

Name ______________________ Class ____________ Date ____________

CHAPTER 48 TEST

INFECTIOUS DISEASES AND THE IMMUNE SYSTEM

MATCHING **Write the correct letter in the blank before each numbered term.**

_____ **1.** mucus

_____ **2.** B cells

_____ **3.** antigen

_____ **4.** autoimmune disease

_____ **5.** interleukins

_____ **6.** cytotoxic T cells

_____ **7.** allergy

_____ **8.** immunity

a. reaction to harmless antigens

b. stimulates an immune response

c. cell-mediated immune response

d. traps pathogens

e. attacks the body's own cells

f. humoral immune response

g. resistance to a specific pathogen

h. activate lymphocytes

TRUE-FALSE **If a statement is true, write *T* in the blank. If a statement is false, write *F* in the blank, and then in the space provided, explain why the statement is false.**

_____ **9.** Koch's postulates are steps used to determine the cause of a specific disease.

____

_____ **10.** Antibodies do not destroy pathogens directly.

____

_____ **11.** B cells identify and then kill infected cells.

____

_____ **12.** A primary immune response involves the recognition of antigens by lymphocytes.

____

_____ **13.** Many people with AIDS die from opportunistic infections.

____

Name ________________________________ Class ____________ Date ____________

MULTIPLE CHOICE Write the letter of the most correct answer in the blank.

______ **14.** Antibodies are produced by

a. T cells.
b. plasma cells.
c. macrophages.
d. antigens.

______ **15.** The skin is an effective nonspecific defense mechanism because it

a. secretes antibodies.
b. has an outer layer of keratin.
c. secretes mucus.
d. is sterile.

______ **16.** Natural killer cells

a. engulf infected cells.
b. are involved in specific defense mechanisms.
c. puncture cell membranes.
d. produce antibodies.

______ **17.** All components of the immune system

a. are ductless.
b. contain white blood cells.
c. are controlled by the nervous system.
d. filter blood.

______ **18.** Cytotoxic T cells are

a. lymphocytes.
b. white blood cells.
c. capable of killing cells.
d. All of the above

______ **19.** In order to be activated, a B cell must recognize its specific antigen and

a. initiate cell division.
b. be stimulated by interleukins.
c. be recognized by interferon.
d. pass through the thymus.

______ **20.** Which of the following is necessary for immunity?

a. fever above 105°F
b. formation of memory cells
c. swelling of lymph nodes
d. release of histamines

______ **21.** In the immune system, macrophages

a. stimulate the inflammatory response.
b. display antigens.
c. produce antibodies.
d. stimulate a secondary immune response.

______ **22.** In an immune response, antigens are recognized by

a. neutrophils.
b. plasma cells.
c. bacteria.
d. cell surface receptors.

______ **23.** AIDS is caused by

a. air borne viruses.
b. a decrease in helper T cells.
c. a DNA virus.
d. All of the above

Name ______________________ Class ____________ Date ____________

SHORT ANSWER Answer the questions in the space provided.

24. What is a primary difference between the body's nonspecific and specific defenses?

25. Briefly describe the steps of the inflammatory response.

26. What is a primary characteristic of an autoimmune disease?

27. Why is a vaccine for HIV difficult to develop?

28. Is being infected with HIV the same as having AIDS? Explain your answer.

29. In the graph of an immune response shown at right, during which time period would the first antibodies to the pathogen be produced? Which period of time would involve the most rapid division of B cells?

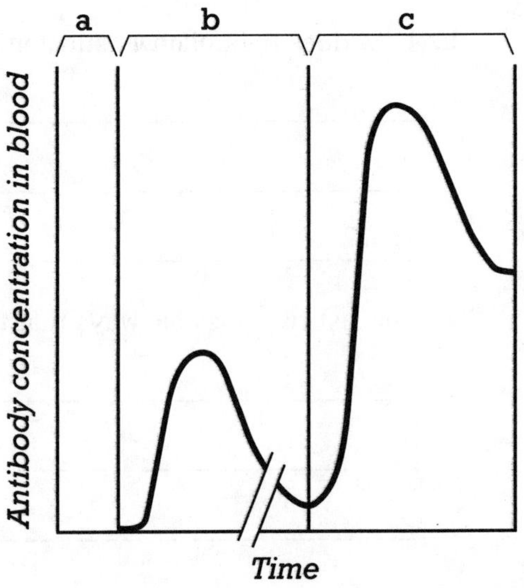

Name ____________________ Class ____________ Date ____________

DRAWING CONCLUSIONS **Follow the directions given below.**

30. You have been asked to perform an experiment to determine the relationship between the secretion of interleukins and the presence of various combinations of macrophages, helper T cells, a specific antigen (called A), and an unknown substance. In your laboratory, you can maintain cells in culture and simulate interaction between cells and substances that occur in the body. You have been supplied with the following:

- antigen A
- purified helper T cells that respond to antigen A
- purified macrophages
- an unknown substance

The results of this experiment are shown in the graph below. Use the graph to answer *a–c*.

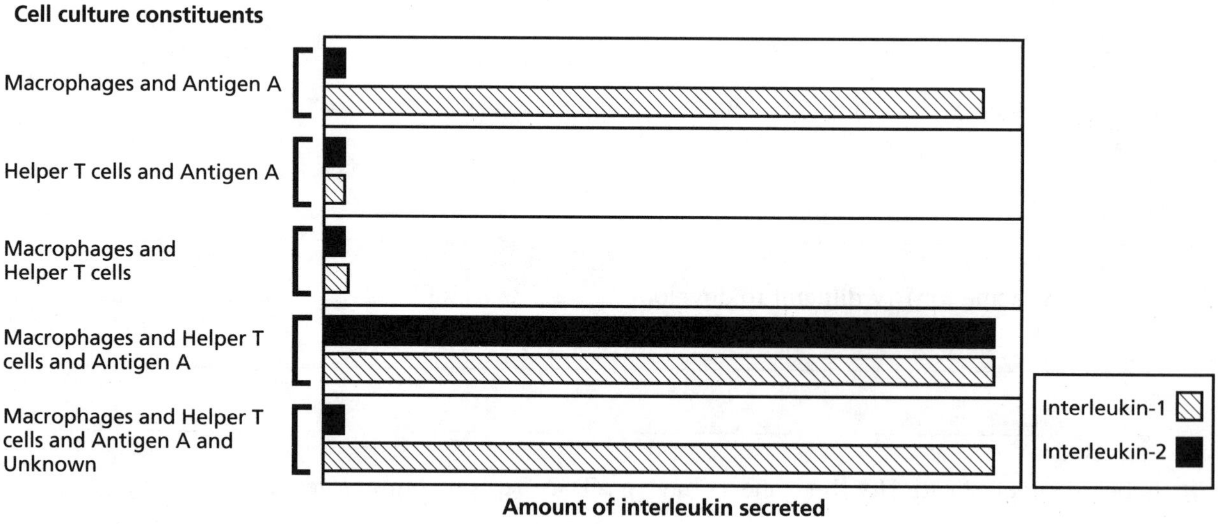

a. What is required for secretion of interleukin-2 by helper T cells? ____________________

____

____

b. How does the unknown substance affect secretion of interleukin-2 by helper T cells?

____

____

____

c. Suggest two possible ways that the unknown substance affects secretion of interleukin-2.

____

____

____

____

Name ______________________ Class ____________ Date ____________

CHAPTER 49 TEST

DIGESTIVE AND EXCRETORY SYSTEMS

MATCHING **Write the correct letter in the blank before each numbered term.**

_____ **1.** proximal convoluted tubule

_____ **2.** peristalsis

_____ **3.** molars

_____ **4.** gastric glands

_____ **5.** liver

_____ **6.** ureters

_____ **7.** nephron

_____ **8.** Bowman's capsule

a. transport urine to urinary bladder

b. collects blood filtrate

c. secretes bile

d. functional unit of kidney

e. secrete hydrochloric acid

f. rhythmic muscle contractions

g. mechanical digestion

h. reabsorption of glucose

TRUE-FALSE **If a statement is true, write *T* in the blank. If a statement if false, write *F* in the blank, and then in the space provided, explain why the statement is false.**

_____ **9.** Food is the only source of vitamins.

____

_____ **10.** The esophagus is not part of the gastrointestinal tract.

____

_____ **11.** A low pH is required for pepsin to be active.

____

_____ **12.** Waste products and non-waste products are separated from each other during filtration.

____

_____ **13.** Dietary proteins are obtained only by eating animal products.

____

Name ______________________ Class __________ Date __________

MULTIPLE CHOICE Write the letter of the most correct answer in the blank.

______ **14.** Bile aids the digestion of

a. carbohydrates. **b.** proteins. **c.** fats. **d.** vitamins.

______ **15.** Which type of nutrient is sodium?

a. vitamin **b.** protein **c.** mineral **d.** fat

______ **16.** Nonessential amino acids

a. are not needed for protein synthesis.
b. are surplus amino acids that can be excreted.
c. can be produced within the body.
d. All of the above

______ **17.** Most absorption within the gastrointestinal tract takes place in the

a. pancreas. **b.** small intestine. **c.** stomach. **d.** large intestine.

______ **18.** Chemical digestion begins in the

a. mouth. **b.** esophagus. **c.** stomach. **d.** small intestine.

______ **19.** Lacteals are

a. excellent sources of thiamin.
b. associated with the large intestine.
c. found within the stomach.
d. required for absorption of fatty acids.

______ **20.** The renal medulla is

a. the outermost portion of the kidney.
b. characterized by the absence of nephrons.
c. the location of the loops of Henle.
d. a source of digestive enzymes.

______ **21.** The structure shown in the diagram at right is a

a. villus.
b. nephron.
c. ureter.
d. urethra.

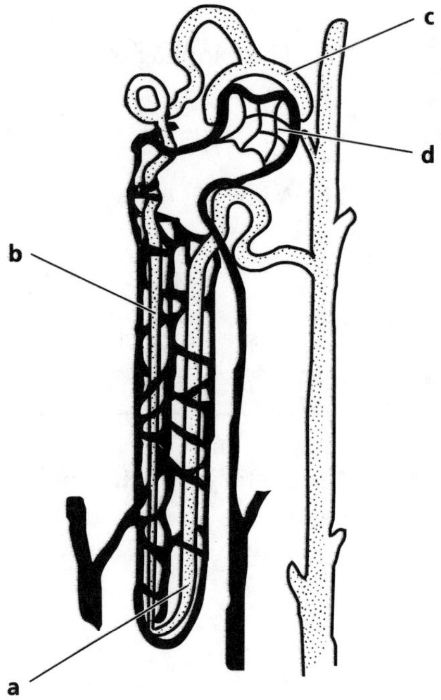

______ **22.** In the diagram at right, most reabsorption takes place at the structure labeled

a. *a.*
b. *b.*
c. *c.*
d. *d.*

______ **23.** In the diagram at right, blood is filtered from the site labeled

a. *a.*
b. *b.*
c. *c.*
d. *d.*

Name ______________________ Class ____________ Date ____________

SHORT ANSWER **Answer the questions in the space provided.**

24. What is a nutrient? ______________________

25. How are carbohydrates absorbed by the body? ______________________

26. Explain why gastric fluid does not harm the stomach. ______________________

27. Why is close interaction of the circulatory and urinary systems important? ______________________

28. Does the gallbladder secrete bile? Briefly explain your answer. ______________________

29. Why is osmotic pressure important for proper kidney functioning? ______________________

Name ______________________ Class ____________ Date ____________

DRAWING CONCLUSIONS **Follow the directions given below.**

30. Refer to the diagram of the human digestive system below to answer *a–e*.

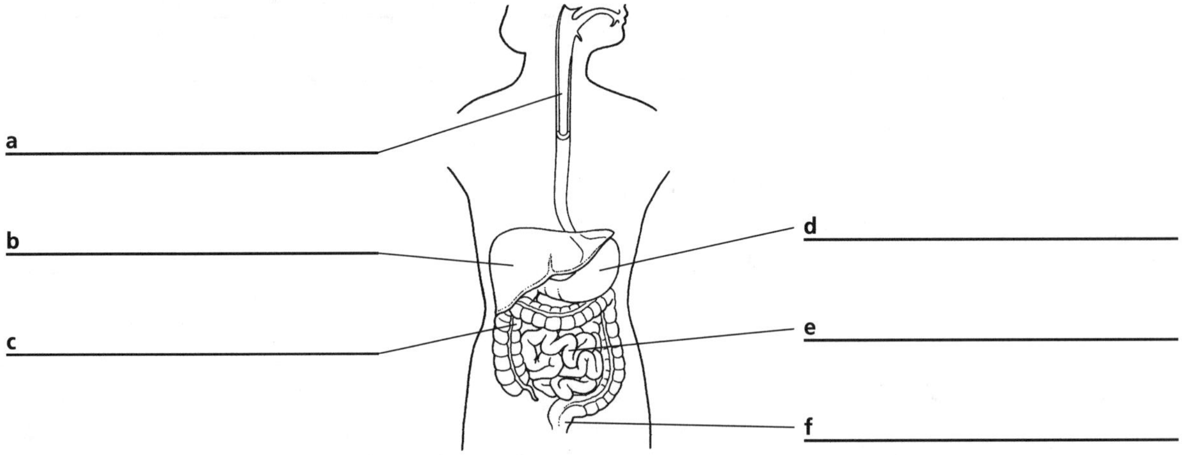

a. Label each structure in the diagram.

b. Which organ is not part of the gastrointestinal tract? What is this organ's role in digestion?

____

____

____

c. Distinguish between chemical digestion and mechanical digestion. ____________

____

____

____

d. Describe how nutrients are absorbed into the circulatory system through the small intestine.

____

____

____

____

e. What is the role of pepsin in digestion? ____________

____

____

____

Name ______________________ Class ____________ Date ____________

CHAPTER 50 TEST

NERVOUS SYSTEM AND SENSE ORGANS

MATCHING **Write the correct letter in the blank before each numbered term.**

_____ **1.** myelin sheath

_____ **2.** diencephalon

_____ **3.** synaptic cleft

_____ **4.** cerebral cortex

_____ **5.** sensory receptor

_____ **6.** spinal reflex

_____ **7.** axon

_____ **8.** tympanic membrane

a. conducts action potentials

b. outer layer of the cerebrum

c. gap between neurons

d. vibrates in response to sound waves

e. a neuron that detects stimuli

f. an involuntary movement

g. increases speed of an action potential

h. contains important relay centers

TRUE-FALSE **If a statement is true, write *T* in the blank. If a statement is false, write *F* in the blank, and then in the space provided, explain why the statement is false.**

_____ **9.** Action potentials stimulate the release of neurotransmitters.

____

_____ **10.** The somatic nervous system of the motor division consists of motor neurons that control the movement of skeletal muscles.

____

_____ **11.** Cones are photoreceptors that detect different colors of light.

____

_____ **12.** Dendrites transmit action potentials to other neurons.

____

_____ **13.** The cerebellum coordinates and smoothes ongoing movements.

____

Name ______________________ Class ____________ Date ____________

MULTIPLE CHOICE **Write the letter of the most correct answer in the blank.**

_____ **14.** Spinal nerves are

a. bundles of dendrites.
b. part of the peripheral nervous system.
c. part of the gray matter.
d. only efferent neurons.

_____ **15.** Auditory information travels to the

a. brain stem.
b. thalamus.
c. cerebral cortex.
d. All of the above

_____ **16.** Neurons that make up the optic nerve are

a. efferent neurons.
b. motor neurons.
c. photoreceptors.
d. afferent neurons.

_____ **17.** The gray matter of the spinal cord consists primarily of

a. cell bodies.
b. dendrites.
c. axons.
d. motor neurons.

_____ **18.** The sympathetic division of the autonomic nervous system

a. stimulates the "fight-or-flight" response.
b. is part of the central nervous system.
c. includes all of the neurons in the patellar reflex.
d. is part of the sensory division of the peripheral nervous system.

_____ **19.** The peripheral nervous system includes

a. the somatic system.
b. the autonomic system.
c. the sensory division.
d. All of the above

_____ **20.** When the voltage across the cell membrane of a neuron is at resting potential,

a. the inside of the cell is positive relative to the outside.
b. there are more sodium ions outside the cell than inside the cell.
c. the cell membrane is not functioning correctly.
d. None of the above

_____ **21.** Which of the following statements about rods is true?

a. Rods are one part of cones.
b. Rods are chemoreceptors.
c. Rods contact the tympanic membrane.
d. Rods are photoreceptors.

_____ **22.** Hair cells are

a. located in the middle ear.
b. found in the olfactory epithelium.
c. important for hearing and balance.
d. found in the cerebellar cortex.

_____ **23.** While sound vibrations are stimuli for hearing, chemicals are stimuli for

a. touch.
b. vision.
c. balance.
d. smell.

Name ______________________ Class ______________ Date ______________

SHORT ANSWER Answer the questions in the space provided.

24. Explain the difference between an afferent neuron and an efferent neuron. ______________________

25. Briefly explain how the relative concentrations of sodium ions and potassium ions inside and outside a neuron change during an action potential. ______________________

26. Briefly describe how the patellar (knee-jerk) reflex operates. ______________________

27. How is taste detected? What type of sensory receptor is involved with the perception of taste?

____

28. What is a neurotransmitter? ______________________

29. Identify the parts of the neuron that are labeled in the diagram below.

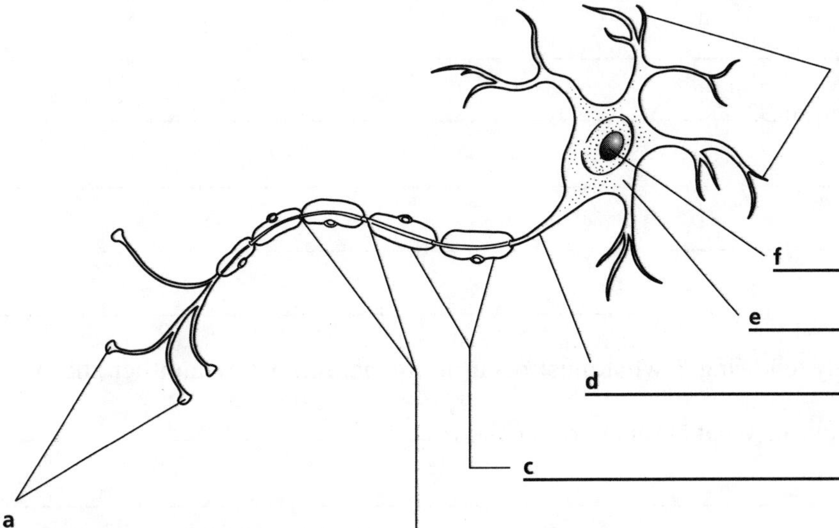

g ______________________

f ______________________

e ______________________

d ______________________

c ______________________

a ______________________

b ______________________

Name ______________________ Class ____________ Date ____________

DRAWING CONCLUSIONS **Follow the directions given below.**

30. Refer to the graph below to answer *a–e.*

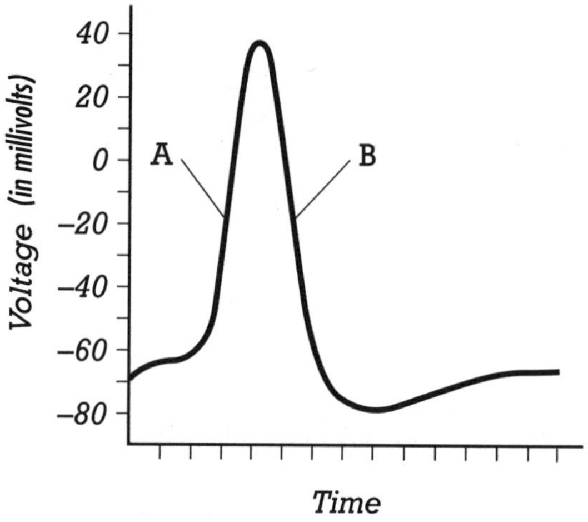

a. What process is illustrated in the graph? ______________________

____

b. What causes changes in the permeability of a neuron's cell membrane that enable this process to occur? ______________________

____

____

c. What is happening in period *A?* ______________________

____

____

____

d. What is happening in period *B?* ______________________

____

____

____

e. In the period immediately following *B,* what must occur in the neuron before another sharp rise in voltage can take place? What is this period called? ______________________

____

____

____

Name ______________________ Class ____________ Date ____________

CHAPTER 51 TEST

ENDOCRINE SYSTEM

MATCHING **Write the correct letter in the blank before each numbered term.**

_____ **1.** steroid hormone

_____ **2.** second messenger

_____ **3.** negative feedback

_____ **4.** diabetes mellitus

_____ **5.** releasing hormone

_____ **6.** pituitary gland

_____ **7.** exocrine gland

_____ **8.** epinephrine

a. regulated by the hypothalamus

b. characterized by insulin deficiency

c. diffuses through target cell membrane

d. secretes its products into ducts

e. last step inhibits the first step

f. amplifies a hormone signal

g. produced by the adrenal medulla

h. produced by neurosecretory cells

TRUE-FALSE **If a statement is true, write *T* in the blank. If a statement if false, write *F* in the blank, and then in the space provided, explain why the statement is false.**

_____ **9.** The adrenal medulla is an endocrine gland.

____

_____ **10.** Hormones are secreted by exocrine glands and affect nearby cells.

____

_____ **11.** Antidiuretic hormone (ADH) increases the amount of water reabsorbed by kidney tubules.

____

_____ **12.** Follicle-stimulating hormone (FSH) does not function in males.

____

_____ **13.** Insulin and glucagon are antagonistic hormones.

____

Name ______________________ Class ____________ Date ____________

MULTIPLE CHOICE **Write the letter of the most correct answer in the blank.**

______ **14.** Which of the following statements is *false?*

a. Hormones are transported in the bloodstream.
b. Amino acids can be hormones.
c. Hormones can act without binding to receptors.
d. Hormones influence the activity of distant target cells.

______ **15.** Second messengers are needed for

a. testosterone.
b. amino acid–based hormones.
c. steroid hormones.
d. sex hormones.

______ **16.** Which of the following is directly involved in the action of most amino acid–based hormones?

a. testosterone **b.** cyclic AMP **c.** glucose **d.** prostaglandins

______ **17.** Iodized salt helps prevent goiter by providing iodine for production of

a. thyroxine. **b.** oxytocin. **c.** prostaglandins. **d.** insulin.

______ **18.** Releasing hormones bind to receptors on

a. posterior-pituitary cells.
b. hypothalamic cells.
c. anterior-pituitary cells.
d. neurons.

______ **19.** Hormones secreted by the parathyroid glands are involved in the

a. metabolism of glucose.
b. metabolism of proteins.
c. regulation of blood glucose levels.
d. regulation of blood calcium levels.

______ **20.** Which of the following endocrine glands secretes hormones that have major effects on body temperature?

a. testes
b. posterior pituitary
c. thyroid gland
d. pancreas

______ **21.** The pituitary gland functions in the negative feedback control of

a. norepinephrine secretion.
b. epinephrine secretion.
c. testosterone secretion.
d. All of the above

______ **22.** The islets of Langerhans contain

a. modified neurons that secrete hormones.
b. endocrine cells that are surrounded by exocrine cells.
c. endocrine cells that store glucose.
d. endocrine cells that are controlled by the pituitary gland.

______ **23.** If the pituitary cells are normal, an abnormally high blood concentration of thyroid-stimulating hormone (TSH) would indicate that

a. the negative feedback mechanism is not working.
b. the negative feedback mechanism is working.
c. too much thyroxine is being secreted.
d. None of the above

Name ______________________ Class ____________ Date ____________

SHORT ANSWER **Answer the questions in the space provided.**

24. What are releasing hormones? Give an example of a releasing hormone and describe its actions.

25. How are positive feedback mechanisms different from negative feedback mechanisms?

26. What characteristic of feedback mechanisms is common to both steroid hormones and amino acid–based hormones? Briefly explain your answer.

27. How might a pancreatic islet cell transplant be more advantageous than daily injections of insulin in treating type I diabetes?

28. What is meant by a "hypoglandular" condition? Give an example of such a condition.

29. How is the solubility of steroid hormones related to their function?

Name ______________________ Class ______________ Date ______________

DRAWING CONCLUSIONS **Follow the directions given below.**

30. Refer to the table below to answer *a–e.*

An 18-year-old male has not experienced puberty. A series of diagnostic tests to analyze hormone levels was performed, and the results appear in the table below.

Diagnostic Test Results

Test	**Result**
Measurement of testosterone level in the blood	Low testosterone level
Measurement of naturally occurring luteinizing hormone (LH) level in the blood	Low LH level
Injection of LH-releasing hormone into the bloodstream followed by measurement of LH level in the blood	No increase in LH level

a. According to the data, why has the young man not experienced puberty? ______________

____

____

b. What are the two structures or glands that control the endocrine function of the testes?

____

____

c. Considering the test results, which gland is probably the primary cause of the low testosterone level? Explain your answer. ______________

____

____

____

d. How does testosterone secretion affect LH secretion? ______________

____

____

____

e. If the third test had resulted in an increase in the blood level of LH, what would be the primary cause of low testosterone levels? ______________

____

____

Name ______________________ Class ____________ Date ____________

CHAPTER 52 TEST

REPRODUCTIVE SYSTEM

MATCHING **Write the correct letter in the blank before each numbered term.**

_____ **1.** flagellum

_____ **2.** epididymis

_____ **3.** scrotum

_____ **4.** vas deferens

_____ **5.** fallopian tube

_____ **6.** follicle

_____ **7.** vagina

_____ **8.** placenta

a. site of fertilization

b. receives ejaculated sperm

c. site of sperm maturation

d. cells surrounding an immature egg

e. passes nutrients from mother to fetus

f. sperm tail

g. transports sperm to urethra

h. temperature is lower than in the abdomen

TRUE-FALSE **If a statement is true, write *T* in the blank. If a statement is false, write *F* in the blank, and then in the space provided, explain why the statement is false.**

_____ **9.** Four sperm cells result from each cell that begins meiosis.

____

_____ **10.** Sperm are not part of semen.

____

_____ **11.** Ovulation is triggered by a sharp rise in luteinizing hormone (LH) secretion.

____

_____ **12.** By the time the zygote implants itself into the uterine lining, it has become a blastocyst.

____

_____ **13.** Estrogen and progesterone secreted by the corpus luteum cause the uterine lining to thicken.

____

Name ______________________ Class ______________ Date ______________

MULTIPLE CHOICE Write the letter of the most correct answer in the blank.

______ **14.** The nucleus of a sperm is found in its

a. tail.
b. midpiece.
c. head.
d. chromosomes.

______ **15.** Seminiferous tubules are located within each

a. ovary.
b. seminal vesicle.
c. epididymis.
d. testis.

______ **16.** The secretions of the prostate gland contribute to

a. the completion of meiosis.
b. the production of semen.
c. sperm maturation.
d. the survival of eggs in the uterus.

______ **17.** Both eggs and sperm

a. are self-propelled.
b. have the haploid ($1n$) number of chromosomes.
c. are produced continuously.
d. All of the above

______ **18.** Which of the following secretes estrogen in response to LH stimulation?

a. uterus
b. fallopian tube
c. ovary
d. blastocyst

______ **19.** When the corpus luteum stops secreting progesterone,

a. menstruation can occur.
b. the uterine lining sloughs off.
c. FSH levels can begin to rise.
d. All of the above

______ **20.** At the instant of sperm and egg fusion, which stage of the menstrual cycle would normally be occurring?

a. ovulation
b. follicular phase
c. menstruation
d. luteal phase

______ **21.** The transformation of a zygote to a blastocyst requires

a. implantation.
b. cleavage.
c. the zygote to be a haploid cell.
d. All of the above

______ **22.** The yolk sac is formed during the

a. first trimester of pregnancy.
b. second trimester of pregnancy.
c. third trimester of pregnancy.
d. formation of an egg.

______ **23.** Which male reproductive organ has functions similar to those of an ovary?

a. seminal vesicle
b. prostate
c. testis
d. penis

Name ______________________ Class ____________ Date ____________

SHORT ANSWER **Answer the questions in the space provided.**

24. How is the corpus luteum formed and why is it important to reproduction? ________________

25. Is menopause a phase of the menstrual cycle? Explain your answer. ________________

26. Describe the function(s) of the epididymis. ________________

27. Does each ovary produce one egg per menstrual cycle? Explain your answer. ________________

28. Describe the relationship between the cervix, the vagina, and the uterus. ________________

29. Identify the labeled structures in the diagram below. What process is illustrated by the diagram?

____

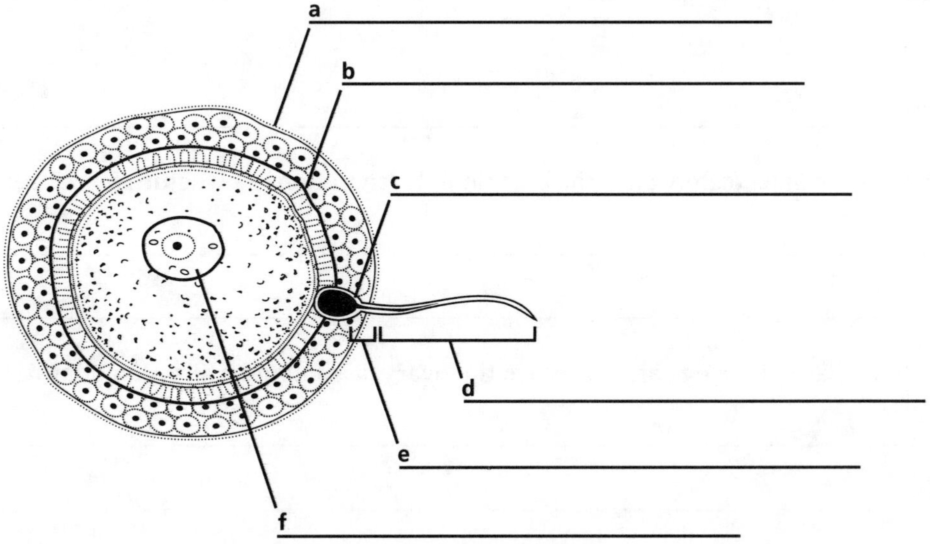

DRAWING CONCLUSIONS **Follow the directions given below.**

30. Use the diagram below to answer *a–e.*

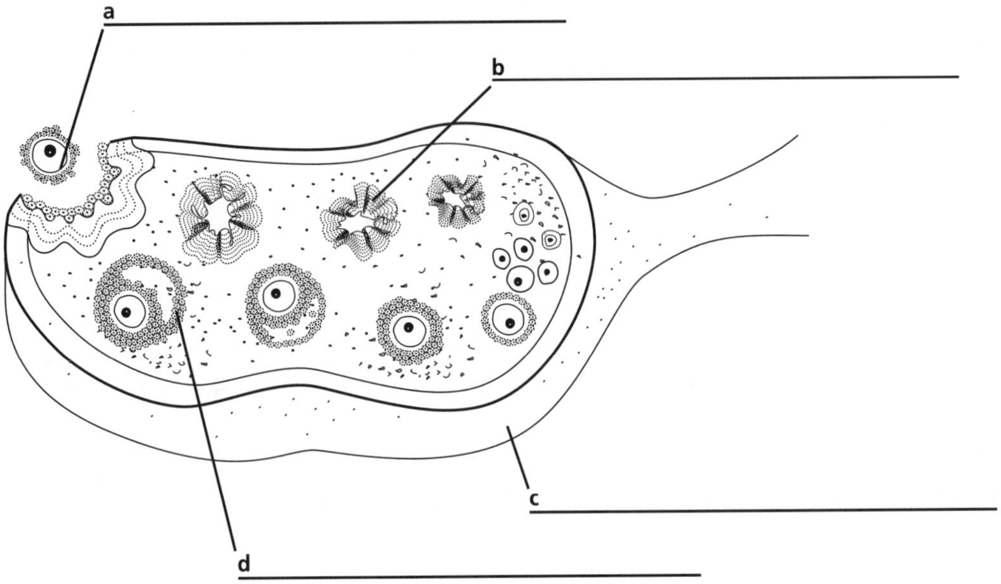

a. Identify the labeled structures in the diagram. What event is illustrated by the diagram?

b. Blood levels of three hormones rise sharply before this event. What are these hormones?

c. How does structure *b* affect the uterine lining?

d. What occurs immediately after the complete degeneration of structure *b?*

e. Trace the path of the egg after it leaves the ovary, assuming fertilization does *not* occur.

Name ______________________ Class ____________ Date ____________

CHAPTER 53 TEST

DRUGS

MATCHING **Write the correct letter in the blank before each numbered term.**

_____ **1.** cocaine

_____ **2.** tars

_____ **3.** marijuana

_____ **4.** cirrhosis

_____ **5.** emphysema

_____ **6.** heroin

_____ **7.** alcohol

_____ **8.** enkephalin

a. associated with amotivational syndrome

b. a depressant

c. degenerative lung disease caused by smoking

d. blocks reuptake

e. painkilling neurotransmitter

f. degenerative disease of the liver caused by alcohol consumption

g. paralyze cilia in lungs

h. a narcotic

TRUE-FALSE **If a statement is true, write *T* in the blank. If a statement if false, write *F* in the blank, and then in the space provided, explain why the statement is false.**

_____ **9.** Drug interactions only occur between prescription drugs.

____

_____ **10.** Drugs can be administered by application to the skin.

____

_____ **11.** Lethal dose only refers to drugs that are injected.

____

_____ **12.** Anyone who uses addictive drugs can become a drug addict.

____

_____ **13.** Blood alcohol concentration (BAC) depends on the sex and weight of a drinker.

____

Name ______________________ Class ____________ Date ____________

MULTIPLE CHOICE **Write the letter of the most correct answer in the blank.**

______ **14.** Alcohol is *not*

a. a drug.
b. psychoactive.
c. addictive.
d. a stimulant.

______ **15.** Nonprescription drugs

a. require a physician's order.
b. cannot be overused.
c. are never psychoactive.
d. can be administered by inhalation.

______ **16.** Strains of bacteria that are resistant to drugs are evidence of

a. errors in diagnosis.
b. addiction to nicotine.
c. overuse of antibiotics.
d. All of the above

______ **17.** A pregnant woman should be aware that

a. she cannot become addicted to drugs while pregnant.
b. the use of drugs affects the fetus.
c. smoking is okay during pregnancy.
d. only nonprescription drugs should be taken during pregnancy.

______ **18.** Which of the following organ systems is involved with *all* drug addictions?

a. respiratory system
b. nervous system
c. digestive system
d. endocrine system

______ **19.** Effective doses of drugs increase

a. with the age of the user.
b. as tolerance increases.
c. during drug interactions.
d. when switching from nonprescription to prescription drugs.

______ **20.** Cocaine increases the amounts of dopamine and norepinephrine in a synapse by

a. blocking receptors on a postsynaptic neuron.
b. increasing the breakdown of norepinephrine.
c. blocking reuptake of dopamine and norepinephrine.
d. stimulating the conversion of epinephrine to norepinephrine.

______ **21.** A drug that increases the activity of the central nervous system is called

a. a depressant. **b.** a narcotic. **c.** illegal. **d.** a stimulant.

______ **22.** Alcoholism is *not* associated with

a. addiction. **b.** lung disease. **c.** hepatitis. **d.** brain damage.

______ **23.** Tars that are released from burning tobacco

a. do not enter the body because cigarette filters capture them.
b. consist of many different chemical compounds.
c. do not cause diseases.
d. All of the above

Name ______________________ Class ____________ Date ____________

SHORT ANSWER **Answer the questions in the space provided.**

24. Why is withdrawal so difficult for drug addicts? ______________________

25. What is a psychoactive drug? Give four examples of a psychoactive drug. ______________________

26. How does nicotine affect the body? ______________________

27. What is the difference between a stimulant and a depressant? ______________________

28. What is the difference between drug addiction and drug abuse? ______________________

29. Figures A and B below show two chronological steps in the effects of a drug on a synapse. Explain what is occurring in the synapse. What aspect of drug use do these figures illustrate?

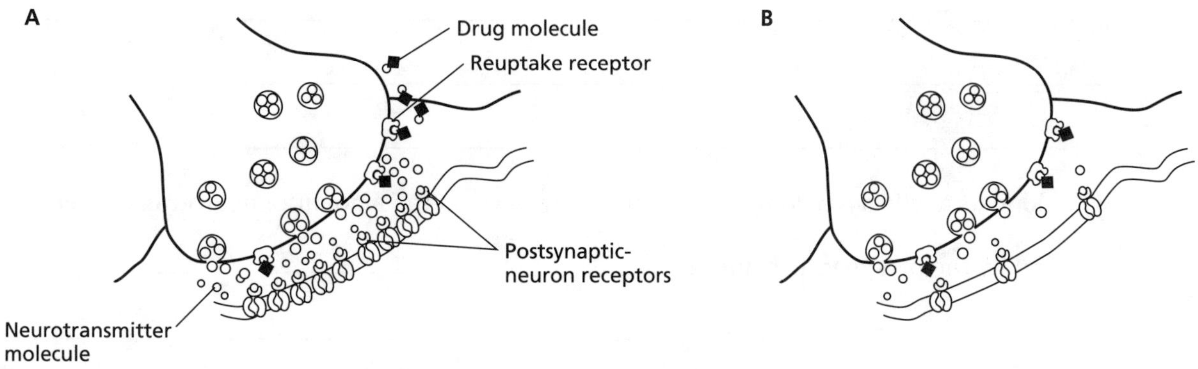

Name ______________________ Class ______________ Date ______________

DRAWING CONCLUSIONS Follow the directions given below.

30. Different drugs can affect neurons in various ways. The drug illustrated in the diagrams below binds at postsynaptic receptors, blocking them. Diagram *A* shows the activity of the drug at the synapse. Diagram *B* shows the same synapse after the drug has been in use for some time. Refer to the diagrams to answer questions *a–e*.

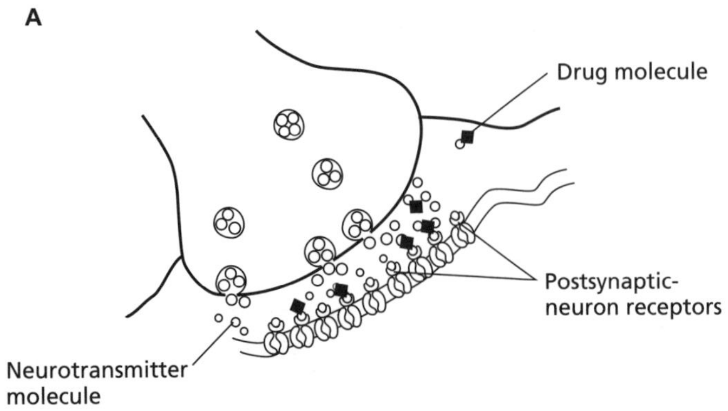

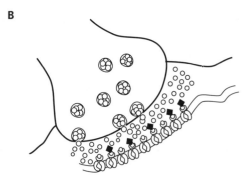

a. How does the drug affect transmission of signals in these neurons? ______________________

____

____

b. Why would the amount of neurotransmitter released increase in diagram *B*? ______________________

____

____

c. What immediate effect would removal of the drug have on the postsynaptic neuron?

____

____

____

d. What long-term effect would removal of the drug have on the amount of neurotransmitter released by the presynaptic neuron? ______________________

____

____

e. Is this an addictive drug? Explain your reasoning. ______________________

____

____

____

The *Modern Biology* Chapter Tests follow a consistent format that makes scoring them an easy task. The recommended point values for the five sections of the tests are as follows: eight Matching items at 2 points each (16 points); five True-False items at 3 points each (15 points); ten Multiple Choice items at 3 points each (30 points); six Short Answer items at 4 points each (24 points); and one multiple-part Drawing Conclusions item at 15 points. The following alternative scoring pattern for the last two sections may also be used: six Short Answer items at 5 points each (30 points); and one multiple-part Drawing Conclusions item at 9 points.

Chapter 1
The Science of Life

1. f
2. c
3. h
4. d
5. g
6. e
7. a
8. b
9. F; only about 2 million species have been identified and named.
10. F; living things are much more structurally diverse than nonliving things.
11. T
12. F; hypothesizing and predicting precede experimentation.
13. F; electron microscopes are much more powerful than light microscopes.
14. d
15. b
16. a
17. a
18. d
19. b
20. d
21. b
22. d
23. c
24. cell structure and function; stability and homeostasis; reproduction and inheritance; evolution; interdependence of organisms; matter, energy, and organization
25. cells; organization; energy use; homeostasis; growth; reproduction
26. No; scientists use scientific methods in a way that is best suited to answer the questions they ask.
27. Communication allows scientists to build on the work of other scientists. Scientists publish their findings in journals or present them at conferences.
28. The SI is a universal, standardized form of measurement.
29. organizing collected data
30. (a) about 24 hours (b) Medium B (c) Medium A (d) The descending part of the curves represents a decline in the growth rate over time because of the depletion of nutrient media. (e) The growth rate should eventually reach zero for the bacteria in both media.

Chapter 2
Chemistry

1. d
2. g
3. f
4. e
5. h
6. a
7. b
8. c
9. F; elements tend to undergo reactions that increase their stability.
10. T
11. T
12. F; dissociation of pure water yields two ions, H^+ and OH^-.
13. F; a solution that contains more hydronium ions than hydroxide ions is acidic.
14. a
15. b
16. b
17. a
18. d
19. b
20. a
21. d
22. d
23. a
24. In redox reactions, electrons are transferred between atoms, so the reactions always occur together.
25. In living things, enzymes act as catalysts for certain chemical reactions.
26. A solute is the substance that is dissolved in a solution. A solvent is the substance in which the solute is dissolved. The concentration is the amount of solute in a fixed amount of the solution.
27. Acids have a sour taste and are highly corrosive in concentrated forms. Bases have a bitter taste and tend to feel slippery.
28. The pH scale is a system of comparing the relative concentrations of hydronium ions and hydroxide ions in a solution. Its values range from 0 to 14, with values less than 7 denoting acidity and those greater than 7 denoting alkalinity.
29. 6; this is a relatively unstable atom because it does not have eight outer-shell electrons.
30. (a) pepsin (b) trypsin (c) The liquid must become alkaline. (d) According to the graph, enzymes function best at certain pH levels. (e) No; according to the graph, a low pH is required for pepsin to function, and a high pH is required for trypsin to function.

Chapter 3
Biochemistry

1. e
2. h
3. f
4. g
5. a
6. c
7. b
8. d

9. T
10. F; a functional group influences the chemical properties of a compound.
11. T
12. F; amino acids become linked during condensation reactions.
13. T
14. d
15. d
16. a
17. b
18. b
19. c
20. a
21. c
22. b
23. b
24. In a water molecule, the two hydrogen atoms bond with the single oxygen atom at an angle because of an uneven distribution of electrical charge. Thus, the molecule is polar.
25. Monomers link to form polymers through a condensation reaction. Hydrolysis is a reversed condensation reaction and causes the breakdown of complex molecules.
26. A monosaccharide is a simple sugar that is a monomer of carbohydrates. A disaccharide consists of two monosaccharides bonded together. A polysaccharide consists of at least three bonded monosaccharides.
27. The shape of a protein is determined by the way the protein's amino acids interact with one another. Amino acid interactions can cause a protein to bend or fold. Protein shape can also be influenced by temperature and the type of solvent in which a protein is dissolved.
28. The polar, hydrophilic heads of phospholipids comprise the interior and exterior surfaces of the cell membrane, and the nonpolar, hydrophobic tails of phospholipids form the middle of the cell membrane.
29. (from left to right) alternating double bonds between carbons; CH_2=CH_2; CH_2=C CH_3–CH=CH_2
30. a. disaccharide; b. fatty acid; c. water; d. dipeptide; e. nucleic acid

Chapter 4
Structure and Function of the Cell

1. g
2. e
3. f
4. c
5. h
6. d
7. a
8. b
9. F; the cell is the smallest unit that can carry out all the processes of life.
10. T
11. F; ribosomes are not membrane bound.
12. F; vacuoles in plant cells are functionally similar to lysosomes in animal cells.
13. T
14. b
15. c
16. d
17. c
18. b
19. a
20. d
21. c
22. c
23. c
24. (1) All living things are composed of one or more cells. (2) Cells are the basic units of structure and function in an organism. (3) Cells come only from the reproduction of existing cells.
25. Answers will vary. Muscle cells are arranged so that they can pull against one another. Neurons are specialized for transmitting electrical impulses.
26. Answers include the following: eukaryotes contain a membrane-bound nucleus and other organelles; prokaryotes do not.
27. (1) a. secondary cell wall; b. vacuole; c. nucleus; d. chloroplast; e. primary cell wall (2) vacuole, chloroplast, and cell wall
28. Answers include the following: The nucleus contains DNA and RNA. Ribosomes are synthesized and partially assembled in the nucleolus. The contents of the nucleus are enclosed by the nuclear envelope. RNA is synthesized in the nucleus and then passes into the cytoplasm through pores in the nuclear envelope.
29. A colonial organism is a collection of genetically identical cells that live together in a closely connected group. It is thought that the organisms in the three kingdoms of multicellular organisms (fungi, plants, and animals) each arose from a colonial ancestor.
30. a. nucleus; b. ribosomes; c. Golgi apparatus; d. cell membrane; e. cell membrane; f. mitochondria; g. cytoplasm and other organelles

Chapter 5
Homeostasis and Transport

1. d
2. b
3. h
4. g
5. f
6. a
7. c
8. e
9. F; the random movement of molecules in diffusion requires kinetic energy.
10. F; when a solution is at equilibrium, molecules move randomly.
11. F; sodium-potassium pumps cause a negative charge to accumulate inside cells.
12. T
13. T
14. c
15. b
16. d
17. a
18. b
19. c
20. d
21. b
22. c
23. b
24. passive: diffusion, osmosis, and facilitated diffusion; active: sodium-potassium pump, endocytosis, and exocytosis

25. Ink molecules at a high concentration in the water would move to an area of lower concentration by a process called diffusion.
26. Carrier proteins do not need to provide additional energy in facilitated diffusion because substances move down their concentration gradients.
27. Ions cross the cell membrane by passing through proteins known as ion channels.
28. During a cycle of the sodium-potassium pump, three sodium ions are actively transported out of the cell and two potassium ions are actively transported into the cell.
29. In endocytosis, cells ingest external substances by folding the cell membrane inward to form a vesicle. In exocytosis, cells release substances by the fusion of a vesicle with the cell membrane and the expulsion of the vesicle's contents into the extracellular environment.
30. a. endocytosis; b. diffusion through ion channels; c. passive diffusion; d. sodium-potassium pump; e. facilitated diffusion; f. exocytosis; g. endocytosis, sodium-potassium pump, and exocytosis

Chapter 6
Photosynthesis

1. f
2. a
3. h
4. e
5. g
6. c
7. b
8. d
9. T
10. F; the electrons move from photosystem II to photosystem I.
11. F; the oxygen atoms that are in the oxygen gas produced in photosynthesis come from water.
12. T
13. F; C_4 plants use the Calvin cycle for carbon fixation, but first they fix carbon dioxide into 4-carbon compounds.
14. d
15. a
16. c
17. a
18. a
19. b
20. b
21. c
22. d
23. c
24. Each chloroplast is surrounded by a pair of membranes. Inside the inner membrane is a system of membranes arranged as flattened sacs called thylakoids. Thylakoids are layered in stacks called grana, and they are surrounded by a solution called the stroma.
25. Four electrons become available to replace those lost by chlorophyll molecules in photosystem II. Hydrogen ions remain inside the thylakoid, while oxygen diffuses out of the chloroplast.
26. Energy from electrons is used to pump a high concentration of protons into the thylakoid. These protons then flow into the stroma and down their concentration gradient, driving the conversion of ADP into ATP, which is catalyzed by ATP synthase.
27. Most of the PGAL is converted back into RuBP, but some PGAL is used to make organic compounds.
28. CAM plants take in carbon dioxide at night and release it into the Calvin cycle during the day. CAM plants lose less water than either C_3 or C_4 plants.
29. It means that the rate of photosynthesis cannot be increased by increasing the CO_2 concentration above a certain level.
30. a. primary electron acceptor; b. primary electron acceptor; c. photosystem II; d. electron transport chain; e. photosystem I; f. electron transport chain; g. ATP synthase

Chapter 7
Cellular Respiration

1. c
2. g
3. a
4. h
5. f
6. d
7. e
8. b
9. F; glucose molecules are converted into pyruvic acid molecules in the process of glycolysis.
10. F; yeasts produce alcohol and CO_2 in the process of alcoholic fermentation.
11. F; in cellular respiration, glycolysis precedes the Krebs cycle.
12. T
13. F; $FADH_2$ and NADH donate electrons to the electron transport chain.
14. a
15. d
16. d
17. b
18. c
19. a
20. c
21. a
22. c
23. d
24. Two ATP molecules are used in step one.
25. When muscle cells are involved in strenuous exercise and the body cannot supply them with oxygen rapidly enough to carry out aerobic respiration, lactic-acid fermentation will occur.
26. Much of the energy originally contained in glucose is held in pyruvic acid.
27. Oxaloacetic acid regenerates coenzyme A when it reacts with acetyl CoA to form citric acid in step one of the Krebs cycle. Coenzyme A is needed to begin the Krebs cycle again.
28. The electrons react with oxygen to form water.
29. the mitochondrial matrix; NADH and $FADH_2$
30. a. glycolysis; b. lactic acid fermentation; c. alcoholic fermentation; d. Krebs cycle; e. electron transport chain

Chapter 8
Cell Reproduction

1. e
2. g
3. h
4. a
5. d

6. b
7. f
8. c
9. F; cells produced by mitosis have an identical copy of the original cell's chromosomes.
10. T
11. F; centrioles are not present in plant cells.
12. T
13. T
14. b
15. a
16. c
17. d
18. c
19. b
20. a
21. c
22. d
23. c
24. A prokaryote would have a loop of DNA attached to the inner surface of the cell membrane. A eukaryote would contain the following structures at some stage of cell division: nucleus, centrosome, mitotic spindle, kinetochore fibers, polar fibers, individual rod-shaped chromosomes, nucleolus, and other organelles.
25. Meiosis results in haploid cells. The cells produced during meiosis differ genetically from the original cell.
26. Mitosis results in two diploid cells. Meiosis II results in four haploid cells.
27. Diagrams should include G_1, S, G_2, M (mitosis), and C (cytokinesis) phases.
28. Spermatogenesis yields four spermatids. Oogenesis yields one egg cell and three polar bodies.
29. Independent assortment is the random separation of the homologous chromosomes. It results in genetic recombination.
30. a. metaphase (2); b. cytokinesis (5); c. prophase (1); d. telophase (4); e. interphase (6); f. anaphase (3); g. mitosis; two diploid cells are produced

Chapter 9
Fundamentals of Genetics

1. g
2. e
3. b
4. h
5. c
6. d
7. f
8. a
9. F; offspring of P_1 are the F_1 generation.
10. T
11. F; alleles for different characteristics are distributed to gametes independently.
12. F; a homozygote would be *QQ* or *qq*.
13. F; pink four o'clocks show incomplete dominance.
14. c
15. d
16. c
17. b
18. b
19. a
20. b
21. b
22. a
23. b
24. Mendel cross-pollinated plants pure for contrasting traits (P generation). He allowed the flowers from the F_1 generation to self-pollinate to produce the F_2 generation. He observed and recorded the results of every cross.
25. Probability equals the number of times an event is expected to happen divided by the number of opportunities for an event to happen.
26. In incomplete dominance, two or more alleles influence the phenotype, resulting in a phenotype intermediate between the dominant trait and the recessive trait, as with four o'clock flowers. In codominance, both alleles are expressed in a heterozygous offspring, as in a roan-coated horse.
27. Use a test cross. Cross the purple-flowering plant (*PP*) with a white-flowering plant (*pp*). Students should draw a Punnett square for each of the following genotypes: *PP* and *Pp*.
28. Students should predict that 100 percent of the offspring will be heterozygous for fruit color.
29. Students should predict a 1 *YY* : 2*Yy* : 1*yy*.
30. (a) The Punnett square represents a dihybrid cross because two traits are compared. (b) green and smooth parent: *QQTT;* yellow and wrinkled parent: *qqtt* (c) *QQTT, QQTt, QQtt, QqTT, QqTt, Qqtt, qqTT, qqTt, qqtt* (d) 1/16 *QQTT*: 1/8 *QqTT*: 1/8 *QQTt*: 1/4 *QqTt*: 1/16 *QQtt*: 1/8 *Qqtt*: 1/16 *qqTT*: 1/8 *qqTt*: 1/16 *qqtt* (e) 9/16 with smooth, green seeds; 3/16 with wrinkled, green seeds, 3/16 with smooth, yellow seeds, and 1/16 with wrinkled, yellow seeds

Chapter 10
Nucleic Acids and Protein Synthesis

1. f
2. c
3. g
4. h
5. b
6. e
7. a
8. d
9. F; replication starts at many replication forks simultaneously.
10. F; transcription ends with a termination signal.
11. T
12. F; mRNA carries the information for protein synthesis from the nucleus to the cytoplasm.
13. F; the genetic code is near universal.
14. d
15. b
16. b
17. b
18. c
19. c
20. d
21. a
22. c
23. a
24. In transcription, RNA is produced from DNA. In translation, polypeptides are assembled from information in mRNA.
25. DNA is a double helix formed from nucleotides that have deoxyribose and a phosphate group as

the backbone. The bases of DNA are cytosine, guanine, thymine, and adenine. RNA is formed from nucleotides that have ribose and a phosphate group as the backbone. The bases of RNA are cytosine, guanine, adenine, and uracil.

26. These codons mark the beginning and ending of a gene that is being translated.
27. mRNA is a single, uncoiled chain of nucleotides that carries genetic information from the nucleus to the site of translation in eukaryotes. tRNA consists of nucleotides folded into a hairpin shape and binds to amino acids. rRNA consists of nucleotides in a globular form. Along with proteins, rRNA makes up ribosomes.
28. (1) Helicases separate the two strands of DNA at replication forks. (2) DNA polymerases construct a complementary chain one nucleotide at a time. (3) Replication ends with two identical copies of the original DNA molecule.
29. A termination signal is a specific sequence of DNA nucleotides that marks the end of a gene during transcription. A stop codon is a sequence of three mRNA nucleotides that causes a ribosome to stop translating mRNA.
30. (a) guanine, cytosine, adenine, and thymine (b) Guanine pairs with cytosine; adenine pairs with thymine. (c) No; the percentage of cytosine is almost double the percentage of guanine, and the percentage of thymine is almost double the percentage of adenine. (d) Yes; DNA of vastly different organisms contains the same four nucleotides. (e) 34.7 percent; the percentage of uracil should match the amount of thymine because uracil replaces thymine in mRNA.

Chapter 11
Gene Expression

1. d
2. g
3. h
4. a
5. c
6. e
7. f
8. b
9. T
10. F; when expressed, exons are translated into proteins.
11. F; benign tumors usually pose no threat to life.
12. F; introns are not translated into proteins.
13. T
14. c
15. c
16. a
17. d
18. c
19. b
20. c
21. d
22. a
23. c
24. By controlling gene expression and making only needed proteins, cells conserve resources.
25. The diagram shows transcription of DNA in to pre-mRNA and of pre-mRNA into mRNA in the nucleus of a eukaryotic cell. Structures labeled *A* represent introns, and those labeled *B* represent exons.
26. Cancer cells divide when densely packed or when they are no longer attached to other cells; they continue to divide indefinitely.
27. Mutations could affect the regulatory abilities of these genes, allowing cells to multiply uncontrolled and leading to cancer.
28. In *Drosophila,* homeotic genes determine where certain anotomical structures will develop.
29. The genomes of eukaryotes are larger than those of prokaryotes and are located on several chromosomes rather than on a single circular chromosome.
30. (a) 6 (b) 2 (c) 7 (d) 5 (e) 4 (f) 1 (g) 3

Chapter 12
Inheritance Patterns and Human Genetics

1. d
2. f
3. a
4. e
5. h
6. c
7. g
8. b
9. F; Down syndrome is called trisomy-21.
10. T
11. F; germ-cell mutations occur in sex chromosomes and can be inherited.
12. F; polygenic traits are controlled by two or more different genes.
13. T
14. a
15. d
16. c
17. b
18. b
19. c
20. a
21. c
22. c
23. a
24. Hemophilia is caused by a recessive X-linked gene. Thus, a female would have to receive two copies of the gene to express the disease. Males only have one X chromosome, so the allele is always expressed if it is present.
25. The principle of independent assortment states that genes separate independently during the formation of gametes. Genes that are linked remain together during the formation of gametes.
26. Chromosome mutations are changes in the structure of a chromosome or loss of an entire chromosome. Gene mutations may involve large segments of DNA or a single nucleotide.
27. Multiple-allele traits are controlled by three or more alleles of the same gene that code for a single trait. Polygenic traits are controlled by two or more different genes.
28. The chromosome map sequence is A—C—B with five map units between A and C, 15 map units between C and B, and 20 map units between A and B.
29. A sex-linked trait is controlled by a gene found on a sex chromosome. A sex-influenced trait is expressed differently in men and women who have the same genotype because of sex hormones.

30. (a) The pedigree should be completed according to the information about cystic fibrosis in the family. (b) A possible key may include the following: □ = male noncarrier; ○ = female noncarrier; ■ = male with cystic fibrosis; ● = female with cystic fibrosis; ◧ = male carrier; ◐ = female carrier. (c) A child born to the F_2 son with cystic fibrosis and a female noncarrier would be a carrier of the trait.

Chapter 13
DNA Technology

1. d
2. e
3. f
4. g
5. a
6. h
7. b
8. c
9. T
10. T
11. T
12. F; PCR is used to quickly make many copies of selected segments of DNA.
13. F; the goal of the Human Genome Project is to determine the sequence of the entire human genome and to map the location of every gene of each chromosome.
14. d
15. b
16. c
17. d
18. a
19. a
20. d
21. d
22. c
23. b
24. A cloning vector is used to clone a donor gene and then transfer the donor gene to another organism. A donor gene is isolated from a specific organism and then transferred to a host organism via a cloning vector. The host organism receives the recombinant DNA.
25. Gene therapy is the treatment of a genetic disorder by introducing a gene into a cell or by correcting a gene deficit in a cell's genome. It differs from traditional treatments in that it attempts to correct the gene defect that causes the disorder.
26. DNA fingerprinting has been used to compare samples of blood or tissue found at a crime scene with those of a suspect, and it has been used to determine whether two individuals are related.
27. DNA fingerprints are very accurate because they compare segments of DNA that tend to vary the most between individuals. Thus, there is a tiny chance that all five sites compared in DNA fingerprints will match exactly between two people who are not identical twins.
28. Advantages include the development of safer, more-effective vaccines and pharmaceutical products and products that will improve agricultural yields. Disadvantages include the development of superweeds and the possibility that genetically engineered foods contain toxins or allergens.
29. a. 3; b. 1; c. 4; d. 2
30. (a) GAATTC—CTTAAG (b) Restriction enzymes are used to cut DNA at specific sites within nucleotide sequences. The pieces of DNA that are cut by these enzymes can bind together to form a new sequence of nucleotides. (c) hydrogen bond (d) The restriction enzyme would cut the DNA at a different nucleotide sequence, and the sticky ends might not match. (e) the plasmid

Chapter 14
Origin of Life

1. g
2. e
3. h
4. a
5. f
6. d
7. b
8. c
9. T
10. F; spontaneous generation does not occur.
11. F; scientists have not yet been able to produce ribozymes that generate other ribozymes.
12. F; it has been suggested that the atmosphere of early Earth was composed largely of carbon dioxide, nitrogen, and water vapor.
13. T
14. b
15. a
16. d
17. d
18. b
19. c
20. a
21. b
22. b
23. d
24. The half-life of carbon-14 is relatively brief (5,715 years) so most of it has decayed by 60,000 years. More accurate measurements of older fossils can be made using isotopes with longer half-lives.
25. The control group consisted of open jars containing meat; in the experimental group, the jars were covered by netting. The independent variable was the presence of adult flies; the dependent variable was the appearance of maggots.
26. Critics held that Spallanzani had boiled his flasks of broth too long, destroying the "vital force" in the air. Pasteur's flasks remained open to the air.
27. Microspheres or coacervates—or structures like them—might have contained early self-replicating RNA molecules.
28. The shapes of both depend on the sequences of their building-block components and on the regions of attraction between those components.
29. Chloroplasts are thought to have originated as photosynthetic bacteria that were housed in a larger, nonphotosynthetic cell. Similarly, mitochondria are thought to have originated as aerobic bacteria.
30. (a) water (b) water vapor, or steam (c) electrode; it provides energy to start chemical reactions (simulates lightning) (d) H_2O, or water vapor, H_2, CH_4, and NH_3 (e) organic compounds

Chapter 15
Evolution: Evidence and Theory

1. g
2. f
3. e
4. h
5. b
6. a
7. c
8. d
9. T
10. F; Lamarck observed that organisms change over time, and he erroneously suggested that organisms acquired traits that they passed to offspring.
11. F; homologous structures suggest common ancestry.
12. F; organisms tend to arise in areas where similar organisms once lived.
13. T
14. b
15. b
16. c
17. d
18. a
19. b
20. b
21. d
22. d
23. b
24. Lamarck wrongly suggested that organisms acquired traits that helped them survive and that they passed these traits to offspring. He was correct in observing that favorable traits tended to be passed on and to increase in frequency.
25. Darwin observed evidence of geological change, including marine fossil deposits high in the Andes mountains; he also observed many similar species of finches on the Galápagos Islands.
26. The breeding of animals by humans—artificial selection—is similar to natural selection in that it modifies the genetic material of a species over generations. It is different in that humans, rather than the environment, select the traits to be amplified.
27. Newer forms of organisms are actually the modified descendants of older species.
28. The environment selects traits that increase an organism's fitness, that is, its reproductive success.
29. same general body shape; backbone; tail; eye; buds of arm/wing and leg
30. (a) A is the oldest; C is the youngest (b) yes (c) different (d) species A and B and species B and C are most closely related; species A and C are least closely related (e) No; the data are insufficient to make that determination.

Chapter 16
The Evolution of Populations and Speciation

1. c
2. f
3. a
4. h
5. e
6. b
7. d
8. g
9. F; populations, rather than individuals, evolve.
10. F; both immigration and emigration result in gene flow.
11. T
12. T
13. F; in stabilizing selection, individuals with the average form of a trait have the highest fitness.
14. c
15. b
16. a
17. b
18. c
19. b
20. d
21. c
22. a
23. d
24. In a small population, an individual accounts for a relatively large fraction of the total number of alleles. Thus, the reproductive success of an individual can have a large impact on allele frequencies in the population.
25. no net mutations; no immigration or emigration; large population; random mating; no selection
26. Gene flow results in changes in allele frequencies.
27. The graphic representation of a trait in a population is a bell-shaped curve because the average form of the trait is found in most members, while extreme forms of the trait are found in few members.
28. In punctuated equilibrium, a species does not change for a long period of time but then changes rapidly over a short period of time. In gradual evolutionary change, a species changes slowly and steadily over a long period of time.
29. allele frequencies: R = 10/16 = 0.625; r = 6/16 = 0.375; phenotype frequencies: red = 3/8 = 0.375, pink = 4/8 = 0.5, white = 1/8 = 0.125
30. (a) stabilizing (b) disruptive (c) about 5.5 cm in 1940; about 3.25 and 8.0 cm in 1980 (d) The fish prefers medium-size (4 cm–7 cm long) leeches (e) Answers will vary. For example, fish in captivity could be offered a number of leeches ranging from 1 cm to 10 cm long, and the fishes' preferences could be noted.

Chapter 17
Human Evolution

1. f
2. e
3. g
4. c
5. d
6. a
7. h
8. b
9. F; toolmaking and language most likely developed in the hominids.
10. T
11. F; bipedalism preceded tool use and language.
12. T
13. T
14. d
15. c
16. b
17. d
18. a

19. b
20. d
21. c
22. b
23. c
24. brain size (cranial capacity), diet, and locomotion
25. Characteristics include a well-developed collarbone, rotating shoulder joints, partially rotating elbow joints, a similar dental formula, and a large, complex brain.
26. *Australopithecus anamensis,* a biped; *Ardipithecus ramidus,* may or may not have been bipedal
27. bipedalism
28. Animal bones bearing tool marks have been found with fossils of *H. habilis* and *H. erectus.*
29. The accumulated mutational differences found in human mitochondrial DNA indicate that modern humans evolved from a small group less than 200,000 years ago.
30. (a) not supported; language is not necessarily related to tool use (b) supported; the animal bone fragment is charred (c) supported; an animal bone fragment is present (d) not supported; tools can be used without clothing (e) supported; shaped stone tools would have required a precise grip and thus an opposable thumb.

27. In vertebrates and echinoderms, the blastopore becomes the posterior end of the digestive tract, and the splitting of an early embryo produces identical organisms. In other orders, the blastopore becomes the anterior end of the digestive tract, and the splitting of an early embryo causes the embryo to die.
28. Animals that have similar embryological development probably shared a relatively recent ancestor.
29. In the three-domain system, domain Archaea consists of kingdom Archaebacteria; domain Bacteria is composed of kingdom Eubacteria; and domain Eukarya is composed of kingdoms Protista, Plantae, Fungi, and Animalia. The three-domain system is based on comparisons of rRNA, which indicates how long ago any two organisms shared a common ancestor.
30. (a) This divergence might have been caused by a decreased availability of food preferred by the ancestral birds. (b) Insects probably were a more plentiful food source than cactus. (c) Their beaks are adapted for cracking seeds. (d) A cladistic taxonomist might use evidence of shared derived characters, such as a beak shape that differed from that of an ancestor. (e) analyses of genetic material

Chapter 18
Classification

1. b
2. h
3. f
4. d
5. g
6. e
7. c
8. a
9. F; Aristotle classified organisms as plants or animals and grouped them by habitat.
10. T
11. T
12. F; modern taxonomists consider the fossil record, the organism's morphology, embryology, and genetic material.
13. T
14. c
15. a
16. d
17. c
18. b
19. d
20. a
21. d
22. d
23. c
24. kingdom, phylum/division, class, order, family, genus, species
25. Aristotle grouped organisms as plants and animals, as did Linnaeus. Aristotle also grouped organisms by habitat. Linnaeus grouped morphologically related organisms into a seven-level hierarchy.
26. Kingdom Protista includes all eukaryotes that are not plants, animals, or fungi. It contains unicellular and multicellular organisms that lack specialized tissues.

Chapter 19
Introduction to Ecology

1. d
2. f
3. g
4. h
5. a
6. c
7. b
8. e
9. T
10. F; the greenhouse effect is a natural phenomenon.
11. T
12. F; regulators maintain a constant internal environment for a specific parameter, such as temperature.
13. T
14. a
15. b
16. d
17. c
18. b
19. b
20. c
21. b
22. d
23. c
24. The human population is growing at a rate that is not sustainable. The use of fossil fuels is contributing to global warming. The release of CFCs into the atmosphere is thinning the ozone layer. Mass extinction, resource depletion, and acid rain are other environmental problems caused by humans.
25. Models help ecologists understand the environment and make predictions about how it might change. Models are limited in their applications because they cannot account for every variable in an environment.

26. A species with a broad niche can live in a variety of places and can use a variety of resources.
27. biosphere, ecosystem, community, population, and organism
28. Trees, grass, animals, flowers, and all other living components of the biosphere are biotic factors. Sunlight, seasonal changes, storms, fires, and earthquakes are some examples of abiotic factors.
29. Each is a method of adjustment that allows organisms to avoid unfavorable environmental conditions.
30. (a) It is a tolerance curve that represents plant growth under varying temperatures. (b) No; improvement in growth will not be observed. Both plants are outside their temperature tolerance range. (c) Plant 2 would begin to grow faster and plant 4 would exhibit slowed growth.

Chapter 20
Populations

1. d
2. g
3. e
4. h
5. f
6. a
7. b
8. c
9. T
10. F; the death rate must equal the birth rate for the growth rate of a population to be stable.
11. T
12. T
13. F; developed countries are modern and industrialized and have high standards of living.
14. c
15. b
16. d
17. a
18. c
19. d
20. d
21. b
22. b
23. c
24. When viewed up close, the individuals in a population may be evenly spaced. When viewed from farther away, however, the individuals may be found to be clustered around a food or water source.
25. Density-independent limiting factors reduce the population by the same proportion, regardless of its size. Examples include weather, floods, and fires. Density-dependent limiting factors are triggered by increasing population density. Examples include resource limitations, such as food shortages.
26. The death rate decreased.
27. The country is most likely a developing country; its citizens are probably poor and have less access to health care and education than people in developed countries.
28. The country is probably a developed country; it is industrialized and relatively wealthy, and its citizens probably have a high standard of living and have access to health care and education.
29. Type I; Type III; Type II
30. Solve the proportions as follows: $\frac{T}{N} = \frac{t}{n}$, $Tn = tN$

    (a) $\frac{6}{N} = \frac{3}{12}$, $6(12) = 3N$, $\frac{72}{3} = N$, $N = 24$ ferrets

    (b) $\frac{6}{N} = \frac{6}{12}$, $6(12) = 6N$, $\frac{72}{6} = N$, $N = 12$ ferrets (half of the original estimate)

    (c) No; *t* would equal zero, indicating an infinite number of ferrets. However, if no marked ferrets were recaptured, it might indicate a very large population; that the method of marking made the ferrets less likely to be recaptured; or that they were harmed in some way or removed from the population.

Chapter 21
Community Ecology

1. c
2. f
3. e
4. d
5. g
6. h
7. b
8. a
9. F; a harmless species that is a mimic of a dangerous species is avoided, just as the dangerous species is avoided.
10. T
11. F; larger land areas usually contain a greater diversity of habitats than smaller land areas and thus can support more species.
12. T
13. F; lichens are common pioneer species because they secrete acids that dissolve rock, releasing minerals for plant growth.
14. d
15. c
16. b
17. c
18. d
19. a
20. d
21. b
22. b
23. b
24. Thorns, tough leaves, and toxins, such as strychnine and nicotine, protect plants from herbivorous predators by providing structures or chemicals that discourage the herbivores from eating the plants.
25. These two species are competitors. *Chthamalus stellatus* grows best in areas exposed to prolonged dry periods. Under these conditions, *Chthamalus* outcompetes *Semibalanus balanoides. Semibalanus* usually grows best underwater. Under these conditions, it outcompetes *Chthamalus.*
26. commensalism; mutualism
27. Humans are reducing the size of natural habitats. This reduction causes a decrease in the number of species (species richness) that can be supported in these habitats. This is the species-area effect.
28. Following retreat of the last glaciers, only barren rock remained. Freezing and thawing gradually broke the rock into smaller pieces. Lichens eventually colonized the barren rock and released

minerals from the rock, forming a thin layer of soil that enabled small grasslike plants and shrubs to grow.

29. plot 1; plot 2
30. (a) plots with both ants and rodents (b) The seed density did not change significantly. (c) The seed density greatly increased (almost tripled).

Chapter 22
Ecosystems and the Biosphere

1. e
2. g
3. h
4. b
5. f
6. d
7. c
8. a
9. F; decomposers break down dead organisms, thereby recycling nutrients contained in their bodies by enabling other organisms to make use of them.
10. T
11. F; carbon moves from the biotic portion of its cycle into the abiotic portion during cellular respiration.
12. F; deserts are unlike other biomes in that they usually have high summer temperatures and very low average annual precipitation.
13. T
14. c
15. b
16. c
17. c
18. b
19. c
20. d
21. a
22. c
23. a
24. A trophic level indicates an organism's position in a sequence of energy transfer levels in an ecosystem that is occupied by one or more types of organisms. An organism's trophic level is determined by whether it is an autotroph, a herbivore, or a carnivore.
25. Some organisms die without being eaten by animals that belong to a higher trophic level, and thus energy from their bodies is not transferred to the next level. Some of the energy in an organism cannot be used by organisms at the next trophic level. Some of the energy in an organism at a higher trophic level is used for maintenance and cannot contribute to biomass.
26. Carbon is converted from an inorganic form into an organic form during photosynthesis.
27. a. nitrogen fixation; b. nitrification; c. assimilation; d. ammonification; e. denitrification
28. Tropical rain forests are located near the equator and have year-round growing seasons, abundant precipitation, tall trees, and the highest species richness of all biomes. Temperate deciduous forests are located farther from the equator and have pronounced seasons, lower annual precipitation, and lower species richness than tropical rain forests do.
29. Lakes and ponds are characterized as either eutrophic or oligotrophic. Eutrophic lakes and ponds are rich in organic matter and vegetation. Oligotrophic lakes and ponds contain little organic matter.
30. (a) There is a smaller loss in numbers of organisms with each change in trophic level, but it is a very large loss for the first two changes in trophic level. (b) There is a smaller transfer of biomass with each change in trophic level. (c) There is a slightly greater transfer of energy with each change in trophic level, but only a very small amount of energy is transferred from the first to the second trophic level.

Chapter 23
Environmental Science

1. c
2. d
3. b
4. g
5. h
6. e
7. a
8. f
9. T
10. F; increased levels of carbon dioxide in the atmosphere correlate with an increase in global temperatures.
11. F; most biologists think there are at least 10 million species of organisms alive on Earth today, and possibly as many as 30 million.
12. T
13. T
14. b
15. d
16. c
17. c
18. c
19. b
20. a
21. d
22. a
23. c
24. Groups of convection cells affect climate all over the world because they generate oceanic circulation patterns.
25. A decrease in the ozone layer would allow more ultraviolet radiation to reach Earth's surface, possibly resulting in an increase in mutations, such as those that cause skin cancer, in humans and other organisms.
26. Upper atmospheric ozone levels are expected to decrease. Atmospheric carbon dioxide levels are expected to increase. Global temperature is expected to increase. Undeveloped land areas are expected to decrease, and various natural resources, such as clean water, fossil fuels, and forested areas, are expected to decrease.
27. tropical rain forests
28. Both debt-for-nature swap and ecotourism originated to help conserve biodiversity in poor countries. In a debt-for-nature swap, a richer country or private organization pays some of the debts of a poorer country in exchange for the poorer country's taking steps to protect its

biodiversity. In ecotourism, national parks are set up to attract tourists.

29. Reintroduction of the gray wolf to Yellowstone National Park is expected to result in a decrease in the large populations of prey that currently exist, an increase in the biodiversity of the park, and an increase in park enjoyment and attendance.
30. (a) release of chemicals into the environment (b) increased atmospheric carbon dioxide levels and global warming (c) biodiversity (d) debt-for-nature swaps and ecotourism (e) conservation efforts (f) reintroducing the gray wolf into Yellowstone National Park

Chapter 24
Bacteria

1. h
2. g
3. e
4. b
5. f
6. c
7. d
8. a
9. F; bacteria that can survive only in the absence of oxygen are called obligate anaerobes.
10. F; many archaebacteria are alive today.
11. F; Gram-negative bacteria appear pink.
12. F; bacteria can also resist antibiotics by secreting enzymes that destroy antibiotics.
13. F; the terms refer to members of two different prokaryotic kingdoms.
14. b
15. d
16. c
17. c
18. b
19. a
20. d
21. c
22. b
23. d
24. Answers include food production or processing by fermentation, digestion of proteins in foods, digestion of carbohydrates in foods, production of industrial and organic chemicals and fuels in mining and petroleum recovery, and the cleanup of chemical and oil spills.
25. Chemoautotrophs extract energy from minerals by oxidizing the chemicals in the minerals, while photosynthetic autotrophs harvest energy from sunlight.
26. Genetic recombination is a nonreproductive means by which bacteria acquire new combinations of genes. Genetic recombination includes transformation, conjugation, and transduction.
27. Bacteria cause disease by secreting endotoxins or exotoxins and by secreting digestive enzymes that allow further invasion of the body.
28. The overuse of antibiotics has encouraged the evolution of resistant strains of bacteria.
29. a. spirillum; b. bacillus; c. coccus
30. (a) Pili allow bacteria to adhere to surfaces and enable conjugation. (b) The cell wall protects and gives shape to bacteria. (c) The chromosome carries genetic information. (d) Plasmid contains genes obtained through genetic recombination. (e) Flagella enable movement.

Chapter 25
Viruses

1. d
2. g
3. f
4. h
5. b
6. c
7. a
8. e
9. T
10. T
11. T
12. F; viruses are smaller than cells.
13. T
14. a
15. b
16. b
17. a
18. c
19. c
20. c
21. c
22. a
23. b
24. Because viruses depend on cells in order to replicate, it is thought that viruses were probably pieces of nucleic acid that were able to travel from one cell to another.
25. A virulent virus undergoes the lytic cycle and causes disease by invading a host cell, producing new viruses, destroying the host cell, and then releasing the newly formed viruses. A temperate virus replicates via the lysogenic cycle and does not kill the host cell immediately.
26. No; viruses do not have all of the characteristics of life, such as cells, metabolism, homeostasis, growth, and reproduction.
27. a. glycoprotein; b. capsid; c. RNA genome; d. reverse transcriptase; e. envelope
28. Viroids and prions are like viruses in that they cause disease, are very small, and are not composed of cells. Viroids are composed of RNA only, prions are made of protein only, and viruses contain DNA or RNA and protein.
29. When humans enter previously undeveloped habitats, they may come into contact with animals that carry previously unknown viruses and become infected through contact. This contact may cause infection and spread of the disease.
30. (a) When the virus was temperate, its DNA became integrated into the host's genome. During viral replication, parts of the bacterial genome were probably replicated with the viral genome and integrated into the viral capsid during assembly. (b) The lysogenic cycle begins with the attachment of the virus to a host cell, injection of viral DNA into the host cell, and integration of the viral DNA into the host genome. As the host cell multiplies, the viral DNA is also replicated and included in each offspring cell. (c) a. 2; b. 5; c. 1; d. 4; e. 3

Chapter 26
Protozoa

1. g
2. c
3. f
4. d
5. h
6. a
7. b
8. e
9. T
10. F; protozoa are thought to have descended from early, unicellular eukaryotes.
11. F; some protozoa are free-living and some are parasitic.
12. F; the process shown is conjugation.
13. T
14. c
15. a
16. d
17. a
18. c
19. d
20. a
21. d
22. d
23. c
24. A motile protozoan; it is able to move toward food sources and to escape harsh environments.
25. Zooplankton constitutes one of the primary energy sources in aquatic ecosystems.
26. Protozoa are a subset of protists.
27. a. gametes; b. sporozoites; c. merozoites; d. gametocytes
28. Conjugation in protozoa involves a mutual exchange of genes. Conjugation in bacteria is a one-way transfer of genes.
29. Pseudopodia are cytoplasmic extensions that enable ameboid movement. Cilia beat in synchronized strokes, causing the protozoan to rotate on its axis. The rapid whipping motion of flagella pushes or pulls the protozoan through water.
30. (a) a. anal pore; b. gullet; c. cilia; d. oral groove; e. food vacuole; f. pellicle; g. contractile vacuole (b) Ciliophora; *Paramecium* (c) Cilia sweep food down the oral groove to the mouth pore and into the gullet, which forms food vacuoles that circulate throughout the cytoplasm. The food is then digested, and waste exits from the anal pore.

Chapter 27
Algae and Funguslike Protists

1. g
2. h
3. e
4. f
5. c
6. d
7. a
8. b
9. T
10. F; algae form gametes in unicellular gametangia, and plants form gametes in multicellular gametangia.
11. T
12. F; it is a member of the phylum Phaeophyta.
13. T
14. b
15. c
16. a
17. c
18. c
19. d
20. a
21. b
22. d
23. b
24. Slime molds have a mobile feeding stage and a stationary reproductive stage, and they live mostly in terrestrial habitats. Water molds reproduce both sexually and asexually, are filamentous, and live mostly in aquatic habitats.
25. Rhodophyta and Phaeophyta; Seaweeds are large, multicellular algae that store food as carbohydrates, live in marine environments, and have structures that resemble leaves, stems, and roots of plants.
26. (from left to right) sexual; asexual
27. Oomycetes form separate sperm-bearing and egg-bearing structures that become connected by a fertilization tube, enabling fertilization.
28. Sporangia from sporophytes produce haploid zoospores by meiosis. The zoospores divide mitotically, forming motile spores that grow into multicellular haploid gametophytes. A mature gametophyte produces gametangia and plus and minus gametes that unite to form diploid zygotes. The diploid zygote divides to form a new diploid sporophyte.
29. Detergents, paint removers, fertilizers, insulators, and toothpaste contain diatom shells.
30. A. Euglenophyta; B. Phaeophyta; C. Oomycota; D. Chlorophyta; E. Myxomycota; F. Dinoflagellata

Chapter 28
Fungi

1. d
2. f
3. c
4. e
5. a
6. h
7. g
8. b
9. F; the cell walls of fungi are composed of chitin.
10. F; some fungi reproduce only asexually.
11. F; mycorrhizae and lichens are both mutually beneficial associations.
12. F; fungi imperfecti reproduce only asexually.
13. T
14. a
15. b
16. c
17. b
18. b
19. d
20. d
21. d
22. c
23. b

24. Some fungi produce sporangiospores on the tips of stalked sporangiophores; some fungi produce conidia on the tips of stalklike conidiophores; some fungi produce cells that dry and fragment off from the parent hyphae; and some fungi produce new cells (spores) by budding.
25. A gametangium is a single cell that contains a haploid nucleus of one mating type. A zygosporangium is a structure that forms when two gametangia of compatible mating types merge and their nuclei fuse to form zygotes.
26. Mycorrhizae are symbiotic associations between a fungus and the roots of a plant. They increase mineral uptake from the soil by plants and thus promote plant growth.
27. Fungi are primarily multicellular, while most protists are unicellular; fungi are heterotrophic, while plants are autotrophic; fungi are nonmotile, while animals are motile.
28. When the environment is favorable, asexual reproduction ensures a rapid spread of the species. When the environment is unfavorable, sexual reproduction enables genetic recombination, increasing the likelihood that offspring will survive in the environment.
29. Both are reproductive structures of fungi, are composed of dikaryotic hyphae, and are large and easily visible. The basidiocarp has basidia, which produce basidiospores. The ascocarp has asci, which produce ascospores.
30. (a) The hypothesis is that symbiotic organisms can grow where the individual organisms cannot grow. (b) location; diameter of organism (c) In location 1, the lichen grew well, but the fungus and the alga grew poorly. In location 2, the lichen grew well, but neither the fungus nor the alga survived. In location 3, all three organisms grew well. (d) The hypothesis is supported by the results; lichens grow where neither the fungus nor the component alga can grow. (e) Lichens contribute to ecological succession by producing soil from bare rock.

Chapter 29
The Importance of Plants

1. e
2. d
3. c
4. g
5. h
6. b
7. f
8. a
9. T
10. F; the aesthetic value of plants is very significant, because people usually avoid foods that are not appealing.
11. T
12. F; plant ecology is the study of the interactions between plants and the environment.
13. T
14. b
15. a
16. d
17. c
18. c
19. a
20. d
21. d
22. c
23. a
24. Answers will vary but may include medicines derived from plants, clothing fibers, fuels, and any other nonfood uses of plants.
25. Answers include the use of irrigation, fertilizers, and pesticides; improvements in cultivars; farm machinery; food preservation techniques; and methods of controlling diseases, weeds, and pests.
26. Scientists hope to find sources of new medicines in wild plants that have not yet been researched, such as those growing in the tropics.
27. Water hyacinth grows in dense populations, impedes the passage of boats, shades underwater plants, and consumes oxygen in the water.
28. The insect on the left can harm the plant by eating it, and the plant might benefit from an insecticide. The insect on the right can benefit the plant by pollinating it. Eliminating the pollinator with an insecticide could affect the plant's reproduction.
29. Answers will vary but may include nitrogen, phosphorus, potassium, iron, magnesium, oxygen, carbon dioxide, and water.
30. (a) tofu (b) millet (c) No; legumes are high in isoleucine and lysine, while grains are high in tryptophan, cysteine, and methionine.

Chapter 30
Plant Evolution and Classification

1. e
2. f
3. h
4. c
5. g
6. a
7. b
8. d
9. F; stomata allow the exchange of carbon dioxide and oxygen.
10. T
11. F; the plant material in peat bogs decomposes very slowly because the bogs are acidic.
12. T
13. F; Cycadophyta, Ginkgophyta, and Gnetophyta also produce seeds.
14. c
15. a
16. c
17. d
18. b
19. a
20. c
21. d
22. b
23. c
24. The primary function of spores and seeds is to protect and disperse the plant's reproductive cells.
25. Green algae require water for dispersal of reproductive structures, and they lack protection from water loss and structural support.
26. Nonvascular plants must live near water because they lack means of transporting water and require water for sexual reproduction.

27. Mosses, liverworts, and hornworts are bryophytes. They are mostly terrestrial; live in moist environments; are nonvascular; lack true roots, leaves, and stems; and have an alternation of generations life cycle.
28. Coniferophyta; seed plants
29. Their leaves are needle-shaped and have a small surface area.
30. (a) meiosis (b) spores; haploid; mitosis (c) gametes (eggs and sperm); haploid (d) fertilization (e) zygotes; seed

Chapter 31
Plant Structure and Function

1. d
2. c
3. f
4. g
5. a
6. e
7. h
8. b
9. F; in dicots primary growth occurs in apical meristems, and in monocots it occurs in apical meristems and may also occur in intercalary meristems.
10. T
11. F; roots are usually found below ground level, but they sometimes begin above ground and then extend underground or are entirely above ground (aerial).
12. F; macronutrients are required in large amounts, and micronutrients are required in small amounts.
13. T
14. b
15. d
16. a
17. d
18. c
19. b
20. a
21. d
22. c
23. b
24. The function of tracheids is to transport water and minerals.
25. The lateral meristems of plants are the vascular cambium and the cork cambium. They cause secondary growth.
26. Root hairs, branch roots, and mycorrhizal associations increase the absorbing surface area of roots.
27. Water moves from the soil to the epidermis, cortex, endodermis, and pericycle of the vascular cylinder, and then into the xylem.
28. Guard cells; they accumulate potassium ions and water, which causes them to swell and bow apart, forming a stoma. In leaves, stomata regulate the exchange of carbon dioxide and oxygen and water loss.
29. Carbohydrates are actively transported into sieve tubes, and water enters the sieve tubes by osmosis. Osmotic pressure pushes the carbohydrates into adjacent sieve tubes and to parts of the plant that lack carbohydrates. Carbohydrates are then actively transported out of the sieve tubes into storage or energy-requiring cells.
30. (a) gas exchange; occurs through stomata (b) photosynthesis; occurs primarily in palisade mesophyll cells of leaves (c) translocation; occurs in sieve tubes of roots, stems, and leaves (d) water pulled upward; occurs in tracheids and vessel elements of roots, stems, and leaves (e) transpiration; occurs through stomata

Chapter 32
Plant Reproduction

1. e
2. g
3. f
4. h
5. d
6. b
7. a
8. c
9. T
10. F; mosses and ferns are homosporous, while conifers are heterosporous.
11. T
12. F; double fertilization is unique to angiosperms.
13. F; the cotyledons of monocots usually remain below the soil surface. The cotyledons of dicots usually emerge above the soil surface.
14. b
15. c
16. a
17. d
18. b
19. c
20. b
21. d
22. d
23. d
24. mature sporophyte, sporangium, spores, mature gametophyte, antheridium and archegonium, egg and sperm cells, zygote
25. Meiosis in megaspore mother cells produces four megaspores. Three of these degenerate and one produces an embryo sac containing an egg cell.
26. Meiosis in microspore mother cells produces four microspores. Each of these produces pollen grains. The tube cell produces a pollen tube leading to an ovule. The generative cell produces two sperm cells, which move into the ovule and fuse with the egg cell and the polar nuclei there.
27. Making cuttings involves growing new plants from pieces of stem, root, or leaf. Layering involves inducing root formation on a stem. Grafting involves attaching two or more plant parts to form a single plant. Tissue culture involves growing new plants from small pieces of tissue in sterile nutrient media.
28. Factors required to break dormancy in certain seeds include light, low temperature, and abrasion by acid or other agents. These help prevent seeds from germinating before environmental conditions are suitable for growth of the plant.
29. water, oxygen, and the appropriate temperature range
30. (a) 1. spores; 2. sperm; 3. eggs; 4. zygote (b) B and C (c) A (d) D (e) spores, male gametophyte, female gametophyte, sperm, and eggs

Chapter 33
Plant Responses

1. e
2. d
3. h
4. g
5. b
6. a
7. c
8. f
9. F; commercial uses of gibberellins include promoting seed germination, increasing the alcohol content of beer, and increasing the size of fruits.
10. F; tropisms are determined by the direction of a stimulus, and nastic movements are independent of the direction of a stimulus.
11. T
12. T
13. F; fall coloration occurs when chlorophyll degrades and different pigments reflect colors other than green.
14. c
15. d
16. d
17. b
18. c
19. d
20. b
21. a
22. c
23. b
24. Ethylene; one rotting apple will produce ethylene gas, which stimulates nearby apples to ripen and spoil.
25. Leaf abscission causes dead, damaged, or infected leaves to drop to the ground rather than shading healthy leaves or spreading disease.
26. Auxins accumulate on the lower sides of horizontally oriented stems and roots. Auxins stimulate stem cells to elongate, resulting in upward growth of the shoot, and inhibit elongation of root cells, resulting in downward growth of the root.
27. Thigmonastic movements; some thigmonastic movements occur within a few seconds of a stimulus.
28. Long-day plants will flower when the number of hours of continuous darkness is shorter than critical night length, or when a period of darkness longer than critical night length is divided into two dark periods each shorter than critical night length.
29. Biennial plants flower in the spring of their second year of growth.
30. (a) auxin (b) step B; the agar block did not contain plant hormones, and no changes in growth were observed. (c) Synthetic auxin could be applied to an agar block and then the agar block placed on one side of a decapitated shoot tip. If the shoot tip were to bend in the direction opposite the location of the agar block, then the results would indicate that auxin causes the results observed in part A of Went's experiments.

Chapter 34
Introduction to Animals

1. f
2. h
3. e
4. a
5. b
6. d
7. c
8. g
9. F; only vertebrates have backbones.
10. T
11. F; the similar development patterns of humans and echinoderms indicate that they are more closely related to each other than they are to other phyla.
12. T
13. T
14. d
15. b
16. b
17. a
18. b
19. c
20. b
21. c
22. b
23. d
24. Scientists have inferred that multicellular invertebrates may have developed from colonies of loosely connected flagellated protists. Colonial protists may have lost their flagella over the course of evolution as individualized cells in the colony grew more specialized.
25. Sponges have no body symmetry and no true tissues.
26. Segmentation refers to a body composed of a series of repeating similar units. It is not found in all animals; some invertebrate phyla are not segmented.
27. The coelom forms from rapid cell division in the blastocoel. The newly differentiated mesodermal cells spread out and completely line the newly formed coelom.
28. a. blastocoel; b. archenteron; c. coelom; d. schizocoely; e. blastocoel; f. coelom; g. archenteron; h. enterocoely
29. A human embryo undergoes radial, indeterminate cleavage; the coelom forms by enterocoely; and the blastopore becomes the anus. In contrast, a clam embryo undergoes spiral, determinate cleavage; the coelom forms by schizocoely; and the blastopore becomes the mouth.
30. a. invertebrates; b. both; c. invertebrates; d. both; e. both; f. invertebrates; g. vertebrates; h. both; i. vertebrates; j. both; k. both; l. invertebrates; m. both; n. both; o. both

Chapter 35
Sponges, Cnidarians, and Ctenophores

1. b
2. d
3. g
4. h
5. a
6. c
7. f
8. e
9. F; some sponge skeletons are composed of spicules.
10. T

11. F; sexual reproduction in sponges produces a swimming larva.
12. F; some cnidarians have only one stage or the other, and some have both stages.
13. F; *Hydra* is an example of a freshwater-dwelling hydrozoan.
14. b
15. a
16. d
17. c
18. c
19. b
20. d
21. a
22. d
23. b
24. The food that a sponge collects is engulfed and digested by collar cells. Nutrients then pass to amebocytes, which spread the nutrients among the sponge's other body cells. Waste products diffuse out of cells and leave the sponge's body through the osculum.
25. Sponges reproduce asexually by budding or by regeneration. When sponges reproduce sexually, sperm from one sponge are released in the water and join with the egg of another sponge, producing a swimming larva that eventually becomes a sessile adult sponge.
26. Both sponges and cnidarians have two cell layers (though only cnidarians have true tissues); the central body cavity of both has one opening, and cnidarians have mesoglea.
27. The dominant body form found in scyphozoans is the medusa, while the dominant body form found in anthozoans is the polyp.
28. Algae; the conditions of shallow equatorial seas allow the algae to live and undergo photosynthesis.
29. a. epidermis; b. gastrovascular cavity; c. mouth; d. medusa; e. mouth; f. gastrovascular cavity; g. epidermis; h. polyp
30. (a) external (b) blastula (c) Planula; it attaches to the sea floor. (d) The polyp forms a stack of medusae that are released into the water. (e) Identical; they are the result of the union of a single egg and sperm.

Chapter 36
Flatworms, Roundworms, and Rotifers

1. a
2. f
3. e
4. c
5. d
6. h
7. b
8. g
9. T
10. F; some flukes are external parasites.
11. F; the intermediate host is a snail.
12. T
13. T
14. a
15. c
16. d
17. d
18. b
19. b
20. b
21. c
22. c
23. c
24. Fertilized eggs are released in the urine and feces of humans, the primary host. In water, ciliated larvae develop and invade the bodies of snails, the intermediate host. The larvae develop tails and become free-swimming. The tailed larvae enter the skin of a human swimming or wading in the water, and the cycle repeats.
25. feeding only cooked meat scraps to animals used for food; inspecting meat for the presence of cysts; cooking meat thoroughly
26. The tegument is composed of cells; the cuticle is not.
27. An acoelomate does not have a body cavity. A pseudocoelomate has a body cavity, and mesoderm lines the outer body wall. Platyhelminthes, or flatworms, are acoelomates with three germ layers.
28. Planaria swim with a wavelike motion. They move over a surface on a layer of mucus they secrete using the cilia that cover their body.
29. a. eyespots; b. excretory tubule; c. nerve; d. pharynx
30. (a) No; horses do not eat meat. (b) after the pig (c) by eating only meat that has been inspected for cysts and by cooking meat thoroughly (d) larval (the larvae are contained in cysts embedded in muscle) (e) Worms are animals, and medicines that kill them can also affect their animal hosts. Bacteria are very different from eukaryotic animal cells, and many antibiotics attack bacterial structures that animal cells do not share, such as the cell wall.

Chapter 37
Mollusks and Annelids

1. c
2. e
3. d
4. a
5. h
6. g
7. b
8. f
9. F; a coelom can be used for blood transport without interference from internal organs.
10. T
11. F; they have a mouth, an anus, and several other digestive organs.
12. T
13. T
14. b
15. c
16. d
17. a
18. b
19. b
20. c
21. d
22. d
23. d

24. Answers include the trochophore larva and the coelom. Annelids are segmented, while mollusks are not.
25. No; an important function of the mantle is secretion of a shell. Annelids do not have a shell.
26. In a closed circulatory system, blood moves more rapidly. Members of Cephalopoda have a closed circulatory system.
27. Oxygen diffuses through the skin of the earthworm. The environment must be moist and cool.
28. Polychaetes differ from other annelids in that polychaetes have antennae and specialized mouthparts. They are also the only annelids that have a trochophore stage of development.
29. There are some differences in habitat: Oligochaeta live in soil or fresh water; Polychaeta are mostly marine; and Hirudinea live in calm, fresh water or in moist vegetation on land.
30. (a) a. shell; b. gill; c. mantle cavity; d. anus; e. heart; f. mantle; g. stomach; h. ganglia (b) The mantle secretes hard shells that protect the mollusk. (c) The evolution of gills has maximized the area available for gas exchange in the mollusk.

Chapter 38
Arthropods

1. b
2. f
3. a
4. h
5. c
6. d
7. e
8. g
9. T
10. F; crayfish use gills for respiration.
11. F; both crayfishes and spiders have eight legs that are used primarily for walking.
12. T
13. T
14. c
15. d
16. c
17. c
18. d
19. c
20. d
21. a
22. c
23. b
24. Segmented appendages and eyes are examples of features associated with cephalization.
25. Before a molt, an arthropod's tissues swell, straining the exoskeleton. A hormone that induces molting is then produced, causing epidermal cells to secrete enzymes that digest the inner layer of the exoskeleton. The old exoskeleton splits, and the arthropod in its new skeleton crawls out.
26. Trilobita (the extinct trilobites), Crustacea (lobsters, crayfishes, sow bugs, pill bugs), Chelicerata (spiders, scorpions, mites, ticks), and Uniramia (millipedes); examples of each subphylum will vary.
27. Abdominal muscles; the telson, which acts as a paddle; and uropods help propel the crayfish during tailflips.
28. Spiders use chelicerae (fangs) to inject poison into their prey. Venom is produced in poison glands in the cephalothorax.
29. Centipedes kill their prey with poison claws and tear the meat apart with mandibles and maxillae.
30. (a) a. stomach; b. poison gland; c. chelicera (fang); d. pedipalp; e. Malpighian tubule; f. silk gland; g. intestine; h. book lung (b) The excretory system of spiders is adapted for life on land because of the Malpighian tubules, which enable spiders to conserve water by reabsorption. The coxal glands also remove waste products at the base of the legs. (c) The main disadvantage of molting is that each new exoskeleton takes a few days to harden, rendering an arthropod vulnerable to predation and desiccation.

Chapter 39
Insects

1. f
2. c
3. e
4. g
5. a
6. h
7. d
8. b
9. T
10. T
11. F; the tracheae transport oxygen to the tissues of insects.
12. F; royal jelly is particularly rich in protein.
13. F; pheromones affect the behavior or development of members of the same species.
14. a
15. b
16. c
17. a
18. a
19. d
20. c
21. b
22. b
23. c
24. The bombardier beetle defends itself by spraying a hot stream of a noxious chemical from an opening on its abdomen that can be rotated.
25. Ants lay a pheromone on the ground to guide other ants to food sources. Female moths secrete pheromone to attract mates.
26. The mouthparts of drones are too short to feed on flower nectar, so drones must be fed by workers. The mouthparts of workers are expected to be functional because workers collect food, work in the hive, and feed the members of the colony.
27. Grasshoppers have two kinds of eyes, simple and compound. There are three simple eyes and two compound eyes. The simple eyes detect light intensity. The compound eyes detect movement and form images.
28. Isoptera (termites)
29. The honeybee has a barbed stinger and displays altruistic behavior. After it stings an animal, the honeybee flies away. The stinger remains in the animal, and the bee's internal organs are ripped out. The wasp has a smooth stinger that can be removed from the victim when the wasp flies away.

30. a. incomplete metamorphosis; b. egg; c. nymph; d. adult grasshopper; e. complete metamorphosis; f. young larva; g. older larva; h. pupa; i. butterfly; j. Larvae and adults do not compete for food and space. k. The pupa and chrysalis protect an insect during the winter and thus enhance the insect's chances of survival.

Chapter 40
Echinoderms and Invertebrate Chordates

1. d
2. g
3. c
4. f
5. h
6. a
7. e
8. b
9. F; many chordates are terrestrial.
10. T
11. F; they can swim.
12. F; most can move around in various ways.
13. T
14. a
15. d
16. b
17. c
18. a
19. c
20. b
21. c
22. b
23. d
24. In vertebrates, it leaves only a trace after the backbone is developed. In cephalochordates, it is retained. In tunicates, it is lost during metamorphosis.
25. notochord, dorsal nerve cord, post-anal tail, and pharyngeal pouches or slits
26. Young tunicates have all four chordate characters, whereas adults have only the pharyngeal pouches or slits.
27. The arms of a sea star can detach and regenerate as a defense mechanism. Regeneration is important to reproduction because each arm of a sea star contains a pair of ovaries or testes.
28. Tunicates are hermaphrodites. Sperm and eggs are released through the excurrent siphon into the surrounding water, where fertilization occurs.
29. Aristotle's lantern is the jawlike feeding structure of sea urchins that consists of teeth and muscles.
30. (a) Cephalochordata (b) Urochordata (c) Vertebrata (d) Cephalochordata and Urochordata; In the water; most sessile animals filter food from water. (e) Cephalochordata: lancelet; Urochordata: tunicates; Vertebrata: answers will vary.

Chapter 41
Fishes

1. d
2. g
3. a
4. e
5. h
6. b
7. c
8. f
9. T
10. F; jaws are thought to have evolved from the first pair of gill arches.
11. F; they tend to lose water and gain ions.
12. T
13. F; lampreys and hagfishes are the only surviving jawless fishes.
14. b
15. a
16. c
17. d
18. a
19. b
20. b
21. d
22. a
23. b
24. The lateral-line system consists of a row of sensory structures that run along each side of the fish's body and are connected by nerves to the brain. The structures detect vibrations in the water.
25. Members of Agnatha and Osteichthyes use external fertilization, where the male releases sperm as the female releases eggs. Members of Chondrichthyes use internal fertilization, in which the male transfers sperm into the female's body with claspers.
26. Answers include the following: sense of smell (detects chemicals with nostrils); lateral-line system (detects vibrations in water); vision; sensitive to electric fields.
27. Deoxygenated blood enters the sinus venosus and then moves into the larger atrium. Contraction of the atrium moves the blood to the ventricle, the main pumping chamber of the heart. The ventricle pumps blood through the conus arteriousus and eventually to the gills.
28. Jaws allow fish to seize and manipulate prey; paired fins increase stability and maneuverability.
29. Cartilaginous fishes either keep moving to maintain a vertical position or store large amounts of low-density lipids. Bony fishes have a swim bladder, which contains a mixture of gases from the bloodstream and regulates the amount of gas in the body to adjust body density.
30. (a) 1. bony fish; 2. mammals; 3. Agnatha; 4. Aves; 5. cartilage; 6. yes (b) all of them (c) Vertebrata (d) aquatic (e) The skeleton is composed of cartilage.

Chapter 42
Amphibians

1. c
2. f
3. a
4. d
5. h
6. e
7. b
8. g
9. F; amphibians have a three-chambered heart.
10. F; the nictitating membrane protects and moistens the eye.

11. T
12. F; most frogs and toads fertilize externally.
13. F; the pulmonary circuit does this.
14. c
15. d
16. a
17. c
18. a
19. b
20. a
21. a
22. d
23. c
24. During inhalation, the floor of the mouth drops and the nostrils open. Air is then pushed into the lungs as the floor of the mouth is raised and the nostrils close.
25. Accept four of the following: metamorphosis; moist, thin skin without scales; feet that lack claws; gills, lungs, and skin for respiration; eggs laid in water or moist places; external fertilization.
26. The moist skin of amphibians is vulnerable to dehydration, so most amphibians live in moist environments and are active at night. Desert amphibians remain in moist burrows deep in the soil, coming out to feed and reproduce only after heavy rains.
27. Answers include a rigid spine to bear the weight of the body; strong limbs to support the body while moving or standing; and a fused lower forelimb (radio-ulna) and hind limb (tibiofibula).
28. The tadpole gradually changes from its aquatic form to its terrestrial form, growing legs, losing its tail and gills, and developing jaws and functional lungs.
29. The male Darwin's frog takes the eggs into his vocal sacs, where the eggs hatch and undergo metamorphosis. Females of some species of frogs sit on their eggs to keep them moist.
30. (a) 5; young frog coming onto land (b) 3; tadpole lives in water (c) 6; adult frog (d) 1; male fertilizes eggs (e) 4; tadpole is growing legs and still living in water (f) 2; fertilized eggs in water

Chapter 43
Reptiles

1. f
2. g
3. a
4. e
5. h
6. c
7. b
8. d
9. T
10. T
11. F; the tuatara is described.
12. F; dinosaurs became extinct 65 million years ago.
13. T
14. b
15. d
16. a
17. c
18. c
19. b
20. c
21. a
22. c
23. d
24. This hypothesis suggests that a huge asteroid hit Earth, sending so much dust into the atmosphere that the amount of sunlight reaching Earth's surface was greatly reduced. The resulting climatic changes led to mass extinction.
25. The body of a turtle is covered by a shell; the pelvic and pectoral girdles lie within the ribs; and turtles have a sharp beak instead of teeth.
26. The upper and lower jaws are loosely hinged and move independently; the lower jaw, palate, and parts of the skull are joined by a flexible ligament that allows the snake's head to stretch around its prey.
27. A crocodile lies waiting until an animal approaches and then attacks quickly. It can see and breathe while it is quietly submerged in water, and it can feed underwater due to a valve that prevents water from entering its air passages.
28. Answers include three of the following: Dinosaurs were a diverse group of reptiles that varied in size, form, and habitat. Icthyosaurs were aquatic reptiles that resembled dolphins. Plesiosaurs were also aquatic, with long, flexible necks and compact bodies. Pterosaurs were flying reptiles.
29. The amnion is a membrane that surrounds the embryo; it encloses the salty fluid in which the embryo floats and develops.
30. (a) Arrows should be drawn from the body to the right atrium, then to the lungs, then from the lungs to the left atrium, then to the ventricle, and back to the body. (b) 1. deoxygenated; 2. mixed; 3. oxygenated; 4. mixed (c) 1. deoxygenated; 2. deoxygenated; 3. oxygenated; 4. oxygenated (d) Crocodilia (e) Bypassing the lungs allows an inactive reptile to conserve energy and raise its temperature quickly.

Chapter 44
Birds

1. e
2. c
3. g
4. d
5. h
6. a
7. f
8. b
9. F; the syrinx is a structure at the base of the trachea used to produce songs.
10. F; contour feathers give birds their shape and color.
11. F; birds are endothermic.
12. T
13. T
14. a
15. c
16. c
17. c
18. d
19. b
20. c
21. d
22. a
23. a

24. Both types of air sacs store air. The anterior air sacs receive oxygen-rich air and send it to the lungs. The posterior air sacs receive oxygen-depleted air leaving the lungs.
25. *Precocial* refers to birds that lay many eggs and incubate them for long periods of time. *Altricial* refers to birds that lay few eggs that hatch quickly.
26. Answers include three of the following: position of stars, topographical landmarks, Earth's magnetic field, changes in air pressure, and low-frequency sounds.
27. Both have a sharp, curved beak and talons, which are used for hunting. Members of Strigiformes hunt at night and rely on their sense of hearing. Members of Falconiformes hunt during the day and use their keen sense of vision.
28. Answers include feathers; wings; a lightweight, rigid skeleton; endothermic metabolism; a beak; oviparity; and an efficient respiratory system consisting of air sacs connected to the lungs.
29. Answers may include that flight evolved in tree-dwellers that jumped between branches, glided, and eventually flapped wings, or that flight evolved on the ground and wings were used to stabilize animals leaping after prey.
30. (a) a. proventriculus; b. gizzard; c. kidney; d. large intestine; e. cloaca; f. crop; g. heart (b) digestive and excretory systems (c) In birds, the passage of food through the digestive system is very rapid. The excretory system is efficient and lightweight; most birds do not store liquid waste. (d) The gizzard often contains small stones that aid in the grinding of food. (e) The crop stores and moistens food.

Chapter 45
Mammals

1. c
2. d
3. f
4. b
5. h
6. g
7. e
8. a
9. F; monotremes are oviparous.
10. F; members of Chiroptera and Cetacea use echolocation.
11. F; the fossil record of therapsids aids scientists in following anatomical changes throughout mammalian evolution.
12. T
13. T
14. b
15. d
16. a
17. c
18. b
19. b
20. d
21. c
22. d
23. c
24. Once dinosaurs became extinct, new habitats and ecological roles became available to mammals without the danger of predation by dinosaurs, allowing mammals to diversify.
25. Both are ungulates, or hoofed mammals. Artiodactyls have an even number of toes and a rumen for breaking down cellulose. Perissodactyls have an odd number of toes and a cecum.
26. Separated ventricles of the heart prevent the mixing of oxygenated and deoxygenated blood. Mammals also have a large internal lung surface area and a diaphragm. These adaptations increase the supply of oxygen, which is needed for the fast metabolism of endothermic animals.
27. All have streamlined bodies similar to those of fish. The forelimbs and hind limbs of pinnipeds are paddlelike for swimming. The forelimbs of cetaceans and sirenians are flippers; a broad tail replaces their hind limbs.
28. All produce milk to feed their young. Monotremes lay eggs, while marsupials and placental mammals give birth to live young. Marsupial females have a pouch in which their young continue early development after birth. Placental mammals nourish their young internally through a placenta.
29. endothermy, hair, a completely divided heart, milk production by mammary glands, a single jawbone, and specialized teeth
30. (a) a. Carnivora; b. Insectivora; c. Cetacea (b) The long canines of carnivores aid in tearing flesh and grasping prey. The baleen serves to filter invertebrates from the water. (c) Skull *b;* the nose is long and pointed and enables probing in soil for insects, worms, and other invertebrates. The teeth are sharp, an adaptation that is useful for catching and grasping insects. (d) Baleen; it is used to filter and trap invertebrates in the water. (e) the cerebrum

Chapter 46
Skeletal, Muscular, and Integumentary Systems

1. f
2. h
3. e
4. g
5. a
6. c
7. d
8. b
9. F; the spinal cavity surrounds the spinal cord.
10. F; the four body tissues are muscle tissue, nervous tissue, epithelial tissue, and connective tissue.
11. T
12. T
13. F; hair and skin color are determined by melanin.
14. b
15. d
16. c
17. b
18. a
19. d
20. d
21. d
22. b
23. b

24. Myosin filaments attach to actin filaments. The myosin filaments bend inward, causing the actin filaments to overlap. This shortens the length of sarcomeres and causes the muscle to contract.
25. The skin provides protection from and interaction with the external environment, retains body fluids, eliminates waste, and helps regulate body temperature.
26. Tissue is a collection of cells that are similar in structure and that work together to perform a particular function. An organ consists of various tissues that enable the organ to perform a specific function.
27. The epidermis, the tough outer layer of skin, consists primarily of dead, keratin-filled cells and serves as the body's protective barrier. The dermis, the inner layer of skin, consists of blood vessels, sensory neurons, hair follicles, glands, and other structures that enable the body to respond to external stimuli.
28. Red bone marrow produces red blood cells and some white blood cells. Yellow bone marrow consists primarily of fat cells and serves as an energy store.
29. a. ball-and-socket joint; b. hinge joint; c. gliding joint
30. (a) biceps; flexor (b) triceps; extensor (c) An insertion is the point where a muscle attaches to a moving bone. The insertion of *a* is the radius, and the insertion of *c* is the ulna. (d) An origin is the point where a muscle attaches to a stationary bone. The origin of both *a* and *c* is the scapula. (e) elbow; hinge joint

Chapter 47
Circulatory and Respiratory Systems

1. b
2. f
3. h
4. g
5. a
6. d
7. c
8. e
9. F; the right atrium collects the deoxygenated blood that returns from systemic circulation.
10. T
11. T
12. F; the circulatory and respiratory systems have independent control systems.
13. F; pulmonary circulation is the movement of blood between the heart and lungs.
14. b
15. d
16. d
17. c
18. c
19. a
20. b
21. c
22. b
23. c
24. No; the problem associated with the transfusion of whole blood is the agglutination of the donor blood cells caused by the antibodies of the recipient. Because there are no donor blood cells if only plasma is being used, there is no need to know the blood type of the donor.
25. Valves in the veins prevent the backflow of blood.
26. Systemic circulation is the circulation of blood between the heart and all other body tissues except the lungs.
27. Mucus decreases friction created by the movement of the lungs during breathing.
28. When a deep breath is taken, the chest expands as rib muscles contract. The rib cage expands and the diaphragm contracts and moves downward. The reduced air pressure in the thoracic cavity causes air from the atmosphere to move into the lungs.
29. a. aorta; b. superior vena cava; c. right atrium; d. right ventricle; e. inferior vena cava; f. pulmonary artery; g. left atrium; h. pulmonary veins; i. left ventricle
30. (a) concentration gradients (b) Carbon dioxide is more concentrated in the blood. (c) The concentration of oxygen in alveoli decreases as the remaining oxygen diffuses from alveoli into the blood. In addition, the concentration of carbon dioxide in alveoli increases, causing the concentration gradient to shift. This shift causes carbon dioxide to diffuse back into the blood from the alveoli. (d) Red blood cells transport oxygen and, to a lesser extent, carbon dioxide. (e) In the lungs, bicarbonate ions combine with a proton to form carbonic acid, which in turn forms carbon dioxide and water.

Chapter 48
Infectious Diseases and the Immune System

1. d
2. f
3. b
4. e
5. h
6. c
7. a
8. g
9. T
10. T
11. F; infected cells are destroyed by cytotoxic T cells.
12. F; a primary immune response is the immune response engaged by the body when it is first exposed to an antigen.
13. T
14. b
15. b
16. c
17. b
18. d
19. b
20. b
21. b
22. d
23. b
24. A primary difference is that the specific recognition of an antigen is required to activate the immune system's specific defenses. Specific recognition is not required for nonspecific defenses.

25. When an injury such as a cut occurs, damaged cells release histamine, which increases blood flow to the wounded area. Phagocytes and neutrophils then engulf and destroy most of the pathogens.
26. In an autoimmune disease, the immune system responds to the body's own cells, attacking them as if they were pathogens.
27. HIV mutates rapidly and suppresses the immune system. These two characteristics make the development of an effective HIV vaccine difficult.
28. No; it is possible to be infected with HIV without showing the symptoms associated with AIDS. Following exposure to HIV, the immune system is able to respond to and control the virus for a limited time.
29. The first antibodies are produced during the time period labeled *b,* or the primary immune response. The most rapid division of B cells occurs during the time period labeled *c,* or the secondary immune response.
30. (a) Presentation of antigen A by macrophages is required for the secretion of interleukin 2 (IL-2) by helper T cells. (b) The unknown substance prevents helper T cells from secreting IL-2 even in the presence of antigen A, which is presented by the macrophages. (c) Answers will vary but may include the following: The unknown substance could bind to or interfere with receptors on the surface of helper T cells that recognize antigen A. It could bind to antigen A as it is presented by macrophages, preventing the helper T cells from binding to the antigen. It could inhibit production of IL-2 by helper T cells. It could also destroy interleukin-1 before it reaches the T cells.

Chapter 49
Digestive and Excretory Systems

1. h
2. f
3. g
4. e
5. c
6. a
7. d
8. b
9. F; intestinal enzymes produce significant amounts of Vitamin D.
10. F; the gastrointestinal tract is defined as the tube beginning at the mouth and ending at the anus.
11. T
12. F; sorting occurs during reabsorption.
13. F; plant products also are a source of dietary proteins.
14. c
15. c
16. c
17. b
18. a
19. d
20. c
21. b
22. b
23. d
24. Nutrients are chemical substances that are necessary for organisms to function and grow properly.
25. Carbohydrates are broken down by a series of enzymes within the digestive system. The final product of carbohydrate digestion, glucose, is absorbed through the wall of the small intestine and transported to blood capillaries.
26. The lining of the stomach is composed of cells that secrete mucus. The mucus lines the stomach lumen and prevents the gastric fluid from contacting the stomach cells.
27. The circulatory system is responsible for removing metabolic wastes from cells throughout the body. Blood transports these wastes to the urinary system, which subsequently excretes them from the body. The intersection of the two systems occurs at the glomerulus–Bowman's capsule complex.
28. No; bile is secreted by the liver and stored in the gallbladder until released into the small intestine.
29. Osmotic pressure in the kidney is necessary for the reabsorption of water from the filtrate into the bloodstream.
30. (a) a. esophagus; b. liver; c. large intestine, or colon; d. stomach; e. small intestine; f. rectum (b) Liver; the liver stores glycogen and breaks down toxic substances, such as alcohol. The liver also secretes bile, which is vital in the digestion of fats. (c) In mechanical digestion, the body physically breaks down chunks of food into small particles that can be digested easily. In chemical digestion, digestive enzymes and fluids change the chemical nature of nutrients so that the nutrients can be absorbed and used by the body. (d) Nutrients are absorbed into the circulatory system through blood and lymph vessels in the lining of the small intestine. Nutrients are absorbed by microvilli through diffusion and active transport. (e) When the pH value in the stomach is low, pepsin splits complex proteins into peptides.

Chapter 50
Nervous System and Sense Organs

1. g
2. h
3. c
4. b
5. e
6. f
7. a
8. d
9. T
10. T
11. T
12. F; dendrites receive input from other neurons.
13. T
14. b
15. d
16. d
17. a
18. a
19. d
20. b
21. d
22. c
23. d

24. An afferent neuron carries information toward the central nervous system. An efferent neuron carries information away from the central nervous system.
25. During an action potential, the inside of a neuron momentarily becomes positively charged as sodium ions rapidly flow into the cell. Potassium ions then flow out of the cell to reestablish the resting potential.
26. When the tendon below the patella is stretched, a sensory neuron detects stretching of the quadriceps. In the spinal cord, the sensory neuron stimulates motor neurons that excite the quadriceps. It also stimulates interneurons that inhibit motor neurons that stimulate the hamstrings. Thus, the quadriceps contract, the hamstrings relax, and the leg rapidly extends.
27. Saliva causes food to release chemicals that can be detected by chemoreceptors in taste buds (the sensory receptors for taste). In response to the chemicals, the taste buds transmit action potentials to the thalamus and then to the cerebral cortex, where taste is interpreted.
28. A neurotransmitter is a chemical released by one neuron that has a specific effect on another neuron. Neurotransmitters diffuse across synaptic clefts between neurons and either increase or decrease the activity of the postsynaptic neuron.
29. a. axon terminals; b. nodes of Ranvier; c. Schwann cells; d. axon; e. cell body; f. nucleus; g. dendrites
30. (a) The graph illustrates the changes in membrane potential that occur in a neuron during an action potential. (b) The permeability of the membrane changes when voltage-gated sodium channels and voltage-gated potassium channels open or close in response to changes in the membrane potential. (c) During period *A* sodium ions rapidly flow into the cell, causing the inside of the neuron to momentarily become more positive than the outside. (d) During period *B* potassium ions flow out of the cell, restoring the resting potential of the cell membrane (about –70 millivolts). (e) The resting potential must be restored before another action potential can occur. The period after an action potential during which neurons cannot fire is called the refractory period.

Chapter 51
Endocrine System

1. c
2. f
3. e
4. b
5. h
6. a
7. d
8. g
9. T
10. F; hormones are secreted by endocrine cells and affect distant target cells.
11. T
12. F; FSH is involved with spermatogenesis in males.
13. T
14. c
15. b
16. b
17. a
18. c
19. d
20. c
21. c
22. b
23. b
24. Releasing hormones are chemicals produced by neurosecretory cells that regulate secretion of the anterior-pituitary hormones. Examples include PRL-releasing hormone, TSH-releasing hormone, LH-releasing hormone, FSH-releasing hormone, GH-releasing hormone, and ACTH-releasing hormone.
25. In a positive feedback mechanism, an increase in the regulated hormone or substance increases the secretion of the regulating, or initial, hormone. In a negative feedback mechanism, an increase in the regulated hormone or substance decreases the secretion of the regulating hormone.
26. The requirement of a hormone binding to a receptor: Without this event, the correct target cell would not be recognized and the hormone would have no effect.
27. Answers wil vary but may include that the transplanted islet cells secrete insulin the way normal islet cells do.
28. "Hypoglandular" refers to a condition of abnormally low gland activity, such as hypothyroidism, type I diabetes mellitus, and pituitary dwarfism.
29. Steroid hormones are lipid-soluble and thus can diffuse through the lipid bilayer of a target cell.
30. (a) The immediate cause for not experiencing puberty is a low level of testosterone. (b) the hypothalamus and the anterior pituitary (c) The anterior pituitary; because the injection of LH-releasing hormone failed to increase LH secretion, receptors on LH-secreting cells of the anterior pituitary could be defective. Alternatively, LH secretion from these cells could be deficient. (d) In the negative feedback mechanism, testosterone secretion inhibits LH secretion from the anterior pituitary. (e) Testosterone-secreting cells in the testes could be unresponsive to LH.

Chapter 52
Reproductive System

1. f
2. c
3. h
4. g
5. a
6. d
7. b
8. e
9. T
10. F; sperm are part of semen.
11. T
12. T
13. T
14. c
15. d
16. b
17. b
18. c
19. d
20. d
21. b
22. a

23. c
24. The corpus luteum forms from the follicle that ruptures during ovulation. The corpus luteum secretes progesterone and estrogen, which cause the uterine lining to thicken.
25. No; menopause occurs when menstruation ceases after a woman's follicles have either ruptured or degenerated.
26. The epididymis conducts sperm from the testis to the vas deferens, stores sperm between ejaculations, and is the site of the final steps of sperm maturation.
27. No; ovulation normally occurs in one ovary during each menstrual cycle. Only one mature egg is ovulated per cycle.
28. The cervix connects the vagina with the uterus.
29. a. outer jellylike layer; b. cell membrane of ovum; c. sperm head; d. sperm tail; e. sperm midpiece; f. nucleus of ovum. The diagram illustrates the fusion of a sperm's head region with an ovum's cell membrane—one of the steps required for fertilization.
30. (a) a. egg cell; b. corpus luteum; c. ovary; d. follicle (b) FSH, LH, and estrogen (c) The corpus luteum secretes estrogen and progesterone, which cause the uterine lining to thicken. (d) menstruation (e) After an egg is ovulated, it is swept into a fallopian tube and travels toward the uterus. If the egg is not fertilized, it dies within 48 hours of ovulation.

Chapter 53
Drugs

1. d
2. g
3. a
4. f
5. c
6. h
7. b
8. e
9. F; drug interactions can occur between prescription or nonprescription drugs.
10. T
11. F; lethal doses apply to all drugs regardless of the administration method.
12. T
13. T
14. d
15. d
16. c
17. b
18. b
19. b
20. c
21. d
22. b
23. b
24. Withdrawal from drugs is difficult because drug addiction causes physiological changes in the nervous system; removal of the drug often results in anguish and pain.
25. A psychoactive drug affects the functioning of the central nervous system. Psychoactive drugs include depressants, narcotics, stimulants, and hallucinogens.
26. Nicotine is an addictive stimulant that increases blood pressure and heart rate, decreases circulation of blood and oxygen, and affects all organ systems.
27. A stimulant is a drug that increases the activity of the central nervous system. A depressant is a drug that decreases the activity of the central nervous system.
28. Drug addiction is the physiological dependence on a drug. Drug abuse includes taking a drug in doses that are greater than prescribed doses or for a longer time than is recommended, as well as taking a drug that is obtained illegally or without a doctor's prescription.
29. In figure *A,* the drug has interfered with proteins that move neurotransmitter molecules back into the presynaptic neuron, causing excess neurotransmitter to remain in the synapse. In figure *B,* the number of postsynaptic-neuron receptors and the amount of neurotransmitter released from the presynaptic neuron have decreased because of overstimulation. These figures illustrate drug addiction caused by a drug that inhibits reuptake of neurotransmitters.
30. (a) The drug binds to neurotransmitter receptors on the postsynaptic neuron, blocking the neurotransmitter from stimulating the postsynaptic neuron. (b) Because the drug blocks the neurotransmitter from stimulating the postsynaptic neuron, the amount of neurotransmitter that is produced and released by the presynaptic neuron increases to compensate for understimulation. (c) If the drug were removed, the postsynaptic neuron would be overstimulated by excess neurotransmitter. (d) Over the long term, the presynaptic neuron would compensate by decreasing production and release of neurotransmitter. The number of postsynaptic-neuron receptors would also decrease. (e) Yes; the drug changes the physiology of the synapse by affecting neurotransmitter release and therefore stimulation of the postsynaptic neuron. Because the immediate effect of the drug's removal is overstimulation—a result of the body's adjustment to the drug—the drug must be administered repeatedly to sustain the desired effect of understimulation.